ORAL LITERATURE OF THE LUO

Also in this series

Gikuyu Oral Literature — Karega Mutahi and Wanjiku Kabira

Oral Literature of the Asians in East Africa — Mubina H. Kirmani and Sanaullah Kirmani

Oral Literature of the Embu and Mbeere — Ciarunji Chesaina

Oral Literature of the Kalenjin — Ciarunji Chesaina

Oral Literature of the Maasai — Naomi Kipury

Oral Literature
of the Luo

Okumba Miruka

EAST AFRICAN EDUCATIONAL PUBLISHERS
Nairobi • Kampala • Dar es Salaam

Published by
East African Educational Publishers Ltd.
Brick Court, Mpaka Road/Woodvale Grove
Westlands
P.O. Box 45314
Nairobi

East African Educational Publishers Ltd.
P.O. Box 11542
Kampala

Ujuzi Educational Publishers Ltd.
P.O. Box 31647
Kijito-Nyama, Dar es Salaam

First published 2001

ISBN 9966 25 086 7

Electronic Typeset by Belbran Enterprises
Nairobi

Printed in Kenya by Printpak Ltd.
Likoni Road, P.O. Box 78354, Nairobi

CONTENTS

PREFACE

The Luo, like many other Kenyan groups, have a wealth of oral literature. This lore principally expressed in oral prose, poetry and song, proverbs and word games such as riddles and puns, is the subject of this book. The purpose of this anthology is to offer representative samples of Luo oral literature in one collection.

There are previous publications which have anthologised Luo narratives and proverbs. But to date, no single text has brought all these genres together. The text does not seek to merely duplicate what is carried in the other anthologies. Rather, it combines material from original field research with samples of what has been published in other texts. Where the latter is the case, it is duly acknowledged.

The text deals with the four main genres of Luo oral literature, namely: riddles, proverbs, poetry and narratives. One can stretch these genres to cover other verbal arts such as tongue-twisters and puns. These four genres are, however, felt to be all-inclusive. The chapters in this book are arranged in the order in which the genres are listed above, with the hope that the text may be used in academic study of Luo oral literature as well as serve as a collection which researchers and students can use to examine the subject.

The second chapter discusses the conventions of riddles as well as the etiquette of riddling among the Luo. It then examines the social functions of riddles (and riddling) before providing a list of riddles in the original Dholuo and their English translations.

Chapter Three examines the nature of the Luo proverb as a socio-ethical genre and thus discusses the world view that emerges from it. The chapter then provides an introductory discussion of the expressive features (style) of the Luo proverb before presenting a collection of items.

The fourth chapter first focuses on the concept of poetry and forms of Luo oral poetry. Unlike the chapters on riddles and proverbs which provide some generic information on the genres, this chapter takes a different approach and provides explanatory notes for each poem presented.

Finally, the last chapter on narratives introduces the conventions of Luo narrative performance, explores their stylistic aspects and provides a summary of the Luo worldview from this genre before presenting samples.

Okumba Miruka
MAY 2001

ACKNOWLEDGEMENTS

I wish to acknowledge the contribution of the following in compiling this anthology:

Susan Awuor Miruka of Asembo Bay, who was the principal informant on the narratives.

Absalom Odhach of Mabinju Village in Asembo, Bondo, who was the principal informant on proverbs.

Steven Owino of Ugolwe Village, Ugenya in Siaya, who provided a lot of insights into the interpretation of proverbs and the understanding of riddles.

Oby Obyerodhyambo of Nairobi, with whom a lot of initial work was done on the manuscript and who provided some poetic pieces for inclusion.

My younger sisters and brothers, who provided the bulk of the riddles published in this anthology.

Asenath Bole Odaga, author of *Luo Sayings* and *Thu Tinda!* from which a number of proverbs and narratives are borrowed.

Paul Mbuya Akoko, author of *Luo Kitgi gi Timbegi*, which was a source of a number of proverbs and useful information on Luo culture.

Shadrack Malo, author of *Sigend Luo Maduogo Chuny*, from which a number of narratives presented in the anthology were taken and translated.

B. Onyango-Ogutu and A.A. Roscoe, authors of *Keep My Words*, which was a source of a number of narratives and other useful information on Luo narratives.

Chapter 1

SOCIO-CULTURAL BACKGROUND: THE PEOPLE AND THEIR CULTURE

Migration and settlement

The people are called *Jo-Luo* (the Luo people) and the language is called *Dholuo* (the Luo language).

Primarily settled in the western part of Kenya in the present Migori, Homa Bay, Kisumu, Bondo, Rachuonyo, Nyando and Siaya Districts, the Luo are a Nilotic group whose progeny includes the Acholi and Jo-Padhola in Uganda and Alur and the Dinka, Anyuak and Shiluk in Sudan.

"Luo" is related to the word *luwo* (to follow). Historically, the Luo are said to have followed the River Nile valley in search of pasture around the Lake Victoria area until they finally settled where they are. Although this can explain why they inhabit areas around Lake Victoria, it is not to say that they have not sought settlement in other areas of Kenya, particularly as a result of formal employment.

According to B.A. Ogot's *The Jii-Speakers*, the first group of Luo-speakers to arrive in western Kenya were the Joka-Jok, "the People of God", who left Tekidi settlement after a major conflict. They headed south, across Uganda, towards Mt Elgon.

They crossed River Sio and entered modern Samia, settling at Ligala. The Bantu-speakers living in this area formed part of the Lake Victoria community, which encompassed Bunyoro and Buganda in the north, to Uvinza in Tanzania to the south. The Samia hills had already attracted many settlers of mixed origin by this time, largely because of the iron ore in the area and the excellent fishing facilities. Residents cultivated crops and their women were excellent potters.

The Joka-Jok remained in Samia for about a century, intermarrying and trading with the Bantu speakers. As more people arrived from the Mt Elgon area to join these prosperous settlements around Samia hills, the Joka-Jok decided to move to the next major centre of activity along the lake shore in Yimbo, leaving behind one group, the Joka-Owidi, who established a large village settlement at Kisumo in Samia. They crossed the river Yala, and settled around Ramogi Hill between 1490 and 1517 AD.

Most Bantu speakers of Yimbo consisted of fishermen, a few hunters and farmers living away from the lake and known as *jobungu* (people of the forest). The farmers also hunted wild game in the forests. From Samia, the women of Yimbo had learnt the art of pottery, for which the Goma clan — found in both Samia and Yimbo — was famous.

They interacted with the newcomers through trade and intermarriage, to the extent that by the end of the 15th century, the region was beginning to witness the emergence of larger settlements and homogeneity of culture which would suggest social organisations capable of integrating diverse ethnic groups over greater geographical areas. By the end of the 19th century, the different economic groups around Lake Victoria had integrated and created larger settlements. These were the communities that the Joka-Jok joined, first in Samia and later in Yimbo and South Nyanza.

Most of the early Joka-Jok settlers preferred to join the *jobungu* instead of the fishermen along the lake shore and on the various islands. And although linguistically, they were a minority living in a sea of Bantu speakers, they nevertheless formed the largest single community in Yimbo. They also intermarried and traded extensively with the Bantu communities and, through marriage and trading alliances, extended their influence over a wide area. A few of the Bantu groups moved away to seek a new home in other lands, while the majority stayed and gradually intermixed with the Luo speakers to produce multi-ethnic and multilingual societies in Yimbo. Similar hybrid societies gradually emerged all along the shores of Lake Victoria and on the various islands such as Sese, Bugaya, Sigulu, Jagusi, Mageta, Buvuma, Kome, Ukerewe, Ukara, Mfang'ano and Rusinga.

These were fluid societies in which the Bantu speakers, the Luo speakers and a few Kalenjin speakers; the cultivators, the herders, the fishermen, the hunters, the blacksmiths and the potters — all combined in different proportions to produce the new societies of the Lake Victoria basin.*

As the Lake Victoria littoral and islands filled up, small groups began to move into the interior of the sparsely populated western Kenya. From Yimbo, groups of the Joka-Jok moved eastwards and southwards to found village settlements in modern Sakwa, Alego, Asembo and Uyoma. These were large multi-lineage or multi-clan agglomerations led by a pivotal figure or family.

---

*B.A. Ogot: *The Jii Speakers.*

This apparently peaceful process of evolution was rudely affected by the arrival of two new groups of Luo speakers — the Joka-Owiny and Joka Omolo. The attempts by the Joka-Owiny to establish political control over western Kenya generated conflicts which split families and villages and also created general insecurity. The arrival of these two Luo-speaking clusters in the area also led to deliberate efforts on their part to create distinctly Luo societies, a move which was resisted by the Bantu and Kalenjin speakers. As more and more people arrived in Uganda and Tanzania to settle on the Lake basin, resources became more scarce, and the struggle for existence intensified. In a sense, such struggles facilitated the process of amalgamation and identity definition and redefinition as well as the creation of larger and more viable polities. It became more difficult for small groups or family units to survive on their own. Some of the pre-Luo population sought new homes eastwards where they settled on higher grounds and southwards across the Winam Gulf to the present-day Homa Bay, Suba and Migori Districts.

By about 1730, the movement of Luo speakers from Central to South Nyanza was almost complete. They had established village settlements along the lakeshore, many of which were multi-ethnic and multilingual trading conglomerations. As the lake region became overcrowded, weaker or more adventurous groups were forced to move inland to find new settlements. This led to greater interaction with non-Luo groups, since they were moving into areas which were already occupied. By the end of the 19th century, Luo settlements had extended into northeastern Tanzania and towards Maasailand and Gusii country.

The concept of divinity

The Luo traditionally believe in God, called *Nyasaye* (one who is beseeched) or *Nyakalaga* (one who spreads out). In fact, it is believed that God lives in a person's bloodstream and is an alienable part of one's being. That is why the Luo talk of *nyasach ng'ato* (one's god) so that if good fortune comes your way, it is said that your god is good. The narrative of Nyamgondho son of Ombare is a case in point.

But the belief in the mystery of God extends to the awesome natural and celestial bodies such as the sun, moon, huge rocks, snakes (especially the python), trees, mountains, etc. which are seen as conduits for divinity. For example, every old man is on waking traditionally expected to recite a prayer direct at the sun: *Thu, iwuogna maber mondo ringa okwe* (*Thu*, appear well for me so my flesh can know peace). The elder then spits and repeats this ritual at sunset when he says: *Thu, ipodhna maber mondo ayudi gweth* (*Thu*, set well for me so I can be blessed). Notice that in the morning prayer, there is reference to the calmness of the body (flesh) in which God is believed to reside.

3

It is also believed that the sun could appear to a person like a vision at night. Such a person gets pretty agitated and has to be physically restrained as he extends an outstretched arm to the sun, requesting blessings. The person also throws cow dung, human excreta and seeds towards the sun and is in return blessed with wealth in the form of a bountiful harvest, large herds of cattle and so on.

A similar treatment is accorded the moon when first sighted. Old men will invoke the moon to enable them get more wives, boys to wish for a bride, girls for a groom and women for satisfaction. The divinity of the moon is explained in the Luo myth about why people die. The myth states that Moon looked with sympathy upon human death and wished to bring it to an end so that people would not die but moon itself appears and reappears. So it asked humanity to send it a morsel of fat. Humanity prepared the morsel and sent off the chameleon to deliver it. But the chameleon arrived with a very dirty morsel which the moon rejected outright. The moon therefore did not only refuse to keep its promise, but it also cursed the chameleon with sluggishness.

The celestial bodies are always used as reference points in predicting weather patterns as well as bad or good tidings. For instance, it is believed that when there is a ring around the sun, an important person will die. Eclipses are viewed with awe and as portentous of a major event. Thus, elders gather, deliberate and decide on an appropriate action to ward off disaster.

Various riddles in this anthology refer to the celestial bodies and allude to the belief in them as manifestations of divinity.

Warfare

One of the most famous Luo stories is that of Luanda Magere, the indomitable warrior who was only vanquished through trickery. His story is not reproduced in this anthology as a narrative, but is represented with a poem that extols the virtues of Magere. Another reference to warfare is in the story of the disobedient wife. A few notes about traditional Luo warfare will assist the reader in understanding the background of this story.

In the past, warfare among the Luo and their neighbours (the Kalenjin and Kisii particularly) or among Luo communities themselves was an expected and usual affair. Young men were always prepared for war. Disputes leading to fights frequently arose from competition for resources (e.g. grazing fields, cattle, etc.). When war was declared, the regiments were arranged according to family lines based on the premise that the motivation to protect kin was stronger. War would be declared by blowing a horn, with the official cheerleader driving the community cattle towards enemy land.

The weapons included spears, bows and arrows, clubs and stones. As a strategy of disabling enemies, the warriors sent the spear earmarked to be the first missile to the elders who would fold its blade. In a similar way, they hoped and believed that their enemies' spears would be useless against them.

Casualties were treated in various ways. The dead would be removed from the battlefields by the enemies who could also take the wounded as prisoners. But the warriors would not recover the bodies of their fallen colleagues. Rather, they would go back home and get the womenfolk to retrieve the casualties (in the story of the disobedient wife, you will notice that the warriors only come back to announce to Obunga that her husband was one of those who fell). The women are sent because the norms of warfare prohibit the killing of women. The women would carry the dead and the wounded back home and would be met with loud wailing. This is a tumultuous but sorrowful affair. A victory is met with a different kind of tumult: joy. In this case, the warriors return in a stampede with their spears pointing skywards as they chant the *Agoro* (victory song).

On reaching home, the warriors who have killed people in the battle stand outside the village fence and do not enter the homesteads through the gate. Instead, a side gate is made for them. Their wives and mothers are all smeared with dust and there is ululation as the warriors are cleansed. This is done by having them swallow the raw lung of a he-goat. The goatskin is split into strands, one of which is tied around a warrior's spear and his wrist. The number of strands received depends on how many people the warrior killed. The he-goat's heart is also cut up and the pieces given to the killer warriors to swallow before they are shaved. The warriors stay the night lying on leaves. They chew a certain herb that makes them sleepless and keep vigil.

Luo cuisine

The Luo traditionally eat a variety of foods, including various meats (wild and tame), fish and vegetables of all kinds. The base of Luo cuisine is *ugali*, a kind of bread made from maize, millet or cassava flour or a mixture of two or all of these. *Ugali* is so important to the diet that if a family has a meal without it, it is said not to have dined. The standard diet consists of *ugali* and stew. The stews are often lavishly embellished with milk, ghee and simsim paste, which makes them very tasty. The community also consumes milk, sweet potatoes, *nyoyo* (boiled mixture of maize grains and beans or peas), blood, mushrooms, termites, various fruits, honey, roots, etc. Because of their proximity to the fresh-water Lake Victoria and their history, the Luo cuisine revolves a lot around fish of all types. The fish is cooked fresh or sun-dried and then stewed or roasted. The fish of choice in Luo cuisine is tilapia (*nilotica* or other varieties). One poem in this anthology celebrates the fish varieties by presenting them as an orchestra.

All meals are made in traditional earthen pots of different shapes. Each pot is used for one particular food variety only. Cooking in earthen pots is a fast disappearing practice and is now only retained in a few rural households. But the Luo will tell you that food made in the earthen pots has a unique taste and aroma quite different from that of food made in the aluminium pans now widely used. One advantage of the earthen pots is their ability to retain heat for a longer period hence keep the food warm long after it has been removed from the hearth.

The traditional hearth consists of three stones arranged in a triangle on which the pots are placed and the firewood built under. In order to retain the heat in the hearth and reduce wastage, one or two sides of the hearth are usually covered with wet cow dung, leaving only one side to allow in air.

Eating times would be around 8.00 in the morning followed by snacks during the mid-morning and another main meal around 3.00 p.m., with supper coming at 8.00 p.m. This pattern has, however, been largely affected by activities introduced with the Western life-style. Children eat in their mother's hut. Male members of the homestead (elders, adults and adolescent boys), eat together in the *duol or abila*, the hut where the patriach confers with his peers and the male fraternity.

Eating is a communal affair. *Ugali* is served in a wide tray or earthen plate from which everyone eats using their fingers. It is often the stew that is served in earthen pots (*tawo*) for individuals, but most often, for two or three people sitting close together. The communal eating helps the community to feed orphans and other disadvantaged children. All wives bring their dishes to the *duol* and these are then shared by the diners. The communal eating is also extremely useful in cementing ties between members of the family.

Traditionally, certain foods were prohibited for certain groups of people. For instance, women would not eat chicken, eggs, elephant and porcupine meat while men would not eat kidneys. Some people choose not to eat certain foods if doing so is believed to be out of character with the person's spirituality. For example, people who are said to be possessed by *juogi* or *lang'o* (spirits) do not eat mudfish. Others do not eat certain foods because of allergy.

Specific traditions dictate how to carve and share an animal's meat. The head of the homestead gets the tongue, heart, liver and chest meat. He invites his fellow elders to share in eating it (this tradition is alluded to in the story of the disobedient wife while the art of slaughtering is celebrated in the poem *Rateng' Oyang'o Dhiang'*). The wives get the intestines and other offals as well as the head. The girls get the vertebrae, kidneys and allied parts. In the past, when skins were still used as clothing and bedding, the old man would tan the skins and distribute them among his wives. Now, they are sold to skin dealers in market centres.

6

Economic activities

In the rural set-up, Luo economic life revolves around subsistence agriculture, animal husbandry and fishing. The agriculture focuses mostly on production of cereals (maize, millet), pulses (beans, peas), other grains (groundnuts, simsim), roots and tubers (potatoes, cassava) and vegetables. These are cultivated in family plots around the homestead or some plot farther afield.

Traditionally, the Luo family has two sets of farmland. One is the kitchen garden known as *orundu* and the farmland proper. *Orundu* basically consists of the area around the huts. It is fenced off and used to grow cereals and vegetables. The *orundu* produce is largely for immediate consumption. The farmland proper, usually a bit of a distance from the homestead, is a larger tract of land dedicated for producing the main crop in terms of cereals and pulses for storage and use over time. Whereas the *orundu* is often cultivated manually using hoes, the farmland proper is cultivated using oxen ploughs and, now, tractors.

Cultivation is launched officially by the eldest male member of the family who announces the occasion to the family the night before. He wakes up very early and goes to his field and strikes down his hoe. That day, everyone in the homestead works on his field. But the next day, each household goes to its own farm. The produce from the man's field is used as a strategic reserve which is only distributed to his wives when there is severe famine. The married sons are also encouraged to have their own granaries and fields. Men, especially married ones, who do not have such reserves have poor social standing among their peers.

The labour for cultivation is largely drawn from the family, but there is also the traditional concept of *saga* in which friends and/or relatives organise themselves into rotating teams to assist one another, especially with weeding on their farms.

In the olden days, the harvesting of crops would involve cutting the stalks or digging the roots and leaving them in the farm to dry before they are removed and taken home. This practice has changed a lot because of increased thievery. Now, people harvest by directly removing the crops and taking them home.

Another dying practice is the storage system. The traditional Luo granary is a structure built of sticks, held together with cow dung plaster and with a grass-thatched roof. There are separate granaries for different crops, for the man and his wives. The granaries have small but open entrances towards the roofs, big enough to allow a human being in. Again, because of thievery and Westernisation, most Luo homesteads now hardly have a traditional granary.

The keeping of livestock is also a traditional economic activity. A homestead without livestock is not quite complete. The animals kept include cattle, goats, sheep and chicken. Cattle are regarded as the main livestock and store of wealth.

In the past, livestock was kept for largely social reasons. Some of this survives to day, but livestock is now being used more and more as an economic asset sold for cash.

Cattle feature prominently in payment of bridewealth, as a source of energy for ploughing and during burial ceremonies as a source of food and sport. Goats are also used for paying bridewealth and as food. The sheep, which is a prized animal among the Luo, is mainly used as a gift to valued friends and as food. But it is never used for payment of bridewealth, perhaps because it is regarded as a dumb animal. Chickens are also mainly used for food and as special food usually prepared only when there are visitors.

The responsibility of tending the livestock is largely a male affair. The sons take turns in grazing and watering the livestock. Traditionally, each son does this for three days and is relieved by another. As would be expected, some like and enjoy the activity while others do not (the story of Kijenje illustrates the kind of relationship that can develop between a herdsboy and the cattle). The father soon realises which son likes the job and takes good care of the animals. This son often gets preferential treatment when it comes to the father giving out cattle to assist him accomplish a cultural requirement, like paying bridewealth. Those who take care of the livestock also have specific parts of the animal reserved for them when it is slaughtered. Today, many homesteads have employed herdsboys because the sons are not available to tend their fathers' cattle due to education and new forms of employment.

The cattle, goats and sheep are all taken away to the fields at around 10 a.m. and brought back at around 5 p.m. for milking (in the case of lactating cows). Heifers, lambs and kids graze by the homestead in the care of the young boys. The cattle are tethered in a designated place within the homestead, usually central enough for the male head of household to monitor any mishaps in the boma at night. Goats and sheep are kept in their special hut, called *abila*.

Chickens are let out from their *osera* (a cone-shaped basket made of sticks) in the morning and locked in at nightfall. The cocks, hens and chicks are kept in their separate baskets to reduce fights, commotion and possible trampling of chicks. During times of plenty, the chickens are fed with grains and leftover *ugali* when they are released in the morning and then left to fend for themselves free range.

Taking care of the chickens is largely a female chore. Cattle, goats and sheep are owned by men while women own the fowls. The man allocates the cows among his wives for milking, with the eldest wife getting the largest share. He can also give out the heifers to his sons, usually to pay bridewealth.

Both livestock and crop agriculture depend a lot on rain. Thus, the availability of rain is central to the Luo economy. In the olden days, therefore, there were revered rainmakers mostly from the neighbouring Luhya community, the foremost of them named *Nganyi*. Rainmaking involved great sacrifices to the ancestors and the divine fraternity whose physical manifestation is seen in awesome features and animals, such as snakes. The story of Oganda, in this anthology, illustrates the length to which communities went to get rain.

Fishing forms another major economic activity among the Luo, whether it is in the lake, river or stream. In the past, the main form of fishing was beach seining, using papyrus mats. This has largely been transformed and now seine nets are used instead of mats. Other forms of fishing involve use of hooked lines (especially in streams, rivers and swamps) and fishing baskets, the latter being popular among women during flash floods.

Currently, fishing is a predominantly male activity for subsistence and income generation. The fish caught is sold to villagers by the lakeside and to traders who then transport it to hinterland markets within and beyond Luoland. Refrigeration now makes it possible for large-scale traders to purchase fish and transport it to major towns in Kenya. On the other hand, local traders also dry the fish as a way of preserving it.

With modernisation, trade has become a major economic activity employing a large population of the Luo. Petty trading in small markets provides people with daily goods and services. A typical trading centre in Luoland will have grocery shops, stalls for selling consumables, a butchery, tailoring services, posho mills and bars.

Before the use of current forms of money, the Luo used to barter goods. There were specific measures of millet for a goat, ram or bull. Sometimes, a person could even slaughter a bull and barter the meat for cereals, each part of the bull being valued differently. People who could not afford to barter would borrow but pawn one item, to be kept and retrieved only when they paid the debt.

A very interesting form of barter is called *singo*. It operates like the promissory note. In the Luo system, if you wish to slaughter a bull but you do not have one, you can get it from a neighbour by giving the neighbour your cow and promising that the neighbour should claim the heifer that your cow begets. As long as the cow does not get a heifer, the neighbour remains with your cow.

Related to this is the practice of loaning animals to a friend to take care of. This is occasioned by the very strong ties between friends or the belief that the friend is one of those people with the *Midas* touch when it comes to rearing cattle. The friend takes care of the cow and benefits from its milk. However, you can retrieve your cow at any time, hence the proverb that the loanee milks as he looks towards the gate (to see whether time has come to let go of the cow).

Together with these primary productive activities, the Luo traditionally engage in other crafts. There are blacksmiths, furniture makers, weavers (of ropes, baskets and fishing equipment), medical practitioners, exorcists, potters, hunters, etc.

Even today, the Luo feature prominently among artisans in towns as tailors, cobblers, carpenters, mechanics, masons and constructors.

A large population of the Luo are also formally employed in the Civil Service and companies as well as in their own enterprises in various towns and cities. Historically, the Luo formed a strong component of the workforce in government corporations such as the railways, posts and telecommunications, ports authority as well as the technocracy and academic services. To date, there are relics of this legacy despite the massive economic transformation going on.

The Luo homestead

The establishment of a new Luo homestead is a ceremonious activity which follows elaborate procedures. It is the pinnacle of a man's life when he has to move from his father's homestead and establish his own. The sons will do this in order of their seniority.

On the eve of the activity, a man sleeps in his eldest wife's hut, from where he emerges the next day to go and establish the new home. Accompanying him are his father (if alive), his eldest wife, his eldest son and a paternal uncle.

The eldest son is not necessarily the senior-most in age. Rather, this is the first son of the eldest wife. The man carries a cock, his son a new axe and its handle, and his wife some fire. They set off very early in the morning to the site of the new home.

The early start has a lot to do with the fact that in the past, establishing a home was a way of laying claim to part of what was then communal land. In these days of land adjudication, one cannot just lay claim to any land. People do not walk long distances to establish new homes. It is becoming common that they just step out of their father's homestead and pitch tent.

Once at the site of the proposed homestead, the man's uncle ties a knot of grass. This is an act of laying claim to the site. It can be compared with another practice related to the mushroom. If someone chances on sprouting mushroom, he/she ties a thatch of grass and puts it at the site. No one can then harvest the mushroom.

The man's son cuts a tree at the site and his father erects a straight pole on which he hangs a cage. Inside the cage are assorted items to attract luck and prosperity. Some of these are a rotten egg (to dispel any sorcery), star grass (for expansion and prosperity) and stalks of maize and millet (to ask for wealth).

Building then begins. The first hut built is a makeshift one-room structure made out of poles, sticks and grass. It is simple because it must be completed the same day and slept in by the builder and his first wife. The cock is tethered inside the hut to crow the next morning. Once the building is finished, food is served and the home is basically established. It is improved later when the man builds proper huts for his wives. The eldest wife's hut is usually the biggest and the central one, with the second wife's lying on the right and the third wife's on the left.

In this anthology, the story of Obong'o, the man who went to build, brings in another dimension. It is apparent that Obong'o (an only son) did not have a living father and, as an only son, had the responsibility of caring for his old mother. It appears that he decided to establish a new home. This is quite in line with traditional Luo culture in which a man would establish his own home. When his father has died and it is clear that his mother is lonely and vulnerable, the son is allowed to move his mother and establish for her a home near his own.

When the sons in the homestead mature, they also build their own huts. The first hut for a son is called *simba*. The first son builds *simba* first. His *simba* becomes the sleeping quarters for all the boys in the homestead until he marries. When he does, the second in the line erects his and the line goes on. The *simba* is the institution in which the boys exchange narratives and riddles. They also learn about sexual relationships and romance. For girls, the contemporary is the *siwindhe*, an old woman's hut in the village where the girls sleep and where they learn about adult life.

There cannot be two *simbas* in the same homestead. A younger son cannot build before an elder one. In fact, if the eldest son of the first wife is younger than the first son of the second or other wife, and is not yet old enough to build a *simba*, law requires that the older son builds a hut which is regarded as the senior-most son's *simba*. The complications that arise from this kind of eventuality, especially when it comes to marriage, is sometimes solved by men establishing separate homesteads for their different wives so that each homestead is independent from the others. But traditionally, the second or other wife's sons would be assured through extra-procedural undertakings like building their *simba* in the uncle's homestead as they wait for the senior-most brother to mature.

When the *simba* owner marries, he stays with his wife in the *simba* for some time. However, he is required to construct another hut and move from the *simba*, which is then demolished. The *simba* is called a boy's hut, the second hut is now called a proper house because it has got its owner, a woman.

The first son builds on the right hand side of the home from his mother's hut, the second on the left, the third on the right, and so on until all the boys have huts. The first son's hut is the nearest to the gate while the youngest son's is the nearest to his mother's. Essentially, the youngest son inherits the father's homestead whereas the others move out and establish their own homes. In Luo parlance, it is said that the youngest son "remains at home".

As is apparent from the description above, the Luo is a patrilineal community. The son is regarded as the pillar of the home and the essence of lineage. Thus if a

11

man only has daughters, he cannot move and establish his homestead. Instead, and in order to allow other brothers after him to build their homes, he would have to go and live in his uncle's homestead until he gets a son.

A special hut in the homestead is the *duol* or *abila*, a kind of office where the male homestead owner confers with his peers, takes his meals, educates the menfolk, holds court, or gives audience to his wives or entertains visitors. The *abila* is constructed in between the hut of the eldest wife and that of the second, with its back to the gate.

Children and their mothers

The Luo birth is attended by an elderly woman who has midwifery skills to supervise the occasion and take appropriate action should complications arise. The midwife will know what to do, including summoning people with medical knowledge to help. But once the child is born, it is detached from the mother using a blade from a dried maize or millet stalk. The umbilical cord is then disinfected using a charcoal paste made with the mother's saliva. The mother smears this paste after pasting it on the baby, on her own umbilicus. The cord is then tied, with three knots for a girl and four for a boy, a ritual which signifies the value attached to the boy. The same practice is repeated with regard to bringing out the child to the light. The mother stays four days and three days before she can bring out the boy and girl, respectively.

The placenta is buried at a different place for the boy and for the girl. The burial of the placenta takes place after approximately twelve hours so that if the birth is in the morning, the placenta is disposed of in the evening. The burying of the placenta is a practice which binds someone to the ancestral land and is often used as an argument in land disputes. People in such cases often challenge their detractors to prove that they own the disputed land by pointing out where the placenta was buried when they were born.

A new mother is treated to a choice of diet, including lots of protein and gruel made from finger millet to rebuild her body and strength. In fact, she is called *ondiek,* a beast, to denote the carnivorous treatment she gets. A standard practice is to slaughter a goat or even a bull for the new mother and make her drink a lot of the soup from the stew.

On the day the mother comes out with the child, she and the child are adorned with feathers from woodpeckers and another bird called *koga* to ward off death from the sounds of such birds' chirrup. These are believed to be birds of bad omen. The child and parents are then shaved after some days as the first form of initiation from the cycle of birth. It is also believed that a woman still in confinement after birth should not respond to a call from outside the house or a curse will befall her.

Traditionally, the birth of twins is treated as a rare and not very pleasant occasion. As soon as it is realised that twins are on the way, young women attending the birth run away lest they also get twins. Immediately after birth, the mother is cleansed by an expert who gives her herbal concoctions to drink. She also has to break the toilet pot using a hoe. The broken pot is buried in a hole at a spot where one or both the twins would be buried should they die.

A messenger is then sent to the woman's maiden home to break the news of twins to her kin. This messenger knows he is not carrying very good news. He will deliver it circumspectly to some children in the village whom he will inform to go and tell the girl's family that their daughter has given birth to twins. The messenger then leaves immediately because should the girl's kin find him, he is in for a rough beating.

Also, the whole village where the birth has taken place is informed so that people do not go to their farms the next day. All villagers are required to come and participate in the *malongo* ceremony, a kind of cleansing, where they recite certain words as they hit a mortar with sticks and touch the mother to discontinue the cycle of misfortune. All this time, both parents are not allowed to leave the house. A ceremony called "freeing the twins" is performed after a month. At this time, beer is brewed, a goat slaughtered and its skin worn by the mother and the twins. The revellers must each bring some grain.

The culmination of the ceremony is a dance in which the parents virtually remain naked as they sing and dance, leaving the hut. The words of the song are said to be extremely obscene. It is a ceremony attended only by people who have no sexual sanction in their relationship. The dance procession leads to the outside of the homestead where the parents are shaved before they return to the house. People drink alcohol and eat then loot the house, leaving only the ritual animal skins earlier given to the mother and the twins.

The final freeing ceremony is a visit by the mother's maiden relatives who come with a bull to be slaughtered on the first day of their visit. They are met at the gate with ululation, music and dance in the same obscene fashion. Drinking and eating takes place that day. The next day, the host homestead also slaughters a bull which is devoured amidst drinking. After this ceremony, the parents of the twins are free to go wherever they wish.

Twins have specific names. The first to be born is always called Apiyo (if a girl) or Opiyo (if a boy) while the second is called Adongo (for a girl) and Odongo (for a boy). *Piyo* means "quick" and *dong'* means "to remain behind". If the twins are of different sexes, say the girl is first and the boy last, the practice is still the same. The girl is named Apiyo and the boy Odongo. Interestingly, the twins also determine the name of the child after them. This child is called Akelo (if a girl) or Okelo (if a boy). To *kelo* means "to bring", i.e. this child escorted the twins.

13

Traditionally, the twins are treated the same way in everything. If one is to be caned, the other also must receive punishment. Otherwise, it is believed, the one not treated like the other will die.

A child's first meal is milk from a sheep. The second is the mother's breast milk until the child is old enough to have gruel and soft foods. Basically, a child is stopped from breastfeeding when it cuts its lower teeth. Alongside the milk and other foods, the child is also fortified and treated using liquid herbal medicine.

Part of the weaning is to have the child stay a whole night or even two without the mother. This is called *nindo ne nyathi oko*. The child is prepared for this by the mother's short absences to do domestic chores. But on the day of *nindo ne nyathi oko*, the mother could travel to her maiden home, leaving the child with a maid who calms the child with lullabies (some examples are provided in the poetry section). When she returns, the mother brings with her several food items and gifts.

An interesting ritual takes place when a mother from a journey intends to breastfeed the child. In olden times, she would bring with her some star grass which she chewed and spat into the child's mouth. She then squeezed her tits in turn, making sure the spurting milk goes past the child like a loop. This last practice is still observed today. It is a form of cleansing, i.e. the mother is expelling whatever evil she might have picked from outside before feeding the child.

Leisure

The Luo's love for entertainment is especially their love for music and dance. This love of leisure and pleasure is not quite unrelated to the fact that the Luo have a strong traditional culture of entertainment encompassing many indoor and outdoor activities.

While now they are known to enjoy disco music, in the past, the community had its sources of music and traditions of using it. Some of this persists to date, especially in the rural community. A lot of it has also become commercial, like itinerant *nyatiti* players who pitch tent wherever patrons wish for entertainment and are ready to pay for it.

Luoland has also produced some of the best modern musicians in Kenya with names like Ochieng' Kabaselleh, Owino Misiani, Okach Biggy, Ochieng' Nelly, Collela Mazee, Orwa Jasolo, George Ramogi, Awino Lawi, Princess Jully and Osito Kalle. The chapter on poetry presents some pieces of *nyatiti* and modern music.

The premier Luo music instrument is the *nyatiti*, a lyre of eight strings converging inside a hide resonator, all housed in a trapezoid wooden frame. The *nyatiti* player is invited to all important ceremonies like marriage, visits, funerals or any other significant event. The *nyatiti* player can be a solo artist, but is usually accompanied by at least one assistant. The assistant carries the instruments but is also the chorus singer. In latter-day *nyatiti* music, many other accoutrements are added like jingles, drums, *ongeng'o* (a metallic ring percussion) and the ringed soda bottle. It is also common to see *nyatiti* players with troupes of dancers, usually female, swirling sisal skirts and shaking their shoulders in the vigorous *otenga* dance.

When a *nyatiti* player is in the village, many people come to witness, dance and socialise. In the process, the *nyatiti* player earns something. In typical style, a *nyatiti* player responds to requests by his audience. If one person is happy with a particular piece, he/she has the right to stop the player and ask him to repeat the number. But he has to make this request with payment to the player. This payment is today made in cash. But in the past, items like chickens and hoes were used. One can also just stop the player to praise himself or herself. The rule still obtains that the player must be tipped. In this case, the *nyatiti* occasion becomes not just a musical session *per se*, but an integrated socialisation process where people announce their virtues and get to learn the art of *nyadhi*, ceremoniousness, a highly valued personal trait.

Other traditional musical instruments include *bu* (horns), *ohangla* (a long drum made from monitor skin), *orutu* (a small stringed instrument), *bul* (drums), *gara* (jingles) *and asilili* (the flute).

Beer drinking is also a great traditional pastime among the Luo. Hardly any ceremony or important gathering of elders goes without beer drinking.

The Luo traditional beer is called *otia*, what is now commonly called *busaa*. It is brewed from sorghum flour that is fermented, sun-dried, cooked and fermented again before it is strained and warmed for drinking. The eldest person in the group is first to taste the drink before passing it on to the others in a calabash or the *oseke* straw.

Traditionally, old men drink the brew from a communal pot into which each of them immerses his straw. As with the other eating activities, this practice of drawing from one source emphasises brotherhood and trust. This is still observed even at drinking occasions today where the straw has been replaced with tin cups which drinkers still pass round to their colleagues asking them to *bil dhoga*, taste my mouth. The tradition requires that whoever is passing on the drink must use their right hand just like whoever is handling a straw must use the right hand. This is regarded as the hand of strength and rectitude so that even left-handed children are categorically trained to use their right hands in greeting people and eating.

The other type of beer is called *mbare*, made from finger millet flour. Unlike *otia*, it is not cooked after fermentation, but just dried and re-fermented.

Beer drinking is mainly a male pastime. But traditionally, the old men go for a beer drinking party with the eldest wife and the old sons. Monogamous men sit closest to the door while polygamous ones sit further inside the room. The logic of this is rather amusing: that monogamous men are likely to upset the beer pot and break the straws if they sit inside and receive some bad news like the death of the wife. The polygamous ones, on the other hand, would first ask which wife before they make any move. It is believed that breaking a beer pot and the straws is an abomination.

At times, an old man only requires to confer with his family or a close friend. Then he asks his wife to make some beer for just the little group. This beer is called *aput,* meaning "small beer" and its consumption is not announced to the whole village.

Beer drinking is often complemented with music and dance by both men and women. Two poems in this anthology "Alcohol Forever" and "The Strainer Goes Jawajawa" are samples of such music.

A third major leisure activity is playing *ajua.* This is a game involving the use of pebble-like oval seeds which are juggled by players on a wooden board with some sixteen holes, eight a side. Into each hole goes three of the seeds, but the number changes once the game gets underway. If a player wins against the opponent in five straight games, he is labelled *ondiek* (a beast). If he beats the opponent a sixth time, the opponent is said to have died and someone else joins the game. When the seeds are configured in different ways, they are called by certain special names. At such points, the winning player praises himself loudly citing his friends and his virtues.

Other leisure activities included wrestling, bhang smoking, pipe smoking and *adhula* (some kind of hockey). Children also have their games and exercises including music, athletics and banter.

Death

In Luo tradition, an elder is expected to die either very early in the morning or late in the evening. A death during the day is not publicly announced by the family until evening. This is the time the eldest wife bursts out wailing and tearing off her clothes. Only after she has done this can the younger wives mourn. The significance of the tearing of clothes is that they are mourning their benefactor or in Luo parlance, the person who dressed them.

The next day, wives and son's smear themselves with dust, with the latter having to go and perform the mock fight with death and expulsion of evil spirits in the ceremony called *tero buru.* In classical Luo tradition, the *tero buru* was performed before burial. But today, this tradition has largely changed and *tero buru* is done even several months or years after the burial.

On such a day, all the cattle in the homestead and the village are collected and taken to graze in the wilderness by the sons and other young men in the village who decorate themselves with leaves, tendrils and dust. They carry clubs, spears and other weaponry as well as whistles. The return is a stampede punctuated by his club dirges, dance and *sira*, a mock fight with death where the mourner enacts spearing or clubbing death. This person runs helter-skelter, chanting and wielding the weapon in a very aggressive fashion. The women meet the *buru* team at the gate and accompany them into the homestead singing their dirges and doing the *sira* in their own fashion.

In times past, Luos used to bury their dead inside their houses. The elder's grave would be dug in the middle of the eldest wife's hut where the body would be laid after being washed by his sisters-in-law. The family members, in order of seniority, throw soil into the grave. But the man's daughters, who are already married, throw their soil afterwards and with their backs turned to the grave. The grave is covered, then there is loud wailing. That night, all members of the family stay in the first wife's hut as a final farewell to the patriarch.

On the third day after the burial, a sporting day is held where traditional games and warfare is practised by young men. Women sing satirical songs and there is generally an atmosphere of freedom, with young men and women meeting their lovers and peers. This is the day, also, when the bereaved family is shaved. The shaving is some form of cleansing from the death and is a practice that is still strong in many Luo families today. In some families, however, the practice has been modified so that instead of clearing all the hair, only a bit of it is cut, usually on the fringes of the head.

Traditionally, the morning of the third day will see a paternal cousin to the deceased remove one of the pillars of the eldest wife's house and give it to women, girls and unmarried men to carry out of the homestead. On their return, they are assembled and escorted outside the homestead by the eldest son who, however, does not step out of the gate. He leaves them out there being shaved by an elderly woman. He returns and, together with the married sons, is shaved within the homestead. When the shaving is over, the eldest son goes for those who were being shaved outside the home. They assemble and have their heads striped with millet flour. A he-goat is brought and all family members hit it with their knees. This goat is then strangled and slaughtered. The meat is cooked by the barber woman. All this time, the mourning family is dressed in leaves and tendrils.

On the morning of the fourth day, the family members leave for the stream at dawn to wash themselves and cast away the dirt of death. They remove their leaves and tendrils and bury them in the water. On their return, the barber smears their necks with simsim oil and they are fed on the head of the he-goat after they have warmed themselves round a fresh fire on a new hearth. Each person is then adorned with a sisal string around the neck to show they are in mourning. The wife on this day starts wearing the deceased's coat until the mourning is over, usually after a year. The grave is also cleared of pebbles, clods, sticks and whatever else in what is called *yweyo liel*, cleaning the grave. This is a task carried out by the eldest sister-in-law of the deceased.

A critical element in Luo mourning is that in the days leading to the shaving, no food is cooked in the home of the deceased. In fact, it is said that no smoke should emanate from that homestead. Instead, the villagers condole with the family by bringing food to feed the family and the mourners. This is in sharp contrast to what happens today in Luo funerals where it is the bereaved family that is loaded with the task of feeding mourners.

On the fourth day, the elderly woman who has been officiating at the mourning activities "teaches" the wives household chores. It is not that they did not know how to do things. Rather, it is a ceremony of re-launching them in their ordinary lives.

In order to signify the death of the male homestead owner, the pointed stick at the top of the traditional huts is broken in each of the deceased's huts. This is a task done by the deceased's grandchild. He is rewarded with a chicken for the task. The sticks are broken before any member of the deceased's family has left. Today, where iron sheets have replaced grass thatch roofing, those who still observe the practice will remove one of the sheets. For women, one of the stones of the hearth is removed.

When the mourning ends, each of the widows brews beer. The eldest widow serves a bit of it to elders who begin deliberating on how the widows will be inherited. Each widow mentions to the eldest the man she hopes will inherit her. The eldest widow is the one who discloses this to the elders. The appointed men are summoned to the meeting and assigned the task. The consummation of the inheritance is met, the next day, with celebration and beer drinking. The person who broke the sticks returns and erects new ones. Mourning officially ends.

Women go back to normal attire and discard the husband's coats. This is the time the first son of the deceased assumes leadership of the homestead, symbolised by having him wear his father's clothes. He is counselled and officially announced to the rest of the family as the head of the homestead.

Not anyone can inherit a widow. It must be a man who, by lineage, is either a brother or a cousin to the deceased and must be younger than the deceased. An inheritor stays with the widow and carries out all the tasks required of a husband. Traditionally he would only move and establish a new home for the widow if there is acrimony in the homestead. Legally, however, the woman and the children from the new union belong to the deceased.

The death of a woman is also given serious treatment and has certain unique practices. The widower has to sleep in the deceased's hut until he dreams that the two of them have had sexual congress. Only then can he stay in the hut of another wife. He does not go back to the hut of the deceased and it is abandoned and left to fall. If the man has only one wife, he has to put up a makeshift structure in which he stays before marrying another woman. He could get this wife through two means. One, he could be provided with a younger sister or cousin to his dead wife. Two, he could get another woman on his own.

Chapter 2

RIDDLES

Introduction

Riddles are called *ngeche* in Dholuo (or *ngero* in singular). The broad meaning of the term *ngero*, however, is any statement or story that has an indirect meaning. It is used to refer to proverbs, parables, allegories, allusions, etc.

The riddle is a very short art form, and very many riddles can be exchanged during each session. Popular riddles are, therefore, frequently repeated. This does not limit the stock of riddles, however. On the contrary, new riddles are coined every day from observations of the environment. The coinage may be based on a new concept in the environment or on a new perception of a common concept. This explains the occurrence of riddles on cups, trains and latter-day utensils as well as those on the egg, for example. Let us look at the following random examples:

CHALLENGE: *Awino jaswa wach.*
Awino the reporter.

RESPONSE: *Nainai.*
Nine-nine (the police van).

This riddle attests to the fact that new concepts in the environment are easily assimilated in folklore. The police van, for example, is likened to the child, Awino, who reports her siblings' misdeeds to the parents. The van's siren is universally understood as a sign of emergency and, therefore, acts as a "reporter".

New riddles are also introduced through the "one to many" or the "many to one" formula. In the former case, one riddle has many acceptable answers as in the example below.

CHALLENGE: *Ding' didi di didi ding' didi*

RESPONSE: 1.   *Wach mandas momiyo opad lemba.*
Because of buns, my cheeks have been slapped.

RESPONSE: 2.   *Dhiang' marateng' manyiedho chak marachar.*
                    The black cow that produces white milk.

And the "many to one" formula may be exemplified by the following riddles.

1. *Adundo hung'unyang'unya Adundo keyo*
   Adundo is l busy, Adundo is harvesting.
2. *Dana luorore e agoche.*
   My grandmother is plodding around her verandah.
3. *Nyanyuok adundo kwayo e got Abom.*
   A hefty kid grazing on Abom Hill.
4. *Polis pangre edho siruari.*
   Police matching along the hem of the shorts.
5. *Seke seke tiend odundu.*
   "Seke seke" under the reeds.

To all these riddles, the answer is 'Lice'.

Riddles are also adapted from the places children go to stay with their relatives, such as uncles and maternal grandmothers. While there, they interact with their peers and gather riddles which they disseminate among their peers on returning home. Narratives and songs, too, are transferred in a similar way. This explains the similarities in the corpus of oral literature material from different regions of Luoland.

Conventions and performance

Riddles are performed in the *Siwindhe* just before the narratives are told. This is not because riddles are inferior. Rather, they introduce concepts which are dealt with in narratives and identify objects which play significant roles as narrative characters.

Luo riddles are delivered as statements, questions or sounds. Riddling usually takes place in the evening at the mother's or grandmother's hut. They may be performed as a warm-up activity to narratives. They also are, however, an autonomous activity on their own. This is particularly so among the pre-puberty youth who often riddle while performing chores or playing.

A riddling session requires at least two participants: one to present the puzzle and the other to attempt solving it. The first party announces the coming of the riddle with the word, *"Mnaye"*. The respondents signal their readiness by saying, *"Kwithe"*.

Shadrack Malo in *Sigend Luo Maduogo Chuny*, says *"mnaye"* means "an enigma" while *"kwithe"* means "set your trap". But Adrian Roscoe and Onyango-Ogutu in *Keep My Words*, say the words mean "Ready?" and "Yes, ready"

21

respectively. These two versions agree on one point: that the first word, *"Mnaye"*, cues the respondents to expect a riddle, and the second, *"Kwithe"*, confirms that readiness.

After the introductory formula, the challenger poses the riddle and the second party suggests the answer. The answer may be accepted if it is right or rejected if wrong. The rejection may go on for as long as the respondents do not get the correct response and want to keep trying. Once they concede defeat, however, the challenger has to offer the solution. And this is done at a cost. If the challenger is a boy, he may ask to be "given" a girl (bride). A girl may ask for a boy (groom), with the idea of a mock marriage being implied. The defeated respondents name their choices first from girls and boys in the village and then even from those further afield known to the challenger. These offers are either rejected or accepted depending on their social acceptability.

This could turn into another game within the riddling one. In order to tease the challenger, the respondents will normally suggest choices he/she will reject to exasperate him or her. This is a test of patience and tolerance. In order to outwit the teasers, the challenger will reject all those proposed until the desired or model person is named.

The challenger then gives the answer and another person poses a new riddle. The person to pose the next riddle can be determined either by the chronological arrangement on the sleeping mat or by who shouts the opening formula first after a challenger is through. The game can go on until the end of the chore, or the play session, or until the riddlers fall asleep, if it is not at the onset of narration.

Stylistic aspects

Structure

Like all short literary forms, Luo riddles are characterised by brevity, so that we have riddles consisting of just one or two words such as:

1. *Mabul* (Umbrella): *Obwolo* (Mushroom).

2. *Kuom lowo* (The earth's hump): *Liel* (An anthill).

3. *Pap adundo* (A tiny field): *Simon* (A fifty-cents coin).

Another structural element of Luo riddles is parallelism, the presentation of balancing parts in the same riddle. An apt example is the riddle:

Adundo hung'unya Adundo keyo.
Adundo is busy, Adundo is harvesting

The first part of the riddle is *Adundo hung'unya* (Adundo is busy) which is some kind of preamble to the declaration of what Adundo is busy doing, which is harvesting. The answer to the riddle is a louse on the head. In which case, variation in the second part presents a totally different case and answer. In fact, there is another proverb *Adundo hung'unya Adundo chweko* (Adundo is 2busy, Adundo is cooking) to which the answer is a burning fire.

Thirdly, it will be noticed that most Luo riddles are expressed as statements of description and hence fall into the class of riddles referred to as *declaratives*. The puzzle in such riddles is implied rather than directly asked for. The above examples conform to this model.

However, there are instances where the riddles are explicit questions and are expressed in the interrogative mode such as in the following:

Agulu ma ok luok iye ni?
Which is this pot whose inside is never washed?

Ich.
The stomach.

Lwang'ni motho e chak ni to en ang'o?
Which is this fly that has died in the milk?

Chiero.
A diseased eye.

Finally, there are epigrammatic riddles, those which correspond syllabically or numerically and present a series of puzzles. A very good example is the riddle:

Nyatiende ang'wen mobet ewi nyatiende ang'wen karito nyatiende ang'wen.
The four-legged sitting on the four-legged waiting for the four-legged.

The focus here is on the number four which characterises different objects and presents some sense of unity and similarity in them. The four objects referred to are the cat sitting on a table waiting for a rat.

Imagery

Essentially, all Luo riddles are metaphors in which one reality is referred to in veiled terms and needs decoding. In majority of cases, the reference is to some physical or behavioural characteristic of what is referred to. For instance, the riddle *Mabul* (Umbrella) makes us imagine the physical structure of the umbrella as well as its function. Logically, we begin to think of items that ressemble the umbrella physically or that fulfil the same functions as it does. Could the answer be a tree, a hat or a bat? Well, the answer is a mushroom. The trick here is in the

23

physical resemblance, especially the one stem of the mushroom plant that makes it more similar to the umbrella than all the other possibilities we could think of.

In some cases, the metaphor is less physically comparative. There is the case of the riddle:

Abolo tong' nyaka loka cha
I have thrown a spear yonder.

Throwing a spear is a physical action but what is referred to is not similarly physical, because the answer is: 'I have swallowed *ugali* into the stomach'. The bolus of *ugali* is referred to as a spear yet the two do not have any physical resemblance, unless we want to see the act of eating as some kind of warfare. Anyhow, when we think of yonder, we also imagine some remarkable physical separation between the one throwing the spear and its destination. In our answer, however, the thrower and the destination are the same. Yet when we hear the answer, it does not only strike us as apt, it is also quite interesting. Which is to say that the references and referents are not so obvious, hence the beauty of riddles.

Even more abstract is this riddle:

Asere mogoyo bungu pile
The ever bushy arrow.

Again, we begin to think of some kind of projectile article. And the riddle challenges us even more when it talks of a bushy arrow. We probably begin to think that the bow is meant rather than the arrow. But when we get the answer, how fascinating it is: the eye. But why should the eye be analogised as an arrow? Well, have we never heard of piercing eyes? Even if we have not, the eye, by the fact that it can see far, resembles the arrow that travels far once thrown. In fact, in Luo language, one can throw his or her eye towards a place. But what about the bush element? We are here referring to the eyelashes which, as it were, form a cordon around the eye.

Incidentally, the question of the bow is not totally irrelevant to this puzzle. When placed horizontally, the traditional Luo bow has a shape which not only resembles the eye socket but even that of the eyelids. If one is not quite familiar with such articles, logically working out the answer to such a riddle is difficult.

Immediacy of derivation and reference

The discussion of the metaphor brings us to another stylistic element: that the riddle derives its imagery from the immediate environment of the parent community, in this case the Luo. The environment here can be physical, political, socio-

24

economic or experiential. This means that by studying the Luo riddles, one is able to develop a clear picture of the community's environment. A look through the riddles listed in this anthology will, for instance, acquaint us with Luo utensils, plants and animals, foods, style of cooking, human physiology, traditional chores, interaction with neighbouring communities, awareness of the cosmic environment, geographical features, weapons, behaviour and so on. Elements of this are covered in the discussion of allusion below.

The immediacy of reference is also illustrated in the fact that the riddles are personalised and personified by the presenter. It will be noticed that most riddles begin with "I" or "My" if not reference to an old man or some other kind of personality. This makes riddling an intimate activity in which people see themselves in oneness with the occasion, activity and one another. They are part and parcel of the environment and their experiences. And the art is theirs too.

Allusion

Many Luo riddles refer to some factual or imaginary people, objects or experiences. There is the riddle *Adundo miel to ifuke* (Adundo dances and she is rewarded), to which the answer is the burning fire (which is fed with firewood as it burns, metaphorised here as dancing). The allusion here would not be obvious to someone not familiar with Luo social behaviour, especially in dancing contexts. Traditionally, a dancer or musician is presented with money or other tokens, first as an appreciation of a job well done, and second, to induce him or her to continue. This is regarded as a crucial practice in what is called *nyadhi* (ceremoniousness). Musicians in Luoland often play at occasions which last the whole night. A person wishing to reward the musician or dancer would actually also praise himself or herself before offering the reward and asking that the music continue. In order to make the night shorter, so to speak, such drama is inevitable. So this is a riddle which refers to a deeply rooted cultural practice.

An example of a historical allusion comes in the proverb *Akadho ka mond Mumia dhaw* (I passed when Mumia's wives were quarrelling). The answer to this is *Osogo* (Weaverbirds). Nabongo Mumia was a famous administrator in the colonial history of the Wanga of western Kenya who neighbour the Luo. He was, as such leaders were, polygamous. To that extent, the riddle presents a historical reality. But whether his wives were known to be quarrelsome or not is something we might not want to vouch for although squabbles in a polygamy are not rare. Mumia is given another mention in the riddle, *Akadho ka mond Mumia yach duto* (I passed when all Mumia's wives were pregnant) to which the answer is: millet heads. Again we do not really want to get into the question of Mumia's virility.

25

A number of the riddles in this anthology refer to policemen and soldiers, places in Luoland (like Kisumu), the coming of western utensils and even colonialism.

Humour

The humour in Luo riddles is inherent in the surprise element of the references and, in some cases, in the veiled satire as well as the bold references to some taboo subjects. Thus, it is difficult to appreciate it in translation and is best in the original language as well as during performance. Examples of humorous Luo riddles are explained below.

> *Gunda ma ibeto ka ji obet piny.*
> A bush cleared while people are sitting down.

In the first place, it is ridiculous for anyone, leave alone a group of people, to clear a bush while sitting down. This is a clear demonstration of laziness. But the real humour comes out when we hear the answer (Eating ugali) which is as surprising as it is graphical. In Luo culture, eating is often a communal activity in which people share the starch from the same plate. The manner of harvesting the *ugali* from the plate is quite like cutting a bush, and in this case, by people sitting down!

Well, the result of gorging, as could be implied in the above riddle, is eventually excretion. And a number of Luo riddles inlaid with humour talk about nothing else but excreta. For example:

> *Ndii nyadundo odonjo e pap.*
> *Ndii!* The short one has entered the field.

On the surface, the entry of the short one is presented as triumphant and one would probably expect the answer to refer to some outstanding athlete whose entry often heralds victory. The answer to the riddle is: a fly has landed on excreta. In an actual performance, this answer is greeted with immediate grunts followed with chuckles because of its graphic anti-climax.

Away from excreta is another riddle with a derisive undertone:

> *Nyar msungu ni e ofis.*
> The white lady is in the office.

This of course is an allusive riddle to the interaction of the community with white people and the culture of office work. But just what could this white lady in the office be? Our first impression is that it must be something important. But when we hear the answer, we are struck by the reverse importance of the reference, in this case, the jigger. While this answer would draw some grins, it also has a message about the Luo perception of colonialism: it was foreign, uninvited, parasitic

26

and a nuisance, which is what the jigger is to the host body. Finally, a look at this favourite humourous riddle:

Piny rach ka koth ochwe.
The earth is ugly when it rains.

The answer to this is: *Jawuoro rach ka taya otho* (The glutton is dangerous, or bad news, when the lights go off/in darkness).

Mnemonics

As oral art, Luo riddles employ sound effects, often in the form of ideophones, for efficacy. These are riddles in which the meaning intended is carried by sound in expressions which are otherwise not semantic at all. In the riddle *Cheke cheke chaluka*, for instance, the riddle imitates the sound of a foot-operated sewing machine. In what is essentially the same riddle except for one sound *(chalula* instead of *chaluka)*, the answer is the sound of a match stick. The difference is that the "k" sound is fricative hence resembles the mechanical movement of the sewing machine while the sound "l" is a lateral sound simulating the continuous sound of a match stick struck into a flame.

One major contribution of mnemonics to art is the creation of a rhythm. This is evident in many Luo riddles. This is not to say that some riddles are not rhythmic. Rather, it is to say that some riddles have more pronounced rhythmic patterns than others because of the way they are structured and the sound patterns they employ. A good example is the ideophonic riddle *Ding' didi di di di ding' didi* which simulates the phrases *Wach mandas momiyo opad lemba* (It is because of buns that my cheeks were slapped) or *Dhiang' ma rateng' manyiedho chak ma rachar* (A black cow which produces white milk). The riddle is actually presented as a metered form, a semi-musical. There is in this riddle direct syllabic correspondence between the riddle and the response. This correspondence is also seen in other epigrammatic riddles.

Parallelism also contributes to the rhythm of riddles as does diction. In the latter case, a riddle that comes to mind is *Osiki kidienya* (A distended stump) to which the answer is *Dhako ma yach* (A pregnant woman). There is an interplay here of assonance and alliteration of "i" and "k" in the two words which also contribute to the rhythm of the piece. But there is also the choice of the word *"kidienya"* which is some kind of coinage. In prosaic parlance people would say *"Osiki modienyre"*. The word *"kidienya"* adds an extra poetic flavour to the ordinary meaning and insinuates that distendedness is inalienable from a pregnant woman. In fact, it moves the word *"dienyruok"* from being a verb to being a noun.

Social functions of riddles

The most important social function of riddles are: socialisation, enhancing memory and education.

Socialisation

Riddles are mainly told among children. They are a very important socialisation tool. They entertain and fit the youth into the normative patterns of the society.

The entertainment value of riddles arises from the variety of objects they refer to, the perspectives from which they are viewed and the inherent humour in them. Let us look at a few examples.

RIDDLE: *Agulu mak luok iye.*
                A pot whose inside is never washed.

ANSWER: *Ich.*
                The stomach.

RIDDLE: *Kar mang'ich moting'o "Hallo Madame"*
                The sleek car carrying "Hallo Madame".

ANSWER: *Chak mawach mogoyo nyambura gi diep.*
                Sour milk which has stricken the cat with diarrhoea.

In the first riddle, the stomach is perceived as a pot that is never washed. Analogically, the stomach is actually a food container, like the pot. Moreso, it is as good a cooking pot as the earthen ones, its cooking process being digestion. The assertion that it is never washed acknowledges its self-sufficiency as far as cleansing is concerned and, therefore, stands above the everyday pot we know. This is not only a fresh view of the stomach but is also a scientific one.

The second riddle is a phonological one in which the sound pattern of the puzzle is repeated in the answer. A sleek car is supposed to be safe and enviable. Ironically, though, the one in the riddle is quite the reverse. One imagines a cat joyfully drinking sour milk only to be rewarded with an attack of diarrhoea! What the riddle could be saying deviously is that appearances can be quite deceiving, but that is after sparking off the laughter.

Riddling, being a group activity, is socialising. The youth learn to relate to each other as doers and receivers. As challengers, they are the initiators of action to test others' wits. But as recipients, their wits are also being tried. The whole activity is, therefore, both inclusive and reciprocal. It demands humility and acquiescence to certain rules. For instance, everyone who poses a riddle must start with a formula. This is a mark and practice of discipline and adherence to social norms.

The offer of a prize to the challenger whose riddle has not been solved also has social value. Prize-giving is a recognition of prodigy and motivates people to excel by coming up with their own riddles. The challenger's refusals of prize offers indicates the value of choice in the community and emphasises patience in the pursuit of goals. The rejection of the prizes is the challenger's statement about what is admired and what is loathed. Such tastes are closely modelled on the tastes of the society itself. Thus, a male challenger will usually reject those girls known to be ugly in appearance, careless, lazy, rude or clumsy in managing their affairs. The female challenger, on the other hand, will refuse boys perceived to be weaklings, cowards, lazy or glutton. Through this, the youth get to appreciate the social norms and aspects of behaviour that are valued and those that are despised. Riddling, therefore, acts as an outlet for those actions that could be disruptive to family life.

In some instances, the themes of the riddles are direct commentaries on life and behaviour. For example:

CHALLENGER: *Machunga ochiek dalawa to onge ng'ama pon.*
There are ripe oranges at our home but no one to pick them.

RESPONDENTS: *Nyiri opong' dalawa to onge ng'ama kendi.*
There are mature girls at our home but no one to marry them.

This riddle makes an important comment on the Luo view of marriage. It laments that a mature girl (of marriageable age) apparently has no suitors. Like the oranges would rot after ripeness, those past their prime for marriage are likely to end up marrying either old men or polygamists. But more importantly, the riddle is asking why these girls have not yet got their matches. Is it that they are not attractive enough or that they are too attractive and therefore frighten off potential suitors? Could the girls be the vain types that reject every offer, waiting for the perfect man? Are they conscious that they are passing their prime or are they just disillusioned with the institution of marriage and choose to ignore it? If the latter is the case, then what is their future in a society which expects them to marry and stay at their husbands' homes?

When this riddle was thrown during a family gathering, there was very knowing laughter from everyone except from the affected girls. The riddle was offered by a boy of about six years, in the presence of his parents and two sisters of marriageable age who were still at their maiden home. The boy was probably voicing the whole family's concern about the fate of the girls, whose agemates had all been married.

Enhancing memory

Riddles also enhance memory. To a large extent, riddles have fixed answers which are memorised and reproduced whenever the particular riddle features.

Unless the answer is obviously off the mark, there is usually little debate about the rationality of the response. This is because many in the group already know the riddle or that the answer offered is self-explanatory.

Education

Riddles are, however, mostly rational. Decoding them reveals that their language is very figurative. The challenges are coined after careful observation of the environment. From this observation are abstracted those distinctive features that characterise an object or concept. For example, the gizzard is peculiarised as *"Gima piene ni iye to ringe ni oko"* (That whose skin is inside but its meat is outside). Indeed, the inner lining of the gizzard is cartilaginous while the outer layer is of softer tissue. This contrasts with the norm where the harder skin is outside to protect the more delicate tissues inside. Riddles also enhance the power of observation of objects in the environment.

The statement of riddles as analogies form a forum for aiding human understanding of the hidden nature of a cultural or natural phenomenon. In this sense, the riddle compares a phenomenon with an object whose nature is better known. Thus, we get, for example, the following riddles about the mushroom.

1. *Jakondo marachar ma koth goyo.*
   The wearer of the white hat who is being rained on.
2. *Jodongo morwako lep rachare.*
   Old men wearing white clothes.
3. *Jodongo mosidho simwata.*
   Old men wearing "simwata" caps.
4. *Mabul.*
   Umbrella.
5. *Ot moger gi yath achiel.*
   A house built on one pole.

All of these riddles focus on either the colour or configuration of the mushroom. Of importance also is the reference to the mushroom as an old man. This probably arises from the "composure" of the mushroom which parallels that of old men.

In conclusion, riddles form a very important facility among the Luo. They entertain, socialise, stimulate the mind and enhance understanding of phenomena. They train the memory, facilitate language use and give a commentary on life.

A Collection of Luo riddles

1. *Abolo tong' nyaka loka cha.*
I have thrown the spear yonder.

   Amuonyo kuon nyaka eich.
I have swallowed *ugali* into the stomach.

2. *Adonj e bungu atur kete ariyo.*
I enter the bush and break two sticks.

   Diel ogo rude.
A goat has given birth to twins.

3. *Adundo girigiri Adundo girigiri.*
Adundo girigiri Adundo girigiri.

   Kit jajuok.
The wizard's stone.

4. *Adundo humo Nyang'unya .*
Adundo is calling Nyang'unya loudly.

   Kulundeng'.
The beetle.

5. *Adundo hung'unyang'unya Adundo chweko*
Adundo is busy, Adundo is cooking.

   Mach liel.
The fire is burning.

6. *Adundo hung'unya Adundo keyo*
Adundo is busy, Adundo is harvesting.

   Onyuogo.
The louse.

7. *Adundo miel to ifuke*
Adundo dances and she is rewarded.

   Mach.
Fire.

8. *Ago del ugwe, ago del imbo.*
I crack the whip in the east, I crack the whip in the west.

   Ndara.
The road.

9. *Ago tang' to atipo.*
I say "*tang*" and I say "*tipo*".

   Apoko njugu to amuodo.
I break open the pod and eat groundnuts.

10. *Agulu mak luok iyeni?*
Which is this pot whose inside is never washed?

    Ich.
The stomach.

11. *Aidh yath kamako tik nyuoga.*
I climb the tree while holding my billygoat's beard.

    Le.
An axe.

12. *Aidh yath to gagi luar.*
I climb the tree as the divination beads fall.

    Olaw.
Saliva.

13. *Akadho ka mond Mumia dhaw.*
I passed when Mumia's wives were quarrelling.

    Osogo.
Weaverbirds.

14. *Akadho ka mond Mumia yach duto.*
I passed when all Mumia's wives **were pregnant.**
Bel.
Millet heads.

15. *Aloo gi Oguna.*
Aloo and Oguna.
Wang'chieng' gi dwe.
The sun and the moon.

16. *An gi onget ma ok two.*
I have a blanket that never dries.
Lep.
The tongue.

17. *Antie e dhogi to ok inyal muonya.*
I am in your mouth but you cannot swallow me.
Lep.
The tongue.

18. *Aonge giko.*
I have no end.
Piny.
The earth (world).

19. *Aora mak dwon.*
A river that never dries.
Pi wang'.
Tears.

20. *Apuoyo matin modak e kind kite*
The small hare living amongst stones.
Lep.
The tongue.

21. *Aring aring adhi ka nera.*
I run and run going to my uncle's home.
Oywo.
The caterpillar.

22. *Aromo gi dana ka tonyore.*
I met my grandmother swaggering.
Oywo.
The caterpillar.

23. *Asere mogoyo bungu pile*
The ever bushy arrow.
Wang'.
The eye.

24. *Askach oyundi.*
The robin's guard.
Pino.
The wasp.

25. *Askache ariyo mochung' gi bunde.*
Two armed soldiers standing guard.
Thomorno.
Brown soldier ants.

26. *Askari man e jela to mor luongo jowadgi.*
An imprisoned policeman happily calling his fellows.
Aluru.
A quail.*

27. *Askari ma pangore e mudho.*
A policeman (soldier) marching in the dark.
Jajwok.
The wizard/night runner.

---

*This riddle is derived from the Luo practice of trapping quails. A trapper cages some quails and stands them on a tall pole from which they sing and attract other quails. At the bottom of the pole are baits and snares for trapping the new arrivals.

28. *Askari moruowo dhi ka lweny.*
Soldiers marching to war.

Olang'o.
Black soldier ants.

29. *Askeche morwako ogute marakwar.*
Police wearing red caps.

Okoko.
Soldier termites.

30. *Awino jaswa wach.*
Awino the reporter.

Nai-nai.
The police 999 car.

31. *Awuotho, aring aringi kinde duto.*
I walk, run and run perpetually.

Pi.
Water.

32. *Baranged mama ok ban.*
My mother's blanket is not folded.

Polo.
The sky.

33. *Bor ma leny e kinde duto.*
An ever shining morsel.

Um guok.
The dog's muzzle.

34. *Bunde joka oyieyo*
The rat family's gun.

Kibrit
Matches.

35. *Bungu ma ataro oyie diere.*
The forest surrounded by a lake.

Tong wang'.
The eyeball.

36. *Bungu ma dongo gi oro*
A bush that grows even during
drought.

Yie wich.
Hair on the head.

37. *Bungu matin to le odakie*
A small bush inhabited by wild
animals.

Wich.
The head.

38. *Bungu mibeto to ok rum.*
A bush that is cleared but it never
gets finished.

Yie wich.
Hair on the head.

39. *Bur mayot witoe kidi kata gi
mudho.*
A hole which is easy to target
with a stone even in darkness.

Dhok.
The mouth.

40. *Bura mochok a tiend lwanda.*
A meeting under a rock.

Yie tik.
The beard.

41. *Bwoywe modhuro edho nam.*
"Bwoywe" grass in abundance at
the lakeshore.

Yie wang'.
Eyelashes.

42. *Cheke cheke chaluka.*
Cheke cheke chaluka.

Charan.
The sewing machine.

43. *Cheke cheke chalula.*
Cheke cheke chalula.

Kibrit.
Match sticks.

44. *Chiemo irenjago to onge kaka achak chame.*
You have given me food but there is no way I can start eating it.
Pany.
The mortar.

45. *Chogo gi kado.*
A bone and soup.
Chieth gi lach.
Stool and urine.

46. *Dak ma malo oromo gi ma mwalo.*
The big pot from the parents' quarters has met the one from the son's quarters.
Jakuo gi jajwok.
A thief and a night-runner.

47. *Dani moguom a kendo cha.*
That grandmother of yours squatting on the fire.
Agulu.
The cooking pot.

48. *Dapi ma kata pi opong'o to ok pukre.*
A water pot that does not spill, however full it is.
Thund dhiang'.
A cow's udder.

49. *Dapi malando ongoro.*
The conspicuous brown water pot.
Wang'chieng'.
The sun.

50. *Dapi moting'o pi eiye to onge dhoge.*
A pot which contains water but has no mouth.
Tong'.
The egg.

51. *Dhako mang'eny gi piende to pielo nyithindo e lo.*
A woman with many bedclothes but lays her children on the bare ground.
Budho.
The pumpkin.

52. *Dhako matin to nyuolo nyithindo mang'eny.*
A small woman who gives birth to many children.
Kal.
Finger millet.

53. *Dhano ma wuotho koda kinde duto.*
A person who walks with me all the time.
Tipona.
My shadow.

54. *Dher Onyango tieko pi e soko.*
Onyango's cow/bull is finishing the water in the well.
Kuon.
Ugali.

55. *Dhiang' achiel ma ywayo nyol.*
A single ox pulling a heavy load.
Kulundeng'.
The dung beetle.

56. *Dhok ma silwende moruowo.*
A column of brown oxen.
Thomorno.
Brown soldier ants.

57. *Ding' didi di di di ding' didi.*
Ding' didi di di di ding' didi.
Wach mandas momiyo opad lemba.
It is because of buns that my cheeks have been slapped.

58. *Ding' didi di di di ding' didi.*
    Ding' didi di di di ding' didi.
    Dhiang' ma rateng ma nyiedho
    chak ma rachar.
    A black cow which produces
    white milk.

59. *Duong' dala.*
    The home's essence.

    Duol.
    "*Duol*".*

60. *Gacha ringo e pap.*
    My train running on a plain/field.

    Ogonglo.
    The centipede.

61. *Gik ma miel to ok wuothi.*
    They dance but do not walk.

    Buya.
    Weeds.

62. *Gima chunye lerni.*
    This thing with an open heart.

    Kom.
    The chair.

63. *Gima dongo kata gi oro.*
    It grows even during the drought.

    Yie wich.
    Hair on the head.

64. *Gima iye ring'o to oko chogo.*
    It is meat inside and bone outside.

Tong' gweno.
The egg.

65. *Gima kata ichiel ichiel to wuok*
    awuoka.
    It will escape even if you make a
    fence.

    Ohula.
    Floods/Moving water.

66. *Gima ok bworngago.*
    It is never sojourned with.

    Osimbo.
    The "osimbo" hat.**

67. *Gima ok idhi.*
    It is never climbed.

    Rabolo.
    The banana tree.

68. *Gima piene ni iye ti ringe ni oko.*
    Its skin is inside but the meat is
    outside.

    Adundo.
    The gizzard.

69. *Gima wuok kodenyo to duogo*
    koyieng'.
    That which leaves hungry but
    comes back satisfied.

    Dapi
    The water pot.

70. *Got Akara.*
    "Akara" hill.

---

*Duol is the hut belonging exclusively to the male head of a home. It is a place where he confers with his peers and entertains friends. Male children have their meals at the "duol" with their father.

**Osimbo is a maroon cap with a black tassel at the tip. It was worn in the olden days when one was on an important mission. A person wearing an *osimbo* would never sojourn anywhere until he accomplished his mission.

35

Um.
The nose.*

71. *Gunda mibeto ka ji obet piny.*
A bush which is cleared when
people are sitting.

Kuon.
Ugali.

72. *Guok migoyo to duogo.*
A dog which is beaten but keeps
on returning.

Jakuo.
A thief.

73. *Huchu hwacha.*
Huchu hwacha.

Rabuon gi riga.
A meal of potatoes and blood.

74. *Hurr bup.*
Hurr bup.

Rabote jajuok.
The wizard's stick.

75. *Hurr lokani hurr lokacha.*
"Hurr" this way and "hurr"
yonder.

Jajuok.
The wizard.

76. *Jaduong' ma got otamo idho.*
The old man who cannot climb a
hill.

Rawo.
The hippo.

77. *Jaduong' ma kok gotieno.*
The old man who crows at night.

Ogwal.
The frog.

78. *Jaduong' ma ok we kabut.*
The old man who never leaves
behind an overcoat.

Opuk.
The tortoise.

79. *Jaduong' ma rang'ede.*
The old man with many ribs.

Dero.
The granary.

80. *Jaduong' morito piny.*
The old man governing the world.

Chieng'.
The sun.

81. *Jakondo marachar ma koth goyo.*
The man with a white hat who is
being rained on.

Obwolo.
The mushroom.

82. *Jawer moyiedhi.*
The special singer.

Hundhwe.
The finch.

83. *Jodongo adek ma ka achiel onge
to ok giti.*
Three old men who, when one is
absent, cannot work.

Kit kendo.
The three fire stones.

84. *Jodongo ariyo ma dhi K'Ogelo.*
Two old men going to K'Ogelo.

---

* The nose is personified in this riddle and given a nominal reference. The name *Akara* is
derived from the word *mokarre* meaning "that which is astride". It therefore depicts the
nostrils.

Oyundi.
Robins.

85. *Jodongo ariyo ma gore mba e pap.*
Two old men hitting one another in the field.

Ngeta.
"Ngeta" seeds.*

86. *Jodongo morwako lep rachare.*
The old men dressed in white.

Obuolo.
Mushrooms.

87. *Jodongo mosidho simwata.*
Old men wearing "simwata" caps.

Obuolo.
Mushrooms.

88. *Ka anindo to oneno, to ka aneno to onindo.*
When I am asleep he is awake but when I am awake he is asleep.

Apuoyo.
The hare.**

89. *Kar mang'ich moting'o "hallo madame".*
The sleek car carrying "Hallo madame".

Chak mawach mogo nyambura gi diep.
Sour milk that has stricken the cat with diarrhoea.

90. *Kar mang'ich motingo' wasunge lilo.*
The saloon car carrying whites only.

Pas.
The charcoal iron.

91. *Kidi man e chuny ataro.*
A stone in the middle of an abyss.

Nyarogno.
The kidney.

92. *Kidiehla kidiehla kom janeko.*
"Kidiehla kidiehla", the mad person's chair.

Yiw rombo.
The ram's tail.

93. *Kisiki man e chuny nam.*
A stump in the middle of a lake.

Tong wang'.
The eyeball.

94. *Koring oring to ong'eng'.*
He runs, then forgets and stops.

Njiri.
The warthog.

95. *Kuom lowo.*
The earth's hump.

Got.
A hill.

96. *Laro man e wi got.*
A verandah on a hill.

Bala/Bondo.
The bald head.

97. *Lokacha huch to lokani huch.*
Yonder "huch" and here "huch".

---

*Used by children who spin them on stools to see which one hits the others.

**In Luo mythology, the hare is reputed to be an animal whose eyes remain open when it is asleep as a way of beguiling hunters that it is awake and is seeing them.

Kuon amara gi riga.
"*Kuon amara*" with blood.*

98. *Lwang'ni motho e chakni to en ang'o?*
Which is this housefly that has died in the milk?

Chiero.
A diseased eye.

99. *Mabul.*
Umbrella.

Obuolo.
The mushroom.

100. *Machunga ochiek dalawa to onge ng'ama pon.*
There are ripe oranges in our home but no one to pluck them.

Nyiri opong' dalawa to onge ng'ama kendi.
There are mature girls in our home but no one to marry them.

101. *Machunga ochiek onego pon.*
Oranges are ripe and should be plucked.

Nyiri opong' onego kendi.
Girls are mature and should be married.

102. *Mama ting'a.*
Mother, carry me.

Kitanda.
A bed.

103. *Mil ka opanga ma Kisumo.*
It shines like the iron roofs of

Kisumu.

Bondo.
The bald head.

104. *Ndii nyadundo odonjo e pap.*
"Ndii" the short one has entered the arena.

Lwang'ni opiyo e chieth.
A housefly has landed on excreta.

105. *Ndii nyaka loka cha.*
"Ndii" upto yonder.

Kulundeng'.
The flying beetle.

106. *Nene adhi to aweyogi bang'a.*
I went and left them behind.

Tielo.
Footsteps.

107. *Noike kende to oduogo gi lewni.*
He was buried alone but returned with clothes.

Oduma.
Maize.

108. *Nyako malando man e odu ni.*
This brown girl in your house.

Ko.
The churning gourd.

109. *Nyako ma pende ogomo moa Ulaya.*
The girl who has come from abroad with a bent navel.

Kikombe.

**Kuon amara* is a type of bread made from dried potato tubers mixed with either finger millet, sorghum or the dregs from traditional beer. "Amara" is actually made from rejected potato — that which is not suitable for boiling. Instead of throwing it away, the Luo keep it for use during famine.

The cup.

110. *Nyako motho gi nyodo achiel.*
The maiden who died after giving
birth only once.

Rabolo.
The banana tree.

111. *Nyanyouk adundo kwayo e got
Abom.*
A hefty kid grazing on Abom Hill.

Onyuogo.
A louse.

112. *Nyanyuok adundo maleng'ore.*
The small child gamboling.

Lwang'ni.
The housefly.

113. *Nyar Alego otwe suka.*
The girl from Alego has tied a
"leso".*

Ng'wen.
White ants.

114. *Nyara ma iye odwe.*
My slim-waisted daughter.

Pino.
The wasp.

115. *Nyara ma ka akalo to nyaka
abolne simon.*
Whenever I pass my daughter, I
must drop her a fifty-cents coin.

Chieth.
Excreta.

116. *Nyara ma ka dongdong to twe
msip.*
My daughter who grows and ties
belts.

Niang'.
Sugar cane plant.

117. *Nyara ma ka nyuol to pielo
nyithindo e lo.*
My daughter who gives birth and
lays her children on the ground.

Budho.
The pumpkin.

118. *Nyara ma ka ochung' to chwo polo.*
My daughter who reaches the sky
when standing.

Ndara.
The road.

119. *Nyara malando.*
My brown daughter.

Mbiru/Ko.
The water pot or churning gourd.

120. *Nyara ma timo gimoro amora ma
atimo.*
My daughter who does everything
I do.

Tipo.
The shadow.

121. *Nyara ma tiyo ma onge yweyo.*
My daughter who works without
resting.

Chuny.
The heart.

122. *Nyara ma wuok duk to duogo gi
law.*
My daughter who leaves naked
but returns dressed.

Oduma.
Maize.

Leso is a wide sheet of garment commonly used as headscarf or tied around the waist by
women in East Africa.

123. *Nyara ma wuok kodenyo to duogo koyieng'.*
My daughter who leaves hungry but returns full.

Dapi.
The water pot.

124. *Nyar amila ma leng'ore ni.*
This naughty girl who gambols.

Olaw.
Spittle.

125. *Nyara morwako sude rachar otamba rateng'.*
My daughter who is dressed in a white suit and black headscarf.

Kibrit.
Match sticks.

126. *Nyara morwako sude ma ratenge.*
My daughter wearing a black suit.

Olang'o.
Black soldier ants.

127. *Nyar Lang'o ma iye odwe.*
The thin-waisted Kalenjin girl.

Pino.
The wasp.

128. *Nyar msungu ma iye odwer.*
The white woman with a thin waist.

Pino.
The wasp

129. *Nyar msungu ni e ofis.*
The white lady is in the office.

Mneme.
The jigger.

130. *Nyarwath adundo okalo aora.*
A bullock has crossed the river.

Lwang'ni.
A housefly.

131. *Nyatiende ariyo mobet ewi nyatiende ang'wen karito nyatiende aboro.*
The two-legged sitting on the four-legged waiting for the eight-legged.

Winyo mobet ewi dhiang' karito okwodo.
A bird sitting on a cow waiting for a tick.

132. *Nyatiende ang'wen mobet ewi nyatiende ang'wen karito nyatiende ang'wen.*
The four-legged sitting on the four legged waiting for the four-legged.

Paka mobet ewi mesa karito oyieyo.
A cat sitting on a table waiting for a rat.

133. *Nyatieng' madundo.*
The tiny "nyatieng."*

Oyundi.
The robin.

134. *Nyatieng' maka odir to chopo loka.*
The "nyatieng" which reaches yonder when thrown.

Wang'.
The eye.

135. *Obambo rachoke.*
"Obambo" the bony.**

Nyatieng is a perfectly round stone used for grinding medicinal herbs. It moves with a lot of speed when thrown.

Obambo refers to tilapia fish that has been split exposing the mid rib and then dried.

Pikipiki.
The motorcycle.

136. *Oboke onywolo nyatieng'.*
A leaf has given birth to a stone.

Rabuon.
Potatoes.

137. *Oda man gi dhoudi adek.*
My house with three doors.

Siruari.
Short trousers.

138. *Oda ma onge dhoot.*
My house has no door.

Tong' gweno.
The egg.

139. *Odheche ariyo ma dongo.*
Two huge winnowing trays.

Polo gi piny.
The sky and the earth.

140. *Odi mula odi mula.*
Patched gold, patched gold.

Pat opuk.
The tortoise's shell.

141. *Oduma ochiek; ing'e nadi? igo kogno.*
The maize is ripe; how do you know? You have clawed it.

Nyako opong'; ing'e nadi? Ipenjo wuongo.
A girl is mature; how do know? You have asked the father.

142. *Ogo pap ataro.*
It has established a huge field.

Biech liech.
The elephant's placenta.

143. *Ogundo jamima.*
Ogundo the petulant.

Janeko.
A lunatic.

144. *Oluoro nyaka K'Omulo.*
It goes round to Omulo's home.

Chiel.
The fence.

145. *Ot moger gi yath achiel.*
A house built on one pole.

Obwolo.
The mushroom.

146. *Ot molor dhoge to ji miel iye.*
A locked house in which people are dancing.

Ko.
The churning milk gourd.

147. *Osiki kidienya.*
The distended stump.

Dhako ma yach.
A pregnant woman.

148. *Pangla kithee.*
"Pangla kithee".

Jatheth.
The blacksmith.

149. *Pap odundo.*
A tiny field.

Simon.
The fifty-cents coin.

150. *Pengle kopi kopia.*
"Pengle kopi kopia".

Bondo.
The bald head.

151. *Pien adila ma iye koni chal gi koni.*
The hide whose inside and outside look similar.

Apet kich.
The beehive.

152. *Piny moting'o jodongo lilo ma yie tikgi boyo.*
A land full of old men with long beards.

Puoth oduma.
A maize garden.

153. *Piny rach ka koth ochwe.*
The earth is ugly when it has rained.

Jawuoro rach ka taya otho.
The glutton is dangerous in darkness.

154. *Polis pangre e dho kanisa.*
Police marching by the church.

Kibrit.
Matches.

155. *Polis pangre e dho siruari.*
Police marching along the hem of the shorts.

Onyuogo.
Lice.

156. *Polo omor ji ringo dwaro arunge.*
Thunder has roared, people are rushing for clubs.

Chiemo ochiek ji dhi e mesa.
Food is ready, people go to the table.

157. *Radhianja nyar ka ruoth.*
Radhianja, the maiden from the chief's place.

Oyoyo.
The duck.

158. *Riga gi kate.*
Blood and its soup.

Chlieth gi lach.
Stool and urine.

159. *Rodh mon.*
Women's side gate.

Dero.
The granary.

160. *Rombe abich ma kwayo e wi got.*
Five sheep grazing on the hill.

Lwedo e wi kuon.
Fingers on ugali.

161. *Sanduk motamo wasunge yawo.*
A box that cannot be opened by white men.

Tong'.
The egg.

162. *Seke seke tiend odundu.*
"Seke seke" under the reeds.

Onyuogo.
Lice.

163. *Simonda ma ok rum.*
My fifty cents that never gets finished.

Olaw.
Spittle.

164. *Sindan tin to tueng'o.*
The needle is small but sews.

Apuoyo tin to go rude.
The hare is tiny but it bears twins.

165. *Thuol ma yweyo iro.*
A snake that exhales smoke.

Gare.
The train.

166. *Thuol oluwo nyinyo.*
A snake slithering along fine metal.

Kong'o oluwo oseke.
Beer in a straw.

167. *Togo man e tiend namni en togo koso chuku?*
Are these reeds along the shore genuine or counterfeit?

Nyathi man eich ni en nyako koso wuoyi?
This child in the womb, is it a girl or a boy?

168. *Wendo ma biro to ikia kata en Onyango kata Anyango.*
A visitor who is coming but you know not whether he is Onyango or Anyango.*

Nyathi man eich.
The baby in the womb.

169. *Winyo ma piyo e yien adek.*
A bird that perches on three trees simultaneously.

Agulu.
The cooking pot.

170. *Wuon ogudu makwarni en ang'o?*
Who is the owner of this red hat?

Thuon gweno.
The cock.

---

*Onyango is the name of a male child born at mid-morning while Anyango is the female.

Chapter 3

PROVERBS

Introduction

The Luo proverb, *ngero*, is a succinct statement full of folk wisdom and is popularly used. The word *ngero* refers to proverbs, riddles, allegory, parables, allusions and any statement or expression that makes indirect references to issues.

Proverbs are integrated into speech to enhance their aesthetic appeal. This is particularly so in the speech of elders — those whose experiences are wider and are regarded as custodians of knowledge about the community's mores and norms. The proverb captures these mores poetically and renders them in an idiom as the embodiment of the community's ethos. Proverbs are like a code of the Luo community's world view and their philosophy of life.

Many of the Luo proverbs are derived from historical experiences. Such proverbs refer to historical characters from whose experiences the Luo derived a general perspective of life. Such proverbs are, therefore, very difficult to understand if one does not know the story behind them. One such proverb is *"Rapemo nokecho obwanda Wamlare"* (Rapemo coveted Wamlare's *obwanda* vegetables). The story behind this proverb is that Rapemo, a chief, desired to share the lowly meal of vegetables belonging to Wamlare, a commoner. By this, he demonstrated unwittingly that social status is skin deep and that human desire is essentially the same.

In general usage then, this proverb comments on a situation where one's fortunes have changed for the worse, in case one was an arrogant person who despised commoners.

Most of the proverbs in this anthology were collected by the author during field research in Asembo, Siaya District, in 1993 and 1994. The key informant on the interpretations of the proverbs was a farmer, Mr Absalom Owino Odhach, then 67 years old. Many other people were contacted to clarify meanings. Other proverbs in the collection were translated from Paul Mbuya's *Luo Kitgi gi Timbegi*.

As much as possible, the nominal explanations of the meaning of the proverbs have been retained in interpretetation. They remain, however, open to varied understanding and further interpretation.

The proverbs are given both in the original language (Dholuo) and in English. The translations are meant to paraphrase the sense of the original proverb. In a number of cases, standard English equivalents have been provided to give the reader additional insights into the meanings of the Luo proverbs with such equivalence. Needless to say, another researcher or interpreter would choose different idioms to capture the same ideas in these proverbs.

They have been arranged in alphabetical order going by the originals in Dholuo, not because this is the way the Luo classify their proverbs, but for sheer convenience.

Social functions

The proverb is used to:
* comment on situations or behaviour as a way of cultivating understanding within the historico-ethical system of thought in the community.
* embellish linguistic communication whether in speech, song or narration.
* state what is considered as unequivocal truth.
* re-state the community's norms, i.e., ridicule deviant behaviour, counsel and advise.

The proverb is a codification of the Luo community's experiences and, hence, accumulated wisdom. It is a commentary on various issues as viewed by the community. Some of the ways of looking at things are analysed below with reference to specific proverbs.

Heredity and kinship

A number of proverbs on heredity and kinship seek to underscore the permanence of these two aspects of human life. Hereditary traits, for example, are indelible and evident in the life of a lineage. This is the point captured in some very graphic proverbs such as:

1. *Awendo ok we yiere.*
   The guinea fowl never abandons its colour/feathers.
2. *Olang'o ng'we gi oro kata koth ochwe.*
   The soldier ants smell both in drought and the wet season.

The first proverb implies that one often takes after one's parents, if not physically, then in character. It is often used to comment on situations where a child does something (often despicable) that reminds people of their kin's character. It supports the view that one's ancestry is a permanent factor in one's life.

45

The second proverb passes the same message using a different perspective. In this proverb, the fact that one tends to be consistent to one's character is stressed, the character having been formed through heredity and experience. The proverb implies that one cannot teach an old dog new tricks. Thus the literal sense that a soldier ant will still reek regardless of weather.

Questions of heredity, of course, link easily with matters of parenthood. In this regard, the Luo have a proverb that says:

Ng'ama nigi nyathi ok nind e thim.
He who has a child does not sleep in the wilderness.

A child is an investment and is expected to be the parents' benefactor in their old age. This belief defines the child's responsibility to the parent and also informs the society's concern with fertility.

Also, kinship is stressed. The Luo worldview, as captured in the proverb, takes a less obligatory tenor from the one it adopts on child-parent relationships. It emphasises the element of individuality in fraternal relations and just falls short of saying that one's brother is not their keeper. Thus, the sibling is told:

Kik ipakri gi mwandu ma kowadu.
Do not boast about your brother's wealth.

And:

Chan man kowadu ok moni nindo.
Your brother's poverty does not make you sleepless.

The first proverb notifies us that despite close blood ties, each individual is responsible for himself/herself. One cannot therefore boast about the success of a sibling. The sibling has, at least, invested time and energy to achieve what he/she has and is not ready to waste it by virtue of kinship to the less successful. This proverb sounds a warning to lazy people who seek glory by associating with the success of their kin but do nothing for themselves. The second proverb puts the case more crudely: One carries one's cross and bothers least with other people's worries, whether they are siblings or not.

Despite this fact, however, the Luo still cherish kinship and recognise its permanence as captured in the proverb: *Wat osiko.* (Kinship is permanent).

Put differently, one can choose one's friends but not one's relatives. This point is emphasised in another proverb: *Wat wat.* (Kinship is kinship). The community, therefore, counsels people to acknowledge kinship and survive within it.

The Luo also notice, nevertheless, that blood ties are essentially redundant if not buttressed by interpersonal relationships. Thus, they say: *Wat imedo gi osiep.* (Kinship is complemented with friendship).

46

Kinship is, thus, the tree but friendship is the manure that fertilises it. Left untended, kinship is as good as dead.

Kinship is protective because in times of trouble, relatives are expected to be sympathetic. This is not necessarily because they are likely to be the most helpful, but because they are the nearest and are assumed to have an intuitive obligation to the preservation and survival of their kin. This is the point expressed in the double-billed proverb: *Ondieg thuru ok chami duto* (A beast from your home does not eat you completely).

This is a rather sharp reminder that intra-kinship feuds abound but should never be destructive. This proverb can be compared to the statement that when a mother canes a child, it is not because she wants to injure him. Rather, it is because she wants to discipline or correct the child. The parent who canes to harm is misguided. Similarly, the relative who seeks to dispense fatality on kin in conflict is admonished. The proverb puts a seal on the kind of hostility permissible between kin. Hostility must be benign!

The individual and others

The emphasis on kinship may create the impression that the Luo are very egalitarian. But as we have already seen, this egalitarianism is defined within certain bounds and leaves a lot of space for individualism.

Individualism and communalism are allowed to co-exist and complement each other. Proverbs expressing this philosophy abound. For example, here is a proverb which warns that collectivism can sometimes cause chaos if not outright strife: *Thuon gwen ariyo ok riw e agulu achiel.* (Two cocks are never cooked in the same pot).

The interpretation of this saying is that in a situation where individuals feel they are contemporaries, the person bringing them together is only laying ground for disaster. In such a case, it is better to keep the two apart — preferably to nurture their own ambitions in separate environments.

Another proverb that celebrates individualism says: *Sindan tin to tweng'o* (the needle is tiny, but it sews). Each individual, despite apparent deficiencies (like the needle's small size), has his/her worth. The proverb is cautioning against prejudice and is similar in vein to *Apuoyo tin to go rude* (The hare is small but it begets twins).

Underlying the celebration of human individuality is the philosophy of rights: that the individual interest cannot be over-ridden with impunity. This is the core of the proverb: *Ong'ino kata tin to ok ma ng'wende.* (Even though it is small, the black ant cannot be robbed of its termite).

This proverb is in counterpoint to another one that seeks to not exactly justify might over right, but to acknowledge that where might is applied, the weak lose, i.e., "*Ng'ama oloyi kiyang' dheri*" (He who is stronger than you does not slaughter your bull"). If he did, he would distribute the carcas as he wishes.

Proverbs derived from the social scene also celebrate individualism. As it were, the Luo are a highly social group which revels in ceremony. Their culture is full of musical extravaganza. From these experiences are gathered the following proverbs:

1. *Ng'at ma miel mamit ema iting'o bade.*
   It's the good dancer whose arms are raised. (Praise goes to those who deserve it).
2. *Ng'at momoso thum ema iwero.*
   He who has "greeted the music"* is the one whose praise is sung.

The first proverb above acknowledges that individuals differ, with some having greater initiative than others. This initiative gives them competitive advantage in the same way as expressed in the saying, "The early bird catches the worm". The same notion is captured in the second proverb which also expresses the concept of self exertion, if not assertiveness, as a requisite individual characteristic. It has the same idea as the saying that seekers get what they want or that one only reaps from where one has sown. The proverb is in fact an invitation for assertiveness and a campaign tool against coyness and procrastination satirised in the proverb: *Wichkuot nonego Apuoyo gono* (Shyness killed the hare in its lair).

But if all the proverbs so far looked at dwell on individualism, it must be pointed out that the Luo also believe in democratic institutions. The best example of this is expressed in the proverb: *Ruoth ok yierre kende* (The chief/king does not elect himself). This epitomises the element that social differences in status should not serve as a source of pride and vanity. The chief cannot afford to ignore or despise his/her subjects because these are essentially the people whose survival gives meaning to his position. While the proverb sends a message to those in privileged positions, it reminds everybody that democratic power lies in their hands and that they can exercise it to gain what they desire of their leadership.

The need for inter-dependence among individuals in the community is also captured in this figurative proverb: *Janeko ema lielore kende* (It's only the madman that shaves his own hair).

The essence of the proverb is that no person is completely independent. It appeals to people to realise that when they are in trouble, help could be sought from a neighbour. In any case, there are some things one cannot possibly do alone. This is metaphorically

---

*"Greeting the music" is a Luo idiom referring to the act of a dancer temporarily stopping the music so that he/she can praise himself or herself. This is not done free of charge. He/she has to pay a token to the musician and can in fact ask the musician to stop what he was singing and instead sing his/her praises.

48

expressed as shaving of one's head. Achieving such a feat is not easy. One who attempts it sends out messages that his/her head is not all right.

The case for inter-dependence is even more vividly portrayed in the realm of economics. The need for this is captured in the proverb: *Dher ariemba wuongo nyiedho to ng'iyo oko* (The keeper of a loaned cow milks it while always looking outward to the gate).

In Luo culture, people give heifers to friends to tend. While the animal is still in the friend's custody, the latter can milk it. There is usually an agreement between the owner and the friend that he inherits some of the heifers born while in his custody. But the owner can come for the original cow any time. This proverb recognises the fact that the custodian is always on the lookout should the owner come to curtail these privileges. One cannot rely on what one does not own.

The egalitarian principle this proverb espouses is that even the poor can generate some wealth through the generosity of others, as long as this generosity does not waive the originator's right over his property. A loan is neither a grant nor a bequest.

Even as one benefits from this communalism, there is still a minimum social expectation. In fact, the Luo believe that those who need help must show a capacity to bear responsibility. If this person is laid back or has no initiative, no one will help lest the helper bear the responsibility. This idea is summarised in this proverb: *Ng'ama nyap tek konyo (*It is difficult to help a weakling).

Egalitarianism and generosity is reciprocated with gratitude. This ideal is, however, not always adhered to. The Luo codify their experience in the proverb: *Wang' mithiedho ema gawi* (The squint-eye that you have treated is the one that looks at you with malice).

This proverb acknowledges the unreliability of human memory. One can often forget a kindness and may even insult his benefactors. This captures the transient nature of human relationships, that friends betray their fellows, a common occurrence in politics, for example. Betrayal is a reality we have to live with, the proverb insinuates, but it is not an ideal.

At a deeper level, the proverb is an indirect warning that people should not only be philanthropic because of the returns they expect from the beneficiaries of their largesse. If one takes the essence of true philanthropy as service without expecting any reward, one would not be bothered by lack of gratitude. But there is a warning in that the days of unleashing misery on others are numbered and that, in the end, justice prevails. This is summarised in the proverb: *Ondong' mitoke ema itokonie* (The same plate you have served others in is the one that is used to serve you).

One should not complain when receiving a dose of one's own medicine. People should do justice to their fellows if they expect the same, the proverb teaches.

The survival instinct is fundamental to the human race. To survive, one needs versatility, shrewdness and sometimes a bit of trickery. Luo proverbs celebrate the human survival instinct. An example is: *Dhano winyo* (The human being is a bird).

Although the proverb is often used to comment on situations where one has employed trickery to achieve a goal, it also celebrates the versatility of human creativity; especially in the face of adversity.

In normal situations, there are also pragmatic strategies for survival. Two such strategies are captured in the following proverbs:

1. *Atonga mayot ema iyombo go koth*
   It is with a light basket that one escapes the rain/downpour. (Cut your cloth according to your size, or do not bite off more than you can chew).

2. *Chako chon loyo dhi ajuoga*
   Starting early is better than seeking a medicineman later. (Prevention is better than cure).

These proverbs declare intuition and insight to be useful human traits for avoiding misery and regret. They put responsibility for one's welfare in one's own hands.

In another proverb, the sense of personal responsibility for one's welfare is drawn from the graphic reality of the hunchback: *Rakuom ong'e kaka nindo* (The hunchback knows how he/she sleeps).

At the literal level, the proverb points to the fact that the hunchback is disabled and hence, cannot sleep as the able-bodied do. The hunchback, however, still has to sleep. The posture he/she adopts is only known to him/her.

The metaphorical sense of the proverb is that despite our shortcomings in life, everyone has a way of surviving.

Closely related to the concept of personal survival is the element of self defence. The Luo record that for the human being, one of the most crucial weapons is the mouth. In the proverb: *Dhok tung dhano* (The mouth is the human being's horn [defence]), the notion that human beings will always talk themselves out of clumsy situations is encapsulated. This proverb is used to refer to a situation, for instance, where a person who is apparently implicated in wrongdoing denies the offence or employs his mouth to manoeuvre a way out. In other words, the proverb states, if lying helps to extricate one from trouble, the human being will lie.

Survival and defence, however, are compromised by the vicissitudes of life. In this regard, the Luo have a series of proverbs which talk about the fluctuations of life and forewarn people. A good example is *Dhier kiyombi* (Poverty can never be entirely eluded).

This proverb warns against arrogance. Some rich people sometimes imagine that they have escaped poverty forever, but fortunes change and they find themselves in dire straits. There is a real life story of a man who was so rich that he used to say he had fenced his home to keep out poverty forever. As fate would have it, however, his wealth consisted mainly of loans and when they were called in at a time he could not repay, the auctioneers did their duty. The man discovered then that he had not fenced out anything. The proverb pleads for humility and warns that there is no fleeing from fate.

A similar message can be found in the proverb: *Gweno uch gi ombij wadgi kiny to mar* (A hen scurries with its kin's entrails but tomorrow is for its own).

When a chicken is prepared and the offal thrown away, living chickens will eat it up unaware that in time, their entrails are also likely to meet the same fate. Like the one before it, this proverb exhorts people to realise that fortunes change and that good luck does not last eternally. It further warns people to avoid despising those who are not as successful as they are: Today me, tomorrow thee. Put otherwise, the proverb says you should not marry when your enemy is in trouble.

The nature of life is such that people are always playing musical chairs. This is the essence of the terse and poetic Luo proverb, *Inind diere inind tung'* (You sleep in the middle, you sleep at the fringe).

Appearances and virtue

One of the most striking things about Bertolt Brecht's *The Caucasian Chalk Circle* is the practical folk wisdom of Azdak, the ordinary sage whose brilliance shines as a matter of accident rather than deliberate design. The moral one draws from the character of Azdak is that wisdom is often shrouded in rags. Appearances cannot be used as a measure of virtue. The Luo are particularly concerned with appearance and reality. They say, *Alot michayo ema tieko kuon* (It is the despised vegetables that eats up the *ugali*).

Nominally, *ugali* (a pastry made from hot water and maize/millet flour that is a staple among the Luo) does not eat up the vegetables. Rather, the imagery is drawn from the reality that the eaters will tend to finish their ugali when it is accompanying a delicacy such as meat or chicken. The Luo do not generally consider vegetables to be a delicacy. The idea then is that people should not despise an object or prejudge it. In conventional English, you could say, "Little strokes fell great oaks".

If one relies entirely on appearances to act and make choices, he/she is likely to make mistakes. Not all that glisters is gold. The Luo have a similar proverb in, *Jaber jaula* (The beautiful one is deceptive).

51

This proverb proclaims the universal truth that physical beauty and human virtue are not automatic bedfellows. Often, the physically attractive turns out to be counterfeit or direly wanting in virtue. This is not only true of human appearance but also in life experiences. For instance, the art of conmanship thrives on the ability of its practitioners to create tempting promises that beguile their target. As one Kenyan newspaper used to put it in a weekly column, when the deal sounds too good, perhaps it isn't.

The derision of physical glister, in the case of human character, is not absolute. The Luo believe that even if one has that facility, it should be complemented with humility and other admirable traits. Thus, they say: *Ber imedo gi ariyo* (Beauty is completed with other virtues).

Ariyo literally means "two", but the idea in this proverb is that physical beauty does not make one a perfect being. One must have other socially desirable traits. In fact, beauty does not entitle one to walk about naked, for example. If one walked naked to show physical beauty, such beauty would be taken to be in bad taste as it contravenes the community's ethic of privacy and decency.

A very interesting proverb to consider on deceptive appearances is: *Bingo iro ok e tedo* (Effusion of smoke is not necessarily cooking). [Big boast, small roast]

This proverb, using a very effective image, counsels that people should be wary of busybodies, as beneath this appearance may be lack of depth. It is a proverb also used to chide extroverts and those who would like to take advantage of appearances. This message is contained in another proverb, *Wacho ok e timo* (To say is not the same as to do, (or Action speaks louder than words).

Caution

In making comments on human nature and behaviour, one very crucial role proverbs play is to advise or caution on what is the best course of action desirable. Two proverbs which come out very strongly on this are: *Jowi mager ema ichuogo piene* (It is the skin of a fierce buffalo that makes the shield), and *Otoyo moluor ema ru.* (It is the timid hyena that lasts the night). [He that goes softly goes safely].

The first proverb warns that the fierce buffalo that will charge at the hunter is the one that will be killed, skinned and its skin made into a shield. It warns against bravado which leads to humiliation. The second proverb contrasts the first by categorically stating that the timid hyena lasts the night because it is not faced with the dangers and uncertainties of those who rush out in blind hunger. Being foolhardy could lead to injury, grave disadvantage and annihilation. This view is presented in another proverb, *Sukruok ne omiyo ong'er yip* (Meddling earned the monkey its tail).

52

In reality, the monkey may not have got its tail as a result of haste or interfering in other people's affairs, but it is very clear that the Luo discourage meddling. Meddling often entwines one in things not meant for him/her. Put another way, the proverb says, "Haste trips up on its own heels".

But caution is not only advisable to discourage hurrying. It is also emphasised in other realms of human action. Thus, even a trait like persistence, which is lauded in other instances, is criticised when in excess, for example in the proverb *Kinda kiteng'a nomiyo opuk ogwaro nyar min Kibogo* (Persistence led to the tortoise scratching the groin of Kibogo's mother).

This proverb is based on an anecdote about a woman called Min Kibogo (Kibogo's mother) who joined other women in basket-fishing on a stream. The other women were satisfied with their catch and left after some time, but she persisted and prospected further. She ventured upon the tortoise who, under the cover of the water, did the uncanny thing. The proverb is similar in meaning to "*Gimoro iweyo gi mitne*" (Too much of something is dangerous).

The same is true for over-confidence, dealt with in these two proverbs:

1. *Kapod in ei pi kik iyany nyang'*
    Do not abuse the crocodile when you are still in the water.

2. *Yie nimo ka dhi gowo*
    A boat capsizes just when it is about to dock.

In the first saying, one is warned to be wary of unfamiliar surroundings and exercise restraint when vulnerable. One should avoid stepping on the toes of those who, in the given context, can break him/her. In the second proverb, people are cautioned against proclaiming success until it is completely certain. As put in the proverb, a boat cannot be said to have completed the journey uneventfully until it has moored and been anchored. In other cultures, the same idea is expressed in a saying to the effect that people should not count chickens before they are hatched.

These are just a few examples of cautionary functions proverbs perform. It should be realised, however, that in almost all proverbs, one can read an element of caution.

Stylistic features

Imagery

The use of figures of speech is a major characteristic of the Luo proverb, whether these figures are metaphors, similes, personifications, allusions or other forms of imagery. As it is with idiomatic expressions, of which proverbs are, images are just

53

a codification of experiences and hence technically exist as references to referents. The proverb has its literal meaning as well as the underlying meaning based on the reality to which it refers.

The figures of speech in Luo proverbs are derived from the community's immediate environment, both physical and abstract.

Similes

Some proverbs are constructed as direct comparisons of one entity to another (otherwise called similes). For example, *Nindo nyamin tho* (Sleep is the sister [kin] of death).

If it were not for the fact that people wake up when they go to sleep, death and sleep would be the same. By comparing the two and calling them sisters, the Luo are acknowledging the withdrawal of human consciousness in sleep and comparing it to withdrawal of consciousness in death, except that the former is temporary. The Luo are perhaps intrigued by the power of sleep (in this proverb comparing it with inevitable death). This is expressed in other proverbs such as: *Nindo tek matero janeko* (Sleep is so strong it overpowers the mad man), and *Nindo otero jater* (Sleep overwhelmed the wife inheritor).

These proverbs point out that despite human intelligence, even mastery of nature, humanity ultimately meets its match in sleep which catches up with the normal and abnormal alike without regard to one's daily cares.

The intrigue with nature is apparent in the proverb, *Piny maru loyo yie rombo gi ng'eny* (Dawning days outnumber the sheep's wool).

The power of this simile lies in the image of the sheep's wool which occurs to the eye as a mass but which in fact is made up of individual strands. One could dare count the strands of wool on the sheep, but it would be a very taxing and absurd exercise. The other element to the image is that the sheep's wool regenerates when sheared just as days follow one another.

· Another proverb which deals with human experience and draws its imagery from the sheep is, *Sembe iporo gi nyamin* (The ram's fatty tail is compared to another).

The Luo use this proverb to refer to a recurring event, what is conventionally summarised in the saying, "History repeats itself". In other words, the proverb is saying that human experience is cyclic.

Metaphors

Metaphors, unlike similes, are more direct in equating one factor with another. They are more brief than the simile which has to use a comparative word or phrase to realise its sense. An example of a metaphor in the Luo proverb is, *Dhano winyo* (The human being is a bird).

When the proverb equates the human being to a bird, it emphasises the nature of humanity, in this case dexterity or shrewdness, just as a bird is versatile in the air. Just as a bird's ability to fly and escape danger is intrinsic to it, so is the art and instinct of survival intrinsic to humanity. Also intrinsic is the self defence instinct, as captured in the proverb, *Dhok tung dhano* (The mouth is the human being's horn [defence]).

The proverb is not saying that the mouth is like the horn, but actually that the mouth *is* the horn. This analogy conjures up the fact that the mouth is useful for the human being's defence. In this case, the proverb personifies humanity and makes it look like a horned animal which, when in danger, pierces its way through. Animals, unlike human beings, do not have the power of speech, just as the human being does not have the brute strength articulated through the animal's horn. If the human being had a horn, the proverb would have no figurative impact.

Another excellently stated metaphor is in the proverb, *Lak chogo* (The tooth is a bone). In its full form, the proverb is stated thus: *Lak chogo ma kata meru otho* (The tooth is a bone even when your mother has died). Teeth, when exposed in laughter, normally indicate excitement or happiness. But this is not always the case because after all, the tooth is a bone which does not reflect people's true feelings. In the event of death, even of people close to us, we still find cause to laugh (hence show teeth) tragic though the occasion is.

Sources of proverbial imagery

The figures used for reference in the proverb are taken from a wide range of sources, including the fauna and flora of the Luo community. Below is an itemisation of some of these.

1. Images derived from the animal world

Different animals are referred to in the proverbs below and their nature or styles of living used to reflect on human nature and experience.

(a) Hare

> *Apuoyo tin to go rude.*
> The hare might be small, but it begets twins. (Everybody has got her/his strengths).

(b) Guinea fowl

Awendo ok we yiere.
The guinea fowl never abandons its colour/feathers. (Like parent like child).

(c) Fish

Fulu bende oro ngege.
Even "fulu" sends tilapia.* (Even a cat looks at a king).

(d) Chicken

Gweno uch gi ombij wadgi kiny to mare.
A hen scurries with its kin's entrails but tomorrow is the turn for its own.

(e) Buffalo

Jowi mager ema ichuogo piene.
It is the skin of a fierce buffalo that makes the shield.

(f) Tortoise

Opuk ogo e pige.
The tortoise has been immersed in its water.**

(g) Frog and cattle

Kwot ogwal ok mon dhiang' modho.
The bloating of a frog does not prevent the cow from drinking. (Might is right).

(h) Elephant

(i)   *Liech ong'iyo gi oporo.*
The elephant is used to the blow-horn. (Familiarity breeds contempt).***

---

*"Fulu" is a small type of fish. The proverb stresses the necessity of co-existence between the mighty and the lowly.

** The proverb is used to refer to a situation where someone has been given a familiar task or put in a situation of his/her liking. The person can only excel in it and enjoy it.

*** The antics of a daily foe should not ruffle one. The blow-horn here is the one used by the hunters to summon one another to an expedition. When the elephant hears it, it knows what to expect and therefore adopts the best strategy of defence or escape).

56

(ii)   *Wich liech turo mana wuongo.*
The elephant's head is its owner's burden. (Every bird must hatch its own eggs. Everybody must bear his/her own cross).

(i) Monitor/lizard

(i) *Ng'ech miyo gi eiye.*
The monitor lizard is fatty from the inside. (Appearances can be deceptive.)

(ii) *Ng'ech ywayo tek.*
It is very difficult to pull a monitor [lizard].*(Let sleeping dogs lie.

(j) Ants

(i) *Olang'o ng'we gi oro kata koth ochwe.*
The soldier ants smell both in drought and the wet season. (One does not leave one's character.)

(ii) *Ong'ino kata tin to ok ma ng'wende.*
Even though it is small, the black ant cannot be robbed of its termite.

(k) Hyena

(i) *Yore ariyo ne otamo ondiek luwo.*
The hyena could not follow two paths.** (Covet all, lose all).

(ii)   *Otoyo moluor ema ru.*
It is the timid hyena that lasts the night).* **(He that goes softly goes safely).

(l) Leopard

Ondiek odak e niang' to kia mit niang'.
The beast [leopard] stays in the sugar cane plantation but does not know the sweetness of cane. (Sleeping foxes catch no poultry).

---

* The analogy of the proverb is that when a monitor lizard digs its feet into the ground, you cannot dislodge it. The proverb is used to comment on unnecessary obstinacy).

** There is a story about the hyena who was invited to a party. As it progressed on its journey, the hyena reached a junction. In trying to determine which road to follow, the hyena used its nose to detect where the party was by the fragrance of food in the air. Both roads seemed to bear the fragrance. The hyena decided to follow the two paths simultaneously. The result was that the hyena walked itself into a split).

*** People living in hyena-infested areas are on the lookout for the animals and have laid traps. A daring hyena which does not check for the traps will obviously be caught in one. But the one which feels its way cautiously will make it round the traps.

57

2. Images derived from the plant world

(a) The green and the dry

Motwo ne owuondo manumu
The dry cheated the green.*

(b) Sausage fruit

Yago ohewo tonde.
The sausage fruit is heavier than its holder/suspender.**

3. Images derived from human experience

(a) The dissector

Jabar bende ibaro.
The dissector is also dissected.***(Today me, tomorrow thee).

(b) Eating with the blind

Ng'ama chiemo gi muofu ema ong'eyo mit bor.
It is he who eats with a blind man that knows the delicacy of fat. (A fool is a lawyer's granary).

(c) The mighty and the minnows

(i) *Ng'ama oloyi kiyang' dheri.*
He who is stronger than you does not slaughter your cow/bull).

---

* There is an anecdote about the dry bundle of firewood inviting the green one for a swim. The green sank but the dry one floated. The proverb refers to those who fool others.

** Used when one is overwhelmed by his/her responsibilities and obligations, the proverb is similar in vein to the one that says "The elephant bears the burden of its head" and should not really complain about it being so heavy.

***The proverb is derived from the practice of breaking the hunch before the hunchback is buried. If the dissector is hunchbacked, then he is only doing what will also be done to him. Every dog has its day.

(ii)   *Ng'ama oloyi onyono kwesi meru.*
         He who is stronger has stepped on your mother's smoking pipe.*

(d) The visitor

   Wendo bade boyo.
   The visitor has long arms.**

(4) Images from domestic items

   (i) *Atonga mayot ema iyombo go koth.*
       It is with a light basket that one escapes the rain. (Cut your coat according to your cloth).
   (ii) *Ondong' mitoke ema itokonie.*
        The same plate you have served others in is the one that is used to serve you. (Tit for tat. Do unto others what you would like them to do to you).
   (iii) *Pand nyaluo dhoge ariyo.*
         The traditional knife has two edges.***

Satire

Satire — poking fun at human folly — is very much an integral part of the Luo proverb. Its greatest element in doing this is, as with many other experiences, the use of humour, exaggeration and understatement. We will illustrate the use of humour and satire in Luo proverbs by looking at a few examples.

   The Luo uphold a culture of authenticity and truth. Pretence is derided in the proverb, *Bingo iro ok e tedo* (Effusion of smoke is not necessarily evidence of cooking).

---

*If such a thing happens, the story goes, you cannot confront the person. Instead, you will chide your mother for carelessly leaving her pipe in the way. You will in essence be looking for an excuse not to deal with the obvious affront.

**As a matter of courtesy, a visitor in Luo homes is not expected to be too eager to eat or overtly display his hunger. When asked to move nearer the table for the meal, a typical visitor will always reply that his position is near enough even when it is not. The derisive conclusion then, is that he must be having very long arms!

***Used to comment on a hypocrite or double dealer. The traditional knife which has two edges can cut both ways. So does a hypocrite or double dealer.

The essence of the proverb is that mediocrity and lack of substance could be hidden under appearances. This proverb intimates that exaggeration does not always present the reality as it is. As it is conventionally put, big boast, small roast. The humour in the proverb lies in the visual image of one who has made a lot of smoke (traditionally, the Luo use firewood for cooking and so the appearance of smoke from a house is indicative of cooking) but is essentially cooking nothing.

An apt example that comes to mind is from school sports. At such meetings, very colourfully dressed athletes who limber all over the place and demonstrate their potential never feature among the winners and are often only substitutes. This proverb can be used to cut such athletes down to size and remind them that vanity, ego and arrogance might just be worthless.

Intrusion in other people's affairs (meddling), gossiping and laziness are also derided by the Luo proverb. Meddling comes in different forms. One very common one among the Luo is self-invitation to a meal. Some people have the habit of appearing just at the time when a meal is being served. The social principle among the Luo is that whoever is present when the meal is set is automatically expected to share in it. By timing his appearance, the intruder (*jahawanya*) gets the benefit of food. However, it is not everybody who appears at meal time that is regarded as "*jahawanya*". Rather, you become "*jahawanya*" if you do this repeatedly so that it's no longer a coincidence.

In traditional society, the "*jahawanya*" would lean on one of the pillars supporting the eave while making sounds to attract those eating inside the house. This way, he would be noticed and invited to the meal. This is the situation satirised in the proverb: *Jahawanya otugore gi siro* (The intruder/unwelcome guest has fallen with the pillar).

The proverb pokes fun at this person who might be unaware of the weakness of the pillar and might go down with it in the process making his presence known.

Laziness is ridiculed through the self-explanatory proverb, *Janyao mor gi jumapil* (The lazy person is happy on Sunday). The lazy person is happy on Sunday because it is a non-working day.

Gossip and rumour-mongering are acknowledged as social cancers among the Luo, like in many other communities. Those who practise it cause disagreements by distorting the content in the transfer of information from one source to another. Such people are symbolised in one proverb as the double-edged traditional knife which cuts both ways. In another proverb, the gossip is presented as the perennial nuisance he/she is, i.e., *Jakuoth ki ti* (The gossip never ages).

The essence of the proverb is that the tool of trade for the gossip is the tongue and this is an organ, unlike others, which gets sharper with repeated use. In other words, an old gossip is perhaps more dangerous than a young one.

The gossip is in the l`same class as the detractor, the person who specialises in planting germs of discord in what are otherwise good relationships. Detraction is very common in marital relationships and is often perpetrated by close relatives. A common scenario is where a person is courting. The detractor comes in and secretly starts informing one of the partners about the ills of the other with the aim of discouraging them from continuing with the relationship. The detractor uses an iota of truth and embellishes it with many untruths for his/her malicious intentions. In order for him to succeed in this, he must spend many hours sitting with the target of detraction. And what is the result of that sitting, literally speaking? This proverb refers to *Jasem piere otuch* (The detractor has holes in the buttocks).

The reference to buttocks here is not literal. Trousers are implied instead. The detractor spends long hours sitting to defame people. This over-sitting leaves its mark on the trousers. At the symbolic level, the proverb points out that the detractor is morally impaired because his actions are harmful.

Finally, there is a satirical proverb about those who do wrong but are very defensive to the extent of being ready for a fist fight. One such character is the person who breaks wind in public, according to this proverb, *Jakuodho oyie dhaw* (He who has broken wind is ready for a fight).

Breaking wind while in company is distasteful. It is received with disdain and a lot of fanning of the nose. The guilty person will often be easy to identify as he/she will not fan the nose, or will do so inconspicuously. When accusing fingers are pointed at the offender, he/she will challenge people to a fight.The proverb is a code of saying that a guilty conscience needs no accuser.

Physical structure of the proverb

The power of the proverb lies in its gnomic nature, characterised by its brevity of expression. There is no better way of illustrating this brevity in the Luo proverb than by looking at some two-word proverbs which encapsulate complex ideas such as, *Lak chogo* (The tooth is a bone).

The brevity of the proverb gives it a unique poetic quality. This poesy is aided by the physical structuring and arrangement of the words that constitute the proverb. The first word or few words in the proverb focus on the subject of expression and the rest on the qualification or description of the first. For example, look at the proverb, *Jakech kimosi* (A hungry man is never greeted).

The word "*jakech*" means "the hungry or poor person". But what about a hungry person? That is the import of the second word "*kimosi*", which is a compound word meaning "is not greeted". But why should one not greet a hungry or poor person? The underlying logic is that doing so could be misunderstood to be an invitation to a meal or material resources. In just two words, the proverb has condensed a lot of information. This is true of many other proverbs presented in the list at the end of this chapter.

It is important to note the parallelism (the presentation of balancing parts) that occurs due to this structuring. One very explicit example is in the proverb: *Inind diere inind tung'*. You sleep in the middle you sleep at the fringe. (Changing fortunes is the lot of life).

This beautifully constructed proverb presents its meaning by contrasts in just two words, *diere* and *tung'*, with one word being repeated. The physical balance of the proverb captures the reality of life: that it is full of ups and downs.

The syntax of proverbs is something that is intrinsic to their power as an aesthetic medium of communication.

Mnemonics

The proverb's syntactical power is greatly complemented by the play on sounds which make the expressions appealing to the ear and, therefore, memorable. Alliteration and assonance are the main mnemonic aspects of Luo proverbs. Consider the proverb, *Jarikni jamuod nyoyo gi kwoyo* (The hasty one eats sand in his "nyoyo").*

On first hearing this proverb, one appreciates its auditory appeal, created by the sheer play on certain consonants and vowels. The critical phonetic consonants here are "j" which alliterates in the first two words and "y" which alliterates in the third and fifth words. The critical vowels on the other hand are "a" and "o" which create assonance in the first two words and the third and fifth words respectively. The critical mnemonics are played in the first three words and the fifth word where the sounds are concentrated, yet dispersed.

The same sense of lexical and phonetic interplay is evident in the proverb, *Jabar bende ibaro* (The dissector is also dissected). Here, the play is on the sound "b" which features in all the words in the proverb. This is bordered by the first three vowels in chronological order as "a" in "jabar", "e" in "bende" and "i" in "ibaro". Note that the vowels in the words are chronological up to the end with "o" as the last. These are aspects one does not notice until one keenly examines the proverb.

It should not now be difficult to see the mnemonics at play in these other proverbs:

1. *Jaou wach jatur bat.*
    He who exaggerates issues breaks arms.

---

*("Nyoyo is a mixture of boiled beans and maize. Haste makes waste or Hurry hurry has no blessing).

2.   *Jabudho e duonde ariyo jabed jamriambo.*
     He who stays in two "duonde"* often becomes a liar.

3.   *Jaber jaula.*
     The beautiful one is deceptive. (All that glitters is not gold.)

Puns

Playing on words and meaning is another poetic feature of the proverb. These two proverbs illustrate this: *Jaraw arawa owaro wi kuon* (The sojourner has scraped the top of *ugali*).

Note the alliteration of the sounds "r" and "w" which, in Luo, results from the diphthong "ou" and the heavy assonance of "a". The mnemonics here create a jarring effect on the ear. But the pun comes into play on the morphemes *"raw"* and *"waro"* which are some kind of syntactic inversions of each other. *"Raw"* means to sojourn or pass by a place. *"Waro"* denotes an aggressive act of hiving off a big part or removing the topmost layer. So *"jaraw"* means a sojourner. *"Arawa"*, on the other hand, is an emphatic word which seeks to demean the sojourner thus *"jaraw arawa"* means "a mere sojourner". By compounding the three words *"jaraw"*, *"arawa"* and *"owaro"*, the proverb becomes a potent tool of expression which satirises the unexpected sojourner who is not very courteous because he scrapes away the last food. The satire is in the fact that when the meal was prepared, nobody had the sojourner in mind. The sojourner's action makes it seem as though the meal was prepared solely for him. Impudence and imprudence are the focal issues here.

The proverb, *Nindo otero jater* (Sleep overwhelmed the wife inheritor) is an idiom which is used to refer to a situation where someone on an important mission has failed to perform as expected because of distractions. *Tero* can mean two things: the act of a man entering a levirite marriage (taking a widow), and sleep overcoming a person. In levirite unions, the inheritor must, on the first night of stay with the woman, have intercourse with her. The proverb deplores a situation where this has not happened because the inheritor (*jater*) has been overcome by sleep *"nindo otero"*. The connotation of the proverb goes further when we consider the double meaning of the word *tero*. If the inheritor (*jater*) has failed to *tero* (have intercourse with the widow) because *"nindo otere"* (sleep has overcome him), then who has *tero* who? The tables have been turned and sleep has *tero* (had

---

*"Duonde" is the plural for "duol" which is the small hut that belongs to the male head of a homestead and where his peers and the male fraternity confer. If one frequents two, meaning that he is a frequenter of two homesteads, he is likely to reveal what is discussed in each of them and may end up antagonising people.

intercourse with) the inheritor. This is the paradox of the hunter and the hunted. When the hunted turns round and hunts the hunter, is it still hunting?

Diction

The proverb succeeds in its aesthetic appeal largely because of its reliance on poetic characteristics. Diction (choice of words for effect) is one of these. Nominally defined, poetry refers to the best combination of words for the desired effect. The combination of words implies first the choice of the best possible words for expressive purposes, both for meaning and appeal.

Diction, when properly executed, leads to depth and authenticity of expression. A few proverbs from the Luo will illustrate the power of this choice of words on their own and the added value due to the arrangement of the words into a syntactic structure. The proverb about the wife inheritor already mentioned above is a good example of effective diction. But here is another example: *Dhogra chi atera* (The inherited wife is a complex/muddle).

In this proverb, there is syntactic inversion which makes what would be an objective verb become a subjective noun. The word *dhogra* is a noun which is taken from the verb *dhogruok* (to be complicated). In ordinary prose, the expression would be: *Chi atera jadhogre* (The inherited woman gets into complications). But when put as "*dhogra chi atera*", the verb has been made into a noun which describes another noun.

The practical sense of the proverb is that in traditional Luo marital practice, a widow can be re-married (inherited) by her husband's brother or cousin. Sometimes, she is married by an outsider to the clan. The import of the proverb is that despite the regulations on who can inherit the widow, it is only she who knows the details of her sex life. She could, in secrecy, be having affairs with people barred by tradition from being intimate with her.

In the next two proverbs, we see a situation where the proverb uses rare words to express an idea: *Ng'ech miyo gi eiye* (The monitor is fatty from the inside). (Appearances can be deceiving).

The word "*miyo*" (is fat) is used rather than the word "*chwe*" of ordinary speech. Whereas the two words mean the same thing, "*miyo*" conjures a fatness which is not inherent to "*chwe*", since the latter describes any form of plumpness while "*miyo*" refers to a rich form of it. The same careful choice of words is seen in the proverb, *Ori diere kuok nego* (The middle one is dying from sweat). (A knave is often caught in his own trap).

Here, focus is on the word "*kuok*" whose prosaic synonym is "*luya*". Again, "*kwok*" conjures up images of an intense form of sweat more than "*luya*" which describes any form of perspiration. The same could be said of the word "*thigo*" in the proverb: *Thigo oyaw ne par* (The door is ajar for the mat) (When the boss is absent, everyone is big). Strictly speaking, *thigo* is a dialectical word from a section of the Dholuo speaking community. The more universal word for door is *"dhoot"*. *"Thigo"* is the rarer word and hence the more poetic because of its phonetic affinity with the next word, *"oyaw"*.

Finally, we can illustrate diction with the proverb: *Yieng'o aila*. (Satisfaction is an excitement). Once basic needs are satisfied, other things like leisure can be sought.

Satisfaction is presented metaphorically as excitement, hence withdrawing th⸱ reference from the excited person to the state. Ordinarily put, the proverb would read, *Ng'ama oyieng jail* (A satisfied person is often excited). But the power of word choice and arrangement makes it possible to avoid the collection of many words and to express the notion in just two words, *Yieng'o aila*.

Allusion

A number of Luo proverbs are abbreviations of larger realities or experiences. They allude to either historical or fictional experiences which have didactic value. But for one who does not know the longer story behind the proverb, the proverb might just be a sentence. Let us examine a few of these allusions.

In Luo history, there is a man called Okal Tako who was very amiable and excellent at accompanying friends to journeys which required fun, a sense of humour and negotiation skills. He became so popular that everyone going on a journey wanted to include Okal in his entourage. Of course there was a lot of eating on these journeys.

Okal went on one journey across the lake when another friend also organised a journey and wanted his services. This person was so particular that he could not take off without Okal. He camped, with his entourage, waiting for Okal's party at the lakeshore. When the canoe carrying Okal moored, they hastily got hold of Okal and interested him in the next journey. Being the hedonist that he was, Okal did not resist but went into the next canoe and proceeded on the journey.

It happened that during the previous journey, Okal and his fellow travellers had been very well fed. On the next journey, the treatment was even better, with delicious food Okal could not resist. The tragedy came, however, when the two varieties of food met in the stomach — they were a poisonous mixture. Okal died before the end of the journey. The Luo reckon that if he had moderated himself and refused to proceed on this journey, Okal would have lived. Greed took him to his death. That is the reality which is alluded to in the abbreviated proverb: *Ich lach nonego Okal Tako*. (Greed killed Okal Tako).

Extremism, like that of Okal, is again the subject of the proverb: *Ikadhogo ka nyar kathomo mane oting'o moo e chieno*. (You have exceeded the limit like the Kathomo woman who carried ghee in the "chieno" skirt).

65

The anecdote behind this proverb is that the Kathomo woman who had gone visiting liked the ghee she was served so much that she hid some of it in her girdle only to be embarrassed when it melted and exposed her. She had overstepped the boundaries of decency by hiding the oil in her skirt. This proverb calls for moderation and resistance to the alluring.

The traditional Luo ghee is a delicacy which any ordinary person would like to have more of. But there are limits to fulfilling one's desires. These limits apply especially when one is among strangers or in a context where personal decency is paramount, like when on a visit, and a modicum of respect is required. Allusion is also used in, *Nitwo ka Nyamgondho* (You will dry like Nyamgondho).

The proverb is used to warn arrogant people that the source of their arrogance might dissipate and leave them in dire straits. The proverb alludes to a Luo legend, Nyamgondho wuod Ombare, who was a poor fisherman until he one day fished an old hag from the depths of the sea. This woman was some kind of fairy who turned his life round and brought him a lot of wealth in the form of cattle. Overnight, Nyamgondho became the village tycoon. But he soon forgot where he had come from and started harassing the woman. As mercurially as she had entered his life, she disappeared with all the wealth she had brought. Nyamgondho followed her as she made her way back to the waters, pleading with her to no avail. He could not believe as he saw the cattle disappear into the water after the woman. He stood on the shores of the lake staring into space and got transfixed to that spot. When the proverb tells us that we might be transfixed like him, it is indeed warning us not to take our fortunes for granted and start getting arrogant. (See the narrative "Nyamgondho wuod Ombare" in the section on narratives).

The foregoing analysis is meant to serve as an introduction to the nature of the Luo proverb as a socio-artistic form. There are numerous other ways of looking at the proverbs for greater perceptions of their semantic and stylistic dynamics.

A collection of Luo proverbs

1. *Acham ayieng' nonego suna.*
   "Let me eat and be full" killed the mosquito. (Greed begets misery).

2. *Adiera en sum.*
   Truth is poison.

3. *Adiera ok tou.*
   The truth never decays.

4. *Agulu mirito ok yieny.*
   A pot being watched over never boils. (Impatience makes the wait longer).

5. *Akuru ok kwodh e iro.*
   The dove is never backbitten in a smoky place.

6. *Alot michayo ema tieko kuon.*
   It is the despised vegetables that eats up the ugali.

7. *Aluru oidho yath.*
   The quail has climbed a tree.*

8. *Ang'e ok tel.*
   "I wish I knew" (or regrets) never precedes (comes first).

9. *Anyam Ny'Othoche, chiemo lone nindo.*
   Anyam Ny'Othoche, for him food is better than sleep.

10. *Apuoyo tin to go rude.*
    The hare might be small, but it begets twins.

11. *Atonga mayot ema iyombo go koth.*
    It is with a light basket that one escapes the rain.

12. *Awayo ojogo lak.*
    "Awayo" (a sour herb) has tired the teeth. (Familiarity breeds contempt).

13. *Awendo ok we yiere.*
    The guinea fowl n ver abandons its colour/feathers. (Like father like son).

14. *Bed uru motang' Hundhwe ni machiegni.*
    Be careful all of you, the chaffinch is around. (Walls have ears).

15. *Ber imedo gi ariyo.*
    Beauty is complemented by other virtues.

16. *Bingo iro ok e tedo.*
    Effusion of smoke is not the same as cooking. (Big boast, small roast).

17. *Bul pek ka ji dwogo.*
    The drum is very heavy on the return journey.**

18. *Bur achiel ok riwie ji ariyo.*
    Two people are never put together into one hole/grave. (Two cats and a mouse, two wives in one house, two dogs and a bone never agree in one).

---

*An impossibility has taken place. Enjoying privileges beyond oneself.

**When people are going for a ceremony or festival, they are excited and do not realise the weight of the drums on which they are playing. This only becomes apparent when the excitement is over. The proverb corresponds to a Swahili proverb "Kupanda mchongoma, kushuka ndiyo ngoma" which means "to climb the thorn tree is easy, climbing down is the dance". There are always two sides to an issue.

19. *Bur ochiek dwaro thinyo.*
    The boil is mature and needs to be squeezed. (It is an opportune time).

20. *Chako chon loyo dhi ajuoga.*
    Starting early is better than seeking a medicine man later.(Prevention is better than cure).

21. *Chako ok e tieko.*
    Starting is not the same as completing.

22. *Chandruok medo rieko.*
    Suffering increases knowledge/wisdom. (Experience is the best teacher).

23. *Chan man kowadu ok moni nindo.*
    Your brother's poverty does not make you sleepless.

24. *Chien kiyany'.*
    The past is never despised.

25. *Chiero mithiedho ema gawi.*
    The squint eye that you have treated is the one that looks at you maliciously. (The thanks of a donkey are kicks).

26. *Chuny midwaro ema ibang'o.*
    The liver you have asked for is the one you eat. (One should be ready to carry one's burden).

27. *Chuth ber.*
    Immediacy is best.*

28. *Dalau kirwenyi.*
    You can never forget your home. (East or west, home is best).

29. *Dhako marach jamocho tung'.*
    The unpleasant woman airs her wares at the edge. (A guilty conscience needs no accuser).

30. *Dhano winyo.*
    The human being is a bird.

31. *Dher ariemba wuongo nyiedho to ng'iyo oko.*
    The keeper of a loaned cow milks it while looking outwards to the gate.

32. *Dhiang' otho od gi Odhera.*
    A cow has been slaughtered at Odhera's home. (Good luck has come to the paupers and miscreants).

---

*This proverb was popularised by a contestant for the Nyakach Parliamentary seat, Mr Dennis Akumu, whose motto during an election was that a candidate promising development to the constituents should show his ability by giving out tangible items during the campaign. The proverb has since been used in other contexts to prompt quick action.

33. *Dhier kiyombi.*
Poverty can never entirely be eluded.

34. *Dhogra chi atera.*
The inherited wife is a complex/muddle.

35. *Dhok e juok.*
It is the word of mouth that is sorcery.*

36. *Dhok tung dhano.*
The mouth is the human being's horn (defence).

37. *Ero koro iomo Nyajwaya gi sere.*
Now you are prodding Nyajwaya** with an arrow.

38. *Ero ti ileny mit ki chieng' itwo.*
Now you are oil-shiny; may you one day be dry!

39. *Fulu bende oro ngege.*
Even *"fulu"* sends tilapia.

40. *Gima ichamo e mari.****
It's what you have already eaten that belongs to you.

41. *Gima ichuoyo ema ikayo.*
You only reap what you have sowed.

42. *Gima ogen jabare.*
What is most anticipated usually fails to materialise. (Do not cry herrings until they are in the net).

43. *Gimoro iwe gi mitne.*
Something is left when it is still sweet.

44. *Guok dhi mana kama oyude chogo.*
A dog only goes where it gets bones.

45. *Gweno uch gi ombij wadgi kiny to mare.*
A hen scurries with its kin's entrails but tomorrow is its turn.

46. *Hera mudho.*
Love is blind.

---

* One may imprecate his fellow with no ill intention. But then something dreadful may well happen to the object of the imprecation.
**Nyajwaya is a mythical character who keeps his cool until provoked. Do not trouble trouble before trouble troubles you.
***This proverb is commonly used by mourners to express the fact that death makes ambitions futile.

47. *Ich lach nonego Okal Tako.*
Greed killed Okal Tako.

48. *Igedo e yo joraw chandi gi wach.*
You've built along the way, sojourners bother you.

49. *Ikadhogo ka nyar kathomo mane oting'o moo e chieno.*
You have exceeded the limit like the Kathomo woman who carried ghee in her skirt.

50. *Inind diere inind tung'.*
You sleep in the middle, you sleep at the fringe.

51. *Iro ok dum mak mach oliel.*
There is no smoke without fire.

52. *Iyieyo kori ka kor opuk madwasi.*
You are over-enthusiastic like the female tortoise.*

53. *Jabar bende ibaro.*
The dissector is also dissected.

54. *Jaber jaula.*
The beautiful one is deceptive. (All that glisters is not gold.)

55. *Jaber puothe tin.*
The beautiful one's garden is small.**

56. *Jabudho e duonde ariyo jabed jamriambo.*
He who stays in two "duonde" often becomes a liar.

57. *Jachan guonyore gi pado.*
The pauper scratches himself using a potsherd.

58. *Jachan nyombo gi wang'e.*
The pauper marries with his eyes. (If you can't get it, you can at least admire/desire it.)

59. *Jachwech chiemo e tago.*
A potter eats in a potsherd.

---

*The imagery is that the tortoise has a hard chest on which one can even grind grains. But if the tortoise over-exposes it to this activity, there is bound to be pain.

**The idea is that she is pre-occupied with her appearance rather than industry and can therefore only manage to cultivate a small plot.

60. *Jagam dhoge ariyo.*
The mediator has two mouths. (In traditional society, the mediator, "jagam", refers to he/she who introduces a bride to a prospective husband or wife.)

61. *Ja hawanya otugore gi siro.*
The intruder/unwelcome guest has fallen with the pillar/post.

62. *Jakech kimosi.*
A hungry man is never greeted.

63. *Jakech kinger.*
A hungry man is never teased (or does not know a joke).

64. *Jakech kiwe e dero.*
A hungry man is never left alone in the granary.

65. *Jakuodho oyie dhaw.*
He who has broken wind is ready for a fight.

66. *Jakuoth ki ti.*
The gossip never ages.

67. *Jakuo wuotho mana gi jakuo wadgi.*
The thief only walks with another thief. (Birds of the same feather flock together.)

68. *Jamak ng'et ok en jang'iepne.*
He who holds/books the ribs during the slaughter is not necessarily the buyer.

69. *Jamneme ng'ute tin.*
The one infected with jiggers has a small neck. (Some things are obvious).

70. *Janeko ema lielore kende.*
It's only the madman that shaves his own hair.

71. *Janeko omi gara.*
The mad one has been given jingles.*

72. *Jang'ol osiki ok ter dhako.*
The stump-cutter (for the funeral fire) does not inherit the widow. (Those who precede are not necessarily the eventual winners).

73. *Janyao mor gi jumapil.*
The lazy/weak one is happy on Sunday.

---

*A comment on a person revelling in an obsession.

74. *Jaote ok go lero.*
A messenger is never stoned.

75. *Jaou wach jatur bat.*
He who exaggerates issues breaks arms.

76. *Jaraw arawa owaro wi kuon.*
The sojourner has scraped the top of *ugali*.

77. *Jarikni jamuod nyoyo gi kwoyo.*
The hasty one eats sand in his *nyoyo*.

78. *Jasem piere otuch.*
The detractor has holes on the buttocks.

79. *Jatelo ogongo gwaro.*
The leader gets pricked by *ogongo*.*

80. *Jaum gwen ema ong'eyo saa donjogi.*
It's the one who covers the chicken who knows when they come to roost.

81. *Jowi mager ema ichuogo piene.*
It is the skin of a fierce buffalo that makes the shield.

82. *Kama gweno ok kogie ikwaye ojeni.*
Leftover ugali is sought from where chicken do not crow.**

83. *Kama ili ema igwonyo.*
It is the itchy part that you scratch.

84. *Kama iluokrie ok ituoe.*
You do not dry where you have bathed.

85. *Kapod in epi kik iyany nyang'.*
Do not abuse the crocodile when you are still in the water.

86. *Kich ithodho to kecho.*
When honey is being harvested, the bees bite. (One goes down fighting).

87. *Kigori gi nyathi to en ema humbe dhi.*
If you fight with a child, he gets all the fame.

88. *Kik ilaw winy ariyo.*
Do not chase two birds at the same time.

89. *Kik ipakri gi mwandu ma kowadu.*
Do not boast about your brother's wealth.

---

*Aqualine thorns.
**If there are chickens, they will be fed the leftovers.

90. *Kik iriemb jaluoro nyaka eode.*
Do not chase the coward right into his house.

91. *Kinda e teko.*
Persistence is strength.

92. *Kinda kiteng'a nomiyo opuk ogwaro nyar min Kibogo.*
Persistence led to the tortoise scratching the groin of Kibogo's mother.

93. *Kinda ne omiyo opuk oyombo Apuoyo.*
Persistence led Tortoise to victory over Hare.

94. *Kodh yamo norwaki.*
A storm will escort/welcome you home. (East or west, home is best).

95. *Kogno achiel ok neg onyuogo.*
One nail does not kill a louse.

96. *Koth go gima oyudo.*
The rain falls on whatever it finds on the way.

97. *Kudho chwoyo ng'ama onyone.*
The thorn only pierces he who has stepped on it.

98. *Kudni achiel ema towo ring'o.*
It is one worm that infects the meat.

99. *Kwot ogwal ok mon dhiang' modho.*
The bloating of a frog does not prevent the cow from drinking.(Might is right.)

100. *Lak chogo.*
The tooth is a bone.

101. *Liech ikuodho ka oloko ng'eye.*
The elephant is backbitten when it has turned its back.

102. *Liech ong'iyo gi oporo.*
The elephant is used to the blow-horn.

103. *Liend nyathini iyweyo ka ihero.*
You clean your child's grave with love. (Love persists even in sorrow).

104. *Ludhi ema ichwado go tho.*
It is your stick that you use to shake off dew.

105. *Lwang'ni ma oheri ema piyo kuomi.*
It is a loving fly that perches on you.

106. *Maliet ema kwe.*
It is that which is hot that gets cold.

107. *Manga oromo gi Magare.*
Manga has met Magare.*

108. *Ma ochomi ka pier matindo.*
This one faces you like thin buttocks. (You cannot escape this situation just like you cannot dispense with your physique.)

109. *Maro oketho Ugunja.*
The mother-in-law has ruined Ugunja.*

110. *Masira kiyombi.*
Misfortune cannot be entirely eluded.

111. *Mbaka nyapong' gi dero.*
The conversation between the grinding stone and the granary.***

112. *Misumba tho arieya.*
The bachelor dies stiff.

113. *Motwo ne owuondo manumu*
The dry cheated the green.

114. *Mudho okonyo ondiek.*
Darkness has helped the hyena.

115. *Ng'ama chiemo gi muofu ema ong'eyo mit bor.*
It is he who eats with a blind man that knows the delicacy of fat.

116. *Ng'ama dwaro ema yudo.*
He who seeks gets. (Knock and the door will be opened.)

---

*Manga and Magare are two mythical figures who are equal in strength. The proverb is used in a situation where there is an epic showdown between powers and the most likely outcome is a stalemate.

*(Ugunja is a small rural town in Ugenya, Siaya District. A story is told of one young man working in Nairobi who met a maiden and they agreed to marry. But he had to visit her home to negotiate the terms of marriage. He and his entourage decided to have a drink at the local bar before proceeding to the girl's home. During the drink, he met a woman who agreed to play pander to his amorous advances. The two retired to a nearby bush. When it was over, the woman excused herself to rush home and attend to some visitors. The man also took off to complete his mission. When the man was introduced to the prospective mother-in-law the two realised that they had met before. The proverb is used to refer to an abomination, such as in this story.

***This abbreviated proverb alludes to the apparently unending struggle.between the grinding stone and the granary, namely: the grinding stone seems all the time to be telling the granary: "I shall finish you, with time", and the latter insists, "I am too large for you". The proverb is used to denote a stalemate.

117. *Ng'ama nigi nyathi ok nind e thim.*
He who has a child does not sleep in the wilderness.

118. *Ng'ama nyap ok ket e kwer.*
A weakling/lazy person is not made to plough.

119. *Ng'ama nyap tek konyo.*
It is difficult to help a weakling.

120. *Ng'ama oloyi kiyang' dheri.*
He who is stronger than you does not slaughter your cow/bull.

121. *Ng'ama oloyi onyono kwesi meru.*
He who is stronger has stepped on your mother's smoking pipe.

122. *Ng'at ma miel mamit ema iting'o bade.*
It's the good dancer whose arms are raised.

123. *Ng'at marach jatang!.*
A bad person is always suspicious. (A guilty conscience needs no accuser).

124. *Ng'at momoso thum ema iwero.*
He who has "greeted the music" is the one whose praise is sung.

125. *Ng'ech miyo gi eiye.*
The monitor is fatty from the inside.

126. *Ng'ech ywayo tek.*
It is very difficult to pull a monitor lizard.

127. *Ngera e awanya.*
Jesting is enough self-invitation.

128. *Ng'wen ne ogalo dhako ka pondo.*
White ants distracted a woman who was deserting a marriage.

129. *Ng'wen ok bodhi e dho bur.*
You do not harvest the white ants from the hole they are flying out of.
(Discretion helps).

130. *Nindo nyamin tho.*
Sleep is the sister (kin) of death.

131. *Nindo otero jater.*
Sleep overwhelmed the wife inheritor.

132. *Nindo tek matero janeko.*
Sleep is so strong it even overcomes the lunatic.

133. *Nine gima ne Olweru oneno Nyayiera.*
You will see what Olweru saw in Nyayiera.*

134. *Nirom gi makolwer.*
You will meet the untrimmed. (Used in the same way as the preceding proverb).

135. *Nitwo ka Nyamgondho.*
You will dry like Nyamgondhɔ.**

136. *Nyabondo moher oyieyo kidek ng'ado.*
The beloved *nyabondo* may be gnawed through by a rat. (What we treasure most is what often gets destroyed.)

137. *Nyaguok modenyo ok tug gi nyaguok moyieng'.*
A hungry puppy does not play with a satisfied one.

138. *Nyaguok ong'iyo kama omuode chogo.*
A puppy frequents where it crunches bones.

139. *Nyang'eya mane ong'eyo ka guok dhi yudo nying'.*
The one who even knew when the dog was going to get a name. (Criticises know-alls or extroverts.)

140. *Nyang' omi amiya.*
The crocodile has just been given.***

141. *Nyar rachiero ogo bul otucho.*
The squint-eyed girl played the drum until it burst.

142. *Nyathi mioro ema chiethne duong'.*
It is the child who accepts to run errands that has big excreta.

143. *Nyathi moyieng' owang'o dero.*
The satisfied child has burnt the granary.****

144. *Nyathi otenga ok cham alot.*
The kite's chick does not eat vegetables.

145. *Nyathi punda kidong' chien.*
The donkey's young one never remains behind.

---

*A warning against bravado.

**See the narrative "Nyamgondho son of Ombare".

***There is a belief that certain deaths are caused by sorcery. One of these is that a sorcerer might set his charms so that you get caught and eaten by a crocodile. In this sense, the crocodile is an innocent messenger of the sorcerer.

****An ignorant person is likely to cause disaster.

146. *Nyodo ne okonyo omboga.*
The offsprings helped the *omboga* vegetables.
147. *Nungo piny kirom.*
One cannot span the waist of the world.
148. *Obaro nyar Wasare ne otero bul e budho simba.*
The deviant girl, daughter of Wasare went to a *simba** meeting with a drum.
149. *Obol ka pany kech.*
He/she is as humble as the mortar during a famine.
150. *Obudha Walunya ne obulo ring'o e kwesi.*
Obudha Walunya roasted meat in a smoking pipe. (The society cannot tolerate extreme deviance.)
151. *Ogwang' chamo to tho rome.*
The mongoose/wild cat eats but it suffers from dew.
152. *Ogwang' itedo gi more.*
A mongoose/wild cat is fried in its cwn fat.
153. *Ogwang' iwito gi lawe.*
A mongoose is thrown away with its clothes/dress/skin.
154. *Ogwang' tho eloj wadji.*
A mongoose dies in the stead of its kin.
155. *Ohigla geto kabange.*
The small pot covets the big pot.
156. *Olang'o ng'we gi oro kata koth ochwe.*
The soldier ants smell both in drought and the wet season.
157. *Ondeyo ngang' to Anyango budho.*
Ondeyo is stretched to breaking point while Anyango is just relaxing.**
158. *Ondieg thuru ok chami duto.*
A beast from your home does not eat you completely.
159. *Ondiek odak e niang' to kia mit niang'.*
The beast stays in the sugar cane plantation but does not know the sweetness of sugar cane.

Simba is the bachelors' hut where they sometimes invite their lovers.
**The idea is that the trickster always takes advantage of his colleague, letting the latter bear the brunt of the task while he waits to reap the benefits. One beats the bush and the other catches the bird.

160. *Ondiek ok nyier nono ma ok oneno wen.*
The hyena does not laugh unless it has seen the offal.(There is no smoke without fire.)

161. *Ondong' mitoke ema itokonie.*
The same plate you have served others in is the one that is used to serve you.

162. *Ong'ino kata tin to ok ma ng'wende.*
Even though it is small, the black ant cannot be robbed of its termite. (Everyone has a right.)

163. *Opuk ogo e pige.*
The tortoise has been immersed in its water.*

164. *Ori diere kuok nego.*
The middle one is dying from sweat. (A knave is often caught in his own trap.)

165. *Osiep maber loyo chiemo mamit.*
Better a good friend than delicious food. (A good friend is a treasure).

166. *Osundu Swaye ringo ka otoyo koneno wen.*
The sycophant runs like a hyena who has seen offal.

167. *Otieno ni opoke?*
Has this Otieno been peeled?**

168. *Otoyo moluor ema ru.*
It is the timid hyena that lasts the night. (He that goes softly goes safely).

169. *Owinjore sare gi remo.*
Matching like the shell and the blood.***

170. *Owiti wuon Akwenda ne ogoyo dero ne bend afula.*
Owiti son of Akwenda built a grain store for gleaned millet. (He was over-optimistic and exceeded the limit.)

171. *Oyieyo achiel ok kuny bur.*
One rat does not dig a hole.

172. *Oyieyo kayi to kudhi.*
The rat bites you and soothes the wound. (A person whom you think is a friend undermines you.)

---

*The proverb is used to refer to a situation where someone has been given a familiar task or put in a situation of his/her liking.

**Said derisively of someone behaving unrealistically elitist. Was this one borne or lowered to earth direct by God?.

***In the past, Luos used shells to scoop and eat boiled blood. This proverb is said of a perfect match, e.g., of an ideal wife and husband.

78

173. *Oyieyo mang'eny ok kuny bur.*
Many rats do not dig a hole.

174. *Pand nyaluo dhoge ariyo.*
The traditional knife has two edges.

175. *Pi luoro togo.*
The water is surrounding the floating island. (One is working his way into trouble naively.)

176. *Piny agonda.*
The world is zigzag. (Change of fortune is the lot of life.)

177. *Piny maru loyo yie rombo gi ng'eny.*
Dawning days outnumber the sheep's wool.

178. *Rabote dhako kileng'.*
A woman's missile never misses its target.

179. *Rachiero okwongo ne owadgi.*
The squint-eyed preceded his brother. (The pot calling the kettle black.)

180. *Rakuom ong'e kaka nindo.*
The hunchback knows how he/she sleeps.

181. *Rapemo nokecho obwanda Wamlare.*
Rapemo coveted Wamlare's vegetables. (The mighty also come down to earth.)

182. *Rasundu thone tek.*
A fool never dies.

183. *Ratego omako dhiang' rachiero logo komiyo wang'e.*
The strong one has held the bull, now the squint-eyed draws the blood with his eyes closed. (Over-confidence can lead to complacency.)

184. *Rieko lo teko.*
Brain is mightier than brawn.

185. *Rienga jawuoth achiel.*
The lone traveller is not to be trusted.

186. *Ruoth ok yierre kende.*
The king does not elect himself.

187. *Rwath tho gi lum e dhoge.*
The bull dies with grass in the mouth.

188. *Sembe iporo gi nyamin.*
The ram's fatty tail is compared to another. (History repeats itself.)

189. *Sindan tin to tweng'o.*
The needle might be tiny, but it sews.

190. *Sukruok ne omiyo ong'er yip.*
Meddling earned the monkey its tail. (Haste trips up on its own heels.)

191. *Tama ga tindo ka mama oa thurgi.*
I cannot savour when mother returns from a visit to her maiden home.(We forget to economise when there is bounty.)

192. *Thigo oyaw ne par.*
The door is ajar for the mat. (When the boss is absent, everyone is boss.)

193. *Thiring'inyi otenga kata nyagweno ng'we.*
The kite does not mind even if the chick is rotten.

194. *Thum wero ng'ama nitie.*
A musician praises only he who is there. (Out of sight, out of mind.)

195. *Thuol odonjo e koo.*
A snake has entered the gourd.*

196. *Thuon gwen ariyo ok riw e a gulu achiel.*
Two cocks are never cooked in the same pot.

197. *Tintin ok midekre.*
A small body is not an ailment.

198. *Tuk goyo odumbo mit ne nyithindo to kuom joka ogwal to en kuyo.*
Throwing objects into the water is fun for children but for the frogs it is sorrow.

199. *Wacho to e timo?*
Is saying the same as doing? (Action speaks louder than words.)

200. *Wang' onge giko.*
The eye has no limits.

201. *Wat imedo gi osiep.*
Kinship is complemented with friendship.

202. *Wat ng'we.*
Kinship smells. (You cannot extricate yourself from your kin.)

203. *Wat osiko.*
Kinship is permanent.

---

*Used in a dilemma when whatever action taken leads to loss of one kind or another.

204. *Wat wat.*
Kinship is kinship.

205. *Wendo bade boyo.*
The visitor has long arms.

206. *Wendo ma pok olimi ok igone chiegi.*
You do not beat up your wife on account of a first-time visitor.

207. *Wichkuot ne onego apuoyo gono.*
Shyness killed the hare in its lair. (Sleeping foxes catch no poultry.)

208. *Wich liech turo mana wuongo.*
The elephant's head is its owner's burden. (Every bird must hatch its own eggs.)

209. *Wuoche achiel ok wuothgo e kudho.*
One shoe is not enough for walking through a thorny patch. (Full measure carries the day. Half measures mean half accomplishments.)

210. *Yago ohewo tonde.*
The sausage fruit is heavier than its holder/suspender.

211. *Yieng'o aila.*
Satisfaction is an excitement. (Once one's basic needs are satisfied, one goes for leisure.)

212. *Yie nimo ka dhi gowo.*
A boat capsizes just when it is about to moor.

213. *Yie ok neg ji duto.*
A boat never kills everyone on board.

214. *Yore ariyo ne otamo ondiek luwo.*
The hyena could not follow two paths.

215. *Yuoro law kwach.*
A sister-in-law is a leopard skin.*

---

*Sisters-in-law are regarded very highly by their brothers-in-law. Their worth is compared in this proverb to the valued trophy, a leopard's skin.

Chapter 4

POETRY

Introduction

Poetry refers to the expression of powerful human feelings, thoughts and ideas through words and sounds arranged in the most effective manner. This arrangement is called verse. Verse is, therefore, the vehicle which carries poetry. But one can have verse that is not poetry, i.e. nonsense rhymes and elocutionary verses. In this chapter, are found various samples of both. In the text, however, the word "poetry" is used broadly to cover both varieties. The reader will notice that examples used in the texts vary from pieces which are sung, others that are rendered in speech, recited, declaimed or dramatised. These are but variable modes of expression. Luo (and other African) poetic performances exhibit a fusion of these different modes. A good example is the Luo *nyatiti* (lyre) tradition where the performer often starts off with a spoken praise name, slides into song, goes into a declamation and reverts to song.

In "West African Voices", *African Affairs 48*, 1949, D.C. Osadebey et al say of African poetry:

> We sing when we fight; we sing when we work, we sing when we make love, we sing when we hate, we sing when a child is born, we sing when death takes a toll.

These words appropriately describe Luo poetry, whether rendered in song, speech or incantation. The Luo are a ceremonious people whose culture is replete with poetic performance both in the public and private realm. The vastness of this poetic panorama makes it impossible for one to capture all of it in the space of an anthology. The Luo do not necessarily have uniform poetic text, although there are similarities from area to area. What is represented here are samples of Luo poetry collected directly from the field, recorded from the author's own memory and adopted from published sources.

The field material was mainly collected during research done in the mid-1980s in Asembo-Bay of Bondo District. For each of the poems in the anthology, brief explanatory notes are given to explain performance, meaning and context. These notes are based on information provided to the author by the field sources and from his own understading of the Luo oral tradition. Readers are, however, encouraged to make their own interpretations from their unique understading of the pieces presented. There is no universal and standard interpretation of any literary material.

Classification of Luo poetry

Luo poetic forms can be classified according to various criteria including function, social context and performer, among others. In this text, we identify the forms of Luo poetry as they are classified by the community or as classified by the informants for the research which resulted in this text. The classes are:

1. *Wende malongo* (Twin birth songs).
2. *Wende hoyo nyithindo* (Lullabies).
3. *Wende nyithindo* (Children's songs).
4. *Wende keny/ndaria* (Nuptial songs).
5. *Wende mon* (Women's songs).
6. *Wende tich* (Work songs).
7. *Wende nyiera* (Satirical verses).
8. *Wende hera* (Love poetry).
9. *Wende kong'o* (Beer-drinking songs).
10. *Wende pak* (Praise songs).
11. *Wende nyatiti* (Lyre poetry).
12. *Wende orutu* (Orutu* songs).
13. *Wende peke* (Songs accompanied by playing an instrument made from bottle tops).
14. *Gajo lep* (Word play/Elocutionary poetry).
15. *Wende lweny* (War songs).
16. *Wende tho kod kuyo* (Dirges and songs of sorrow).

    The community classifies its poetry according to a multiplicity of criteria including:

- Performers (2, 4).
- Context (1, 5, 6, 7, 9).
- Function (3, 8, 13, 14, 15).

---

*Orutu is a one-stringed instrument.

83

- Instrumentation (10, 11, 12).
- Style (16).

It should be noted that these are not rigid and exclusive classes of poetry. For instance, a song sung during a beer drinking party may be a praise song as well.

In terms of formalisation of performance and popularity, the *nyatiti* poetry is what can be easily classified as the major traditional Luo oral poetic form. The text presents two *nyatiti* songs with brief notes.

Performance and style

The samples of Luo oral poems presented in this anthology reveal various stylistic features characteristic of oral poetry. The main features are discussed below with examples from the different classes of poetry covered in the anthology. But as a general note, it is worth mentioning that the pervasive modes of delivery of Luo oral poetry are: song, recital, declamation and drama. The poems could be either solo, choral or antiphonal as explained below.

Solo performance: This mode of performance is characteristic of specific genres like lullabies, love songs and work songs (where the chore is solitary). But there are also solo performances with regard to all other genres like panegyric and the dirge.

Choral performance: This form of performance is particularly evident in children's play poetry. It involves a group simultaneously voicing the poem, usually rendered in the song mode. In fact, most of the children's play poetry in this anthology is choral performance.

Antiphony or strophe: It will be noticed that most choral poems are also antiphonal, i.e. there are two parties alternating in voicing the words with a soloist calling the tune and a chorus answering. The poem, *Owang' Winyo ma Nyasure* (the Crested Crane Bird), is a classic example of antiphonal performance.

Drama: The word "drama" is used here in the sense of "non-verbal" articulation in a performance. This may be quite limited or elaborate. In a lullaby, the drama includes the swaying and rocking of the child to and fro. And in the self-praise poem, there is a lot of head shaking, hand gestures and body movements in the arena. In the dirge, the drama is quite intense as the mourner mounts a mock fight with death and scavenges around for imaginary enemies who he spears.

We see drama in the children's dance songs, *Ng'ielo* (Python), and *Nyarombo Mee*. We also see it in *Min Aloo*, which is actually a dramatised recital in which the children parody a meeting with a woman with varicose veins. The drama, therefore, involves the child acting *Min Aloo* and the others taunting her. Drama is also quite explicit in *The Crested Crane Bird* as the singers and players demonstrate the attributes of the crane bird.

The dirge is another poetic form that illustrates drama. A woman singing a dirge performs some kind of involuntary dance plodding the compound where the corpse lies in state. She holds her waist or head in disbelief, hits her hands against her thighs, wipes tears from her eyes and blows phlegm from the nose while shrieking in tantrums that may also include rolling on the ground. At the end of it all, she is red-eyed, physically tired and her voice husky.

The man can alternatively be heard voicing his dirge from afar as he approaches the funeral. He carries a huge club, blows a horn and wears headgear. As he nears the homestead, the outburst becomes more dramatic as he breaks into short sprints in a mock-fight with death.

Simplicity, elasticity and spontaneity

In oral performance, especially of song, the text is often not fixed. It may be shortened or lengthened depending on the requirements of the moment. The lengthening may be done by repeating certain lines or inclusion of other ideas. Often, an oral performer takes stock of his audience in the performance and uses it as a source of reference by including their names and other things observed during the performance, as classically exemplified in a *nyatiti* session. It means that as he performs, he also creates; it is not a mere reproduction of rehearsed material.

But this is an aspect that is also evident in poetic forms such as lullabies, children's play poetry and elocutionary poems. Take the case of the lullaby, *Nyandolo*. The first key characteristic of this lullaby is its structural simplicity ensured by the use of repetitive lines and words. In *Nyandolo*, we see a poem that basically consists of three structural segments repeated over and over with variation only in the person referred to. The first segment introduces the subject of the song (let sleep overcome the child). The second calls on the source of the sleep and the third asks sleep to move over. The second and the third segments are then repeated over and over again.

Elasticity can also be exemplified with the elocutionary poem, *Nyako*, which can be recited indefinitely as it keeps ricocheting to some earlier section from where the series is repeated. This element of elasticity is obvious even in lullabies and panegyrics which can be extended for as long as there is need, with the singer adding names of people or other references.

Repetition

As mentioned above, repetition is a common feature of Luo oral poems of all categories. In the children's play song, *Python*, for instance, we see a poem that is structurally static with syllabically similar lines sung by the soloist and a refrain echoed by the chorus. The only change is in the last line where the poem uses onomatopoeia (*sesegere*) to bring the song to a climactic end.

Apostrophe

Apostrophe refers to addressing absent subjects. For instance, in *Nyandolo*, sleep is addressed by the child minder; in *Oombe,* the beast is also called upon to devour the crying child while in *Mama Nyaka Nende Idhi e Chiro* (Mother Since You Went to the Market), the child minder calls on the mother to somewhat intervene vicariously and quieten the crying child. In the work song, *Akuru Ny'Obondo,* the dove is addressed by the worker as if it were present. Dirges are also strong in their use of apostrophe where mourners address death and the deceased as if they were able to hear and respond.

Allusion

Two poems in this anthology illustrate the use of allusion. *Min Okumu* ends with a refrain "*Abakunda kunda kunda*" which is historically allusive of the Ugandan group of drummers, *Abakunta,* who enthralled audiences with their drums in the late 19th century. The second allusive poem is *Mumi Gocho* in which the orchestra of fish is arranged. This ditty reminds us of the fact that the Luo, who live around Lake Victoria, are familiar with different types of fish and, in this case, personify them with different characteristics. There is a double allusion in this ditty. While the obvious one is the reference to the 'Twist' dance style which was a rave in the 1960s and 1970s, there is also the element of live bands or orchestras as indicated in the fact that there is a conductor. It is conceivable that this poem was composed during this era.

Satire (irony, humour, symbolism)

Satire is often a result of use of other devices like irony, sarcasm and the like. The satirical poems presented in this anthology reflect various devices already discussed. But three outstanding aspects of style that need to be mentioned here include imagery, irony and parody. The poem, *Oyundi*, satirises the lazy person

86

by parodying a conversation between two sparrows in which the first, ostensibly an elder to the second, asks the latter to undertake certain chores. The second sparrow is ready with all kinds of excuses for not doing so. Ironically, however, this sick sparrow has a burst of healthy energy when it is told that the food is ready. At this time, it is no longer sick and speeds to the table as ideophonically represented in *sesese*. Of course the sparrow is personified by being given speech abilities and human duties and stands out as a symbol.

Noticeable in the poems, whether they are sung, recited or dramatised, is the inlaid satire in a number of them. In *Ng'ielo*, there is a slight satire on the son-in-law who blasted his way into the mother-in-law's house; in *Min Okumu*, the woman who cannot dance is lampooned just as *Min Aloo* is laughed at because of her varicose veins.

The use of humour is integral to satire and we see this vividly in the *Nyatiti* song *Msonga Odhil* in which the player reels out one humourous situation after another. First, he talks about how a mute illustrates that he is ready for marriage by nestling his sister. Secondly, there is the case of the beer brewer (a woman) who is so infatuated that she has forgotten she is brewing beer for a living and has surrendered all the beer to her lover to share with his friends. Thirdly, we have the pauper who has such ravenous appetite that when he gets money, it all ends up in delicious food rather than on other needs. The fourth is one with a sexual undertone. The poet talks of everything being delicious in nakedness. He goes ahead to count the items like groundnuts, maize cobs and sugar cane. But what the poet actually means, but does not state, is that even human beings are delicious when naked! By not explicitly stating this and using circumlocution, the poet actually makes obvious what he means.

Hyperbole

Hyperbole is another stylistic element typical particularly of panegyric. A notable example is in the *J. Oreng'* poem where the poet claims that the host slaughtered a fowl and the guests "ate soda". By this kind of exaggeration, the poet underlines the abundance of food and therefore stresses the magnanimity of his host. In another instance, he refers to his subject as the god of vehicles, i.e., a consummate mechanic who, like the creator, knows the vehicle inside out.

Elocution

By their very nature, elocutionary poems thrive on punning and coinage; for instance in the poem *Nyako* (Girl), but the response changes this into a verb "*Inyaka*" (you yield "e" which has totally no semantic relationship with the noun.

87

This gives rise to another coinage where the response is linked to another noun "rabuon" (potatoes). The third line then takes the last part of the second line, which is a noun, potatoes, for the next construction of a verb *"ibuona"* and so on. This kind of play on words illustrates the linguistic versatility of Dholuo.

This kind of coinage is also seen in the *nyatiti* poem, *J. Oreng'*, where the poet takes words and coins others out of them to create a new sense but also to have rythmic conformity. This is the case of the word "carrot" which the singer uses to construct a verb "rado" (crushes) as he names the ingredients of the meal they had. There is even some intricate reversal where the poet talks of the carrot crushing their mouths when the reality is that it is their mouths which crushed the carrots. In other words, the poet is saying that the interaction of the food and mouth was so intense and reciprocal one could not distinguish which was doing what.

Circumlocution

Luo poetry also abounds in circumlocution, especially in praise poetry. A person is not referred to just by his name and left at that. Reference to him is embellished with names of his relatives, friends, deeds and places of origin, material as well as paternal. This is an element we could probably call contextualisation: that a person is not an island but part of a wider context.

Social functions

Poetry, whether recited, declaimed or sung, has certain objectives. It is these ends that we call social functions. In this text, we have divided the functions into:

(a) socialisation,

(b) aesthetics,

(c) social commentary, and

(d) cultural and historical record.

Socialisation

Socialisation can be understood in two ways: as a way of fitting one into a social fabric or as a way of deriving pleasure through entertainment. The sense in which poetry is a socialiser encompasses both these as we obviously derive pleasure from poetry, since it is an art, but also derive some information intended to cultivate in us the sense of the social fabric from which the poetry is created.

To illustrate, let us take the occasion of the children's play song, *Nyarombo Mee*. In this song, the children sing as they pass under a bridge of arms formed by their leaders. At the end of each cycle of the song, a player is held and asked to name his or her food preference. If it is a vegetable, the player queues behind the leader whose trademark is the vegetable and if it is a carcass, the player queues behind the other leader. At the end, when all players have taken sides, there is a tug of war.

This occasion socialises in several ways. There is a division of labour and recognition of leadership, hence an element of organisation among the players. The social organisation is ensured by the rules of play (i.e., having to go through the bridge, be held, name one's preference, line up and then pull for one's side in the tug of war). The player is conditioned to accept the rules and more so to accept that anybody could join his or her group by virtue of choosing the type of food preferred. This is because the players do not know what each leader has chosen and each has to whisper the choice when held at the bridge. The vigour of movement, dance and pulling becomes an interactive process which is also a vent for release of pent-up energies and creation of pleasure.

Of course the pleasure derived from a poetic performance is for both the audience and the players as well — whether it emanates from the play on words, movement and dance, attire, humour and so on.

Aesthetics

Poetry is often defined as the arrangement of words in the best possible order. Inherent in this definition is the element of beauty. But that beauty is not only in the order of the words. It is in the choice of those words (diction), their arrangement (syntax) and the layers of meaning that accrue from their usage (polysemy, ambiguity) as well as the licence with which poets create new words (coinage) as comes out in *nyatiti* songs.

There is also the aspect of play on sounds which comes out so powerfully in the ideophones, alliteration, assonance, rhyme and rhythm. As well, there are the poems in which the words are not expressly meant for semantic communication but more as artistic expressions. This is the category of elucotionary poems. A detailed discussion of these aspects appears under the section on stylistic aspects.

Social commentary

Through oral poetry, the Luo express different thoughts and ideas often focusing on social life. Several examples can be cited of such commentary whether direct or indirect.

The play poem, *Python*, ends with the son-in-law shooting his way into the mother-in-law's house. This is an abominable intrusion because Luo customs prescribe a big physical and social distance between a son-in-law and his mother-in-law. By commenting on this unexpected behaviour, the poem is acting as an educator against such wayward behaviour, and is in fact laughing at it.

In *Min Okumu*, we also find criticism of those who are unable to dance, hence get to learn about the premium the Luo place on such social abilities. The other satirical poem, *Oyundi*, clearly illustrates that the community loathes laziness just as the poem, *J. Oreng*, indicates the value placed on magnanimity and expertise at one's job. Whether they are lullabies, work songs, play songs, elocutionary songs or dirges, Luo poems are almost always laced with some form of commentary on daily life.

Cultural and historical record

The poems in this anthology serve as examples of historical and cultural record, e.g., *Mumi Gocho* and *Min Okumu* which allude to certain periods in history. As discussed under stylistic aspects, *Min Okumu* ends with a refrain "*Abakunda kunda kunda...*" which is historically allusive of the Ugandan group of drummers (the Abakunta) who enthralled audiences with their drums in the late 19th century in western Kenya. *Mumi Gocho*, on the other hand, parodies an orchestra with fish as the members of the team. While the poem records for us the fact of Luo lacustrine environment, its reference to the 'Twist' style of dance, which was a rave in the 1960s and 1970s, leads to the inference that this poem was composed during this era when well organised live musical bands were a common feature on the entertainment scene.

A collection of Luo poems

Lullabies (Wende hoyo nyithindo)

Nyandolo

Nyandolo
Nindo otere
Nindo man e wang' baba
Obi mana ka
Nindo man e wang' mama
Obi mana ka
Nindo ma e wang' ...

Nyandolo

Nyandolo,
Let sleep overwhelm him/her.
The sleep in father's eyes,
Let it come here.
The sleep in mother's eyes,
Let it come here.
The sleep in ....

This lullaby is sung to a child by its nurse, who could be the mother, a sibling or other minder. It invites all the sleep to come and fill the child's eyes. It can continue indefinitely with the singer adding in as many names as possible.

Oombe

Oombe

Oombe oombe
Oombe oombe

Oombe oombe
Oombe oombe.

Nyathi ma ywak,
Ondiek chame!

A child who cries,
The beast eat it up!

Nyathi ma ywak,
Ondiek chame!

A child who cries,
The beast eat it up!

Nyathi marach,
Otoyo chame!

A child who cries,
The hyena eat it up!

Nyathi ma ling',
Ondiek weye.

A child who is quiet,
The beast spare it.

Nyathi ma ling',
Ondiek weye.

A child who is quiet,
The beast spare it.

Nyathi ma ling'
Otoyo weye.

A child who is quiet,
The hyena spare it.

The child in this lullaby is being prepared to sleep by being warned that it will be devoured by beasts if it does not keep quiet. The lullaby is mostly used when the child is crying but can also be sung when the child is quiet to help it appreciate behaving well by not crying unnecessarily. The word *"Ondiek"* generally refers to beasts such as the hyena (also called *"otoyo"*) and the leopard (also known as *"kwach"*). Some people would say *"Ondieg Otoyo"* for the hyena and *"Ondieg Kwach"* for the leopard.

Mama nyaka nende idhi e chiro   **Mother since you went to the market**

Mama nyaka nende idhi e chiro,   Mother since you went to the market,
To iweya gi leloni.   You left me with this "lelo"*.
Ng'ama rite to ng'a?   Who is nursing it?

Mama nyaka nende idhi e kulo,   Mother since you went to fetch water
To iweya gi leloni.   You left me with this "lelo".
Ng'ama rite to ng'a?   Who is nursing it?

Mama nyaka nende iwuog awuoga,   Mother since you just left,
To iweya gi leloni.   You left me with this "lelo".
Ng'ama rite to ng'a?   Who is nursing it?

(*Source*: Collected from Asembo-Bay, Siaya).

In this lullaby, the child minder is tired of soothing the child. The tone is therefore apostrophic as it addresses the absent mother who seems to have forgotten that the minder can only take care of the child for so long. For instance, if the child is breast-feeding, the minder cannot satisfy this need.

Children's play poetry (Wende nyithindo mag tugo)

Ng'ielo   **Python**

Solo: *Ng'ielo ng'ielo*   Solo: Python, python.
Chorus: *Ng'ielo jadhogre.*   Chorus: Python the meanderer.
Solo: *Ng'ielo ng'ielo*   Solo: Python, python.
Chorus: *Ng'ielo jadhogre.*   Chorus: Python, the meanderer.

---

*The word "lelo" refers to a person who is noisy, capricious, uncompromising and stubborn.

Solo:	Kata kuma oaye	Solo:	Whence he comes.
Chorus:	Ng'ielo jadhogre.	Chorus:	Python, the meanderer.
Solo:	Kata kuma odhiye	Solo:	Where he goes.
Chorus:	Ng'ielo jadhogre.	Chorus:	Python, the meanderer.
Solo:	Ka omako ng'ato	Solo:	If it catches one.
Chorus:	Ng'ielo jadhogre	Chorus:	Python, the meanderer.
Solo:	Ne opowore e od maro	Solo:	He burst into the mother-in-law's house.
Chorus:	Rateng' sesegere powe.	Chorus:	The black one "sesegere powe".

In this play song, the children make a snake-like formation by holding each other's waists. They then move sinuously as they sing. In the final refrain, the formation jumps back one step as a demonstration of the kind of restraint expected of a man who is going into his mother-in-law's house. In Luo culture, a son-in-law keeps a conspicuous distance from the mother-in-law.

Wadwaro osiepwa

We want our friend

Group A:	Wan wadwaro osiepwa	Group A:	We want our friend
	Wan wadwaro osiepwa		We want our friend
	Ma wanyalo ywayo		Whom we can pull.
Group B:	Osiepu en ng'awa?	Group B:	Who is your friend
	Osiepu en ng'awa?		Who is your friend
	Ma mondo obi olimu		Who should come and visit you?
Group A:	Osiep wa en Achieng'	Group A:	Our friend is Achieng'
	Osiepwa en Achieng'		Our friend is Achieng'
All:	Achieng' oriti	All:	Achieng' goodbye
	Dhi ited kuon ma odhiek.		Go and cook soft ugali.

There are two groups of children in this song. The first one represents suitors asking for a girl's hand in marriage while the second represents the girl's kinsmen. Once the second group is told who the target of the "suit" is, it "releases" her to join the suitors much in the same way as the bride moves over to the groom's family after marriage.

This exchange goes on until the groups are satisfied with their composition and none calls for a friend. Then they perform a tug of war as the finale.

The derisive remark, "go and cook soft ugali", is a warning that a girl must be a good cook. Ugali is an important staple dish among the Luo. It accompanies virtually every meal. In Luo cuisine, the ugali is made quite stiff and cooking is done by girls or women. A girl or woman who is unable to make adequately stiff ugali is deemed to be a poor cook. In the song, therefore, the remark is a tongue-in-cheek warning that the bride who fails to perform this task satisfactorily (since the ability to cook well is regarded as a key qualification for a wife) is a liability and an embarrassment.

Nyarombo		**The lamb**	
Leader:	*Nyarombo mee.*	Leader:	The lamb *mee.*
Players:	*Mee.*	Players:	*Mee.*
Leader:	*Miya nyithinda.*	Leader:	Give me my children.
Players:	*Mee.*	Players:	*Mee.*
Leader:	*Acham godo obuolo.*	Leader:	So we can eat mushrooms.
Players:	*Mee.*	Players:	*Mee.*
Leader:	*Obuolo ma milambo.*	Leader:	Mushrooms from the south.
Players:	*Mee.*	Players:	*Mee.*
Leader:	*Acham godo opuge.*	Leader:	So we can eat tortoises.
Players:	*Mee.*	Players:	*Mee.*
Leader:	*Opuge ma milambo.*	Leader:	Tortoises from the south.
Players:	*Mee.*	Players:	*Mee.*
Leader:	*Acham godo odielo.*	Leader:	So we can eat Odielo*.
Players:	*Mee.*	Players:	*Mee.*
Leader:	*Odielo ma milambo.*	Leader:	Odielo from the south.
Players:	*Mee.*	Players:	*Mee.*
Leader:	*Tel-tel ma liyo.*	Leader:	The whistling woodpecker.
	Tel-tel ma liyo.		The whistling woodpecker.
	Otieko nyithindo duto.		Has finished all the children.

In this play song, two children stand facing one another with their hands forming an overhead bridge under which the other players pass. At the end of each cycle of the song, they get hold of the player just passing under the bridge at that particular time. This victim is asked to name what he/she prefers as a meal (vegetables or meat).

Each group has a leader who has chosen either vegetables or meat as their preferences. According to the choice made, the player is asked to line up behind either of the leaders. When all the players have been posted, there is a tug of war to determine the winner.

---

*Odielo is a succulent weed commonly used as vegetables.

Mumi Gocho	The catfish plays
Mumi gocho	The catfish plays,
Kamongo kondakta	The mudfish conducts,
Sire kapten	"Sire" is captain,
Omena chodho twisti.	"Omena" dances the twist.

This is a children's ditty sung at play. It is a simulation of an orchestra, in this case an orchestra of fish. The catfish, which is big, is the musician while the mudfish, equally big but with whiskers, conducts the orchestra. A smaller fish, *sire*, acts as the master of ceremonies while the tiny and swift *"omena"* dances. The word *"chodho"* which means "to scoop", denotes the immense enjoyment with which the "omena" dances.

Min Okumu	Okumu's mother
Solo: *Min Okumo watemnie miel otami?*	Solo: Okumu's mother, shall we try for you, you can'ı dance?
Chorus: *Amil wang'.*	Chorus: Amil wang'.
Solo: *Min Okumu watemnie miel otami.*	Solo: Okumu's mother, shall we try for you, you can't dance?
Chorus: *Amil wang'.*	Chrus; Amil wang'.
Solo: *Abakunda.*	Solo: Abakunda.
Chorus: *Abakunda kunda kunda. Amil wang'.*	Chorus: Abakunda kunda kunda Amil wang'.
Solo: *Abakunda*	Solo: Abakunda
Chorus: *Abakunda kunda kunda Amil wang'*	Chorus: Abakunda kunda kunda Amil wang'.

Usually performed by female children at play, this song teases a woman, Min Okumu (Okumu's mother), who cannot dance well. The soloist, who mocks at the woman's clumsiness, sings the first and every other alternate line while the others chorus as they dance on Min Okumu's behalf to demonstrate to her how to dance. "Amil wang" which means "in the shining of the eye", denotes the dexterity with which people should dance. And "abakunda", which simulates the sound of drums and adds to the rhythm of the play, is the Luo version of the name Abakunta. The allusion here is that the drums to which the children are dancing sound like a call to the Abakunta musical group.

95

Min Aloo	Aloo's mother
Heh Heh yaa, uu, uu	Heh heh yaa, uu, uu.
Iw guok otimo choke	The dog's tail is bony.
Cherekorua.	Cherekorua*.
Nyithindo gi unyiero ang'o?	You children, what are you laughing at?
Wanyiero tiend min Aloo motimo leche	We're laughing at the varicose leg of Aloo's mother.
Tang' ane	Show it then.
Atang'o ang'o?	Show what?
To kare di	Then press it.
Adiyo dich.	I have pressed, "*dich*".

(*Source:* Oby Obyerodhyambo)

In this song, the playing children get one among them to act as Aloo's mother. They then ridicule her legs which have varicose veins, regarded as a form of ugliness. Her asking what they are laughing at is meant to show her pretence that she should not be the object of any derision. But she eventually relents and exposes the veins, challenging the players to press them. When the children simulate this, the subject of the song changes to someone else.

Although the Luo child is taught never to tease adults, the song gives them poetic licence to do just that.

Owang' winyo ma nyasure	The crested crane-bird
Solo: *Winyo ma nyasure,* *Owang' winyo ma nyasure.*	Solo: The crested bird, Owang' the crested bird.
Chorus: *Ka dhano.*	Chorus: Like a human being.
Solo: *Winyo ma nyasure,* *Owang' winyo ma nyasure.*	Solo: The crested bird, Owang' the crested bird.
Chorus: *Ka dhano.*	Chorus: Like a human being.
Solo: *Ah!*	Solo: Aah!
Chorus: *Owang'.* *Owang' winyo ma nyasure.* *Ka dhano.*	Chorus: Owang', Owang' the crested bird. Like a human being.
Solo: *Winyo go buombe,* *Owang' winyo go buombe.*	Solo: The bird flaps its wings, Owang' the bird flaps its wings.
Chorus: *Ka dhano.*	Chorus: Like a human being.

*"Cherekorua" is an ideophone to fill in the rhythm while "dich" is an onomatopoeic word for pressing. Like *Min Okumu*, this song is also an example of a drama with definite roles to be played.

Solo:	Winyo go buombe.	Solo:	The bird flaps its wings,
	Owang' winyo go buombe.		Owang' the bird flaps its wings.
Chorus:	Ka dhano.	Chorus:	Like a human being.
Solo:	Eeh!	Solo:	Eeh!
Chorus:	Owang',	Chorus:	Owang',
	Owang winyo go buombe.		Owang' the bird flaps its wings.
	Ka dhano.		Like a human being.
Solo:	Winyo ma jasunga,	Solo:	The proud bird,
	Owang' winyo ma jasunga.		Owang' the proud bird.
Chorus:	Ka dhano.	Chorus:	Like a human being.
Solo:	Winyo ma jasunga,	Solo:	The proud bird,
	Owang' winyo ma jasunga.		Owang' the proud bird.
Chorus:	Ka dhano.	Chorus:	Like a human being.
Solo:	Ooh!	Solo:	Ooh!
Chorus:	Owang',	Chorus:	Owang',
	Owang' winyo ma jasunga.		Owang' the proud bird.
	Ka dhano.		Like a human being.

This is a song for general entertainment sung by both children and adults. It may have more stanzas if the soloist decides to include more attributes of the bird.

The song glorifies and praises the beauty of the crested crane by comparing it with the human being, arguably the ultimate creation in the universe. In the perfomance of this song, the soloist simulates the bird's pride or whatever it is he/she wishes to attribute to the bird while the chorus replies, replicating the soloist's act. In recent times, this song has become very popular in the fusion of various tunes by schools participating in music and drama festivals.

Stylisitcally, the song is a good illustration of certain characteristics of the Luo poem namely:
- antiphony: the call and response pattern (solo and chorus).
- Repetition: lexical, phonological and structural.
- Imagery: the simile, in this case comparing the bird to the human being.

Work songs (Wende tich)

Akuru Ny'Obondo   **Pigeon daughter of Obondo**

Akuru Ny'Obondo   Pigeon daughter of Obondo,
Kimiya mo   Please give me some cream
Aketie ko   To put in a churn
Ko olodhi   So the churn can yield,
Kidhe, Kidhe, Kidhe   Kidhe, Kidhe, Kidhe.

This is a work song performed by one person as she churns butter from milk in a gourd. This task is performed by girls and women (sometimes boys, too). The milk is preserved in a gourd until there is an adequate quantity accumulated. The gourd is shaken and hit against the lap repeatedly for some 30 minutes or so. Periodically, the gourd is then opened to check the progress of the yield. After some time, all the milk is poured out and the butter (which is subsequently added to cooking food or melted to produce ghee) separated from it. The milk, which is now sour, is drank directly or added to other foodstuffs to improve their taste. Churning is done in the evening.

The imagery of the pigeon in this poem conforms to the character of the bird as a quasi-magical being. In certain Luo narratives, for instance, the pigeon plays the role of a saviour to individuals who face danger and probable death at the hands of ogres. In this song, the pigeon is hailed as the custodian of cream. In essence, the poem is some kind of invocation. In Luo prayer, the being to whom a plea is directed is loaded with a lot of positive attributes. In this case, the pigeon is hailed as the "daughter of Obondo". The expression "daughter of..." in Luo linguistic culture is an endearing appreciation of the object of description.

The last expression in the poem (kidhe, kidhe, kidhe) is an ideophonic descriptipon to simulate the sound of the gourd knocking against the lap.

Satirical poems (Wende nyiera)

Oyundi   Sparrow

Oyundi ni dhi ing'weti.   Sparrow go and gather vegetables.
Oyundi ni tienda lit.   Sparrow my leg is sick.

Oyundi ni dhi imoti.   Sparrow go and collect firewood.
Oyundi ni tienda lit   Sparrow my leg is sick.

Oyundi ni dhi iluoki.   Sparrow go and wash.
Oyundi ni tienda lit.   Sparrow my leg is sick.

Oyundi ni dhi kulo.   Sparrow go and fetch water.
Oyundi ni tienda lit.   Sparrow my leg is sick.

Oyundi ni dhi iregi.   Sparrow go and grind flour.
Oyundi ni tienda lit.   Sparrow my leg is sick.

98

Oyundi ni dhi itedi.	Sparrow go and cook.
Oyundi ni tienda lit.	Sparrow my leg is sick.
Oyundi ni bi ichiem.	Sparrow come and eat.
Oyundi ni "sesese".	Sparrow "sesese"

This song could be sung by anybody as long as the occasion demands it. It is, however, mostly sung by children to lampoon the lazy. It simulates a conversation between two sparrows, the first asking the second to help with chores and the latter waxing about its sick leg. Ironically though, the sparrow makes a dramatic recovery when called upon to eat and rushes to the meal as ideophonically captured in "sesese".

Bet angewa	**Sitting exposed**
Bet angewa	Sitting exposed
Jochiro odagi	Is prohibited by market traders
Lwang'ni fuyo	Flies buzz (it)
To guogi nang'o.	And dogs lick (it).

This is a song discreetly sung by one who has spotted someone, often a female, sitting carelessly and hence exposing her private parts. It prompts all within earshot to adjust themselves. "Market traders" is an allusion to fishmongers whose merchandise attracts a lot of flies. They are, therefore, unamused by the possibility that the same flies that have perched on the exposed genitals will also land on their fish.

Ratong akwaya		**The borrowed machete**	
Solo:	*Wach kode,*	Solo:	Talk with it,
	Aa, ni wach kode.		Aa, talk with it.
Chorus:	*Ratong akwaya.*	Chorus:	The borrowed machete.
Solo:	*Wach kode,*	Solo:	Talk with it,
	Aa, ni wach kode.		Aa, talk with it.
Chorus:	*Ratong akwaya.*	Chorus:	The borrowed machete.
Solo:	*Mach otho e nyoyo,*	Solo:	Fire has died under "nyoyo",

	Mach otho e nyoyo.		Fire has died under "nyoyo".
Chorus:	*Ratong akwaya.*	Chorus:	The borrowed machete.
Solo:	*Mach otho e nyoyo,*	Solo:	Fire has died under "nyoyo",
	Mach otho e nyoyo.		Fire has died under "nyoyo".
Chorus:	*Ratong akwaya.*	Chorus:	The borrowed machete.

This song is meant to ridicule those who rely on borrowing. In the song, the borrower is unable to replenish the hearthfire for boiling the "nyoyo", a traditional dish of beans mixed with maize, because he does not have his own machete with which to go and cut more firewood as he has returned the borrowed machete to its owner. The song may be performed solo or chorally by children or adults, male or female as long as it is relevant.

Min luongo nyathine / Mother calls her child

Solo:	*Mini luongo nyathine,*	Solo:	Mother calls her child,
	Mini luongo.		Mother calls.
Chorus:	*Othuone.*	Chorus:	The headstrong.
Solo:	*Mini luongo nyathine,*	Solo:	Mother calls her child,
	Mini luongo.		Mother calls.
Chorus:	*Othuone.*	Chorus:	The headstrong.
Solo:	*Ero, ero.*	Solo:	There, there.
Chorus:	*Owe bel mak oyieko gi chunge.*	Chorus:	She has left the millet unwinnowed.
Solo:	*Ero, ero.*	Solo:	There there.
Chorus:	*Owe bel mak oyieko gi chunge.*	Chorus:	She has left the millet unwinnowed.

In this song, children criticise the disobedient ones who do not finish their work and whose mothers have to keep calling them to complete their chores. In another version, a rather cheeky one, it is performed as a work song by women putting mud on rafters to make a wall. The tune remains the same but the words change. Here is the second version.

Dayo luongo "nyathina" / Grandma calls "my child"

Solo:	*Dayo luongo "nyathina",*	Solo:	Grandma calls "my child",
	Dayo luongo.		Grandma calls.

Chorus:	Othuone.		Chorus:	The headstrong.
Solo:	Dayo luongo "nyathina", Dayo luongo.		Solo:	Grandma calls "my child", Grandma calls.
Chorus:	Othuone.		Chorus:	The headstrong.
Solo:	Nii, nii.		Solo:	Like this, like this.
Chorus:	Owe bel mak oyieko gi chunge.		Chorus:	She has left the millet unwinnowed.
Solo:	Nii, nii.		Solo:	Like this, like this.
Chorus:	Owe chul mak osoyo e dho there.		Chorus:	She's failed to insert the phallus into her vagina.

Here, the women censure the favourite son who has failed to perform his marital duties because he has been so pampered that he has failed to learn how to love independently and to do what is required of him. Through the song, the young women then have a chance to express dissatisfaction with the poor performance of husbands and to indirectly tell the owner of the house they are making to take his sexual obligations seriously. On such occassions, taboo words are mentioned liberally because the company is adult.

In Dholuo, the word "grandmother" also means "mother-in-law", i.e., a woman calls the mother of her husband by that title and the mother-in-law refers to her as her child. There is therefore a double meaning to the words "my child".

Elocutionary poetry

(a) Nyako

Call: Nyako!
Response:Inyaka arabuon
Ibuona atin?
Itinda aring'o?
Iringa ajaneko?
Inega agwendi?

Igwena achogo?
Ichoga aguogi?

Ikuoga arabolo?
Ibola asuka?
Isuka awich?
Iwiya athol?
Ithola aring'o?

(a) Girl

Call: Girl
Response: You yield me, am I potatoes?
You despise me, am I small?
You savour me, am I meat?
You avoid me, am I a lunatic?
You slaughter me, am I your chicken?
You scrape me, am I a bone?
You reprimand me am I your dog?
You ripen me, am I bananas?
You wrap me, am I a sheet?
You plait me, am I hair?
You weave me, am I a rope?
You roast me, am I meat?

101

The chain rhyme above, mostly recited by adolescents, is a simulation of the response of a recalcitrant girl to the advances of a boy. She makes nonsense of his efforts by coining all sorts of words out of the original. The rhyme is actually a pun in which the root of the word is retained but the meaning is varied by the introduction of different prefixes and suffixes. For example, the word "nyako" means "girl" but "nyak" means to yield or come to fruition.

Notice that the rhyme is repetetive after a certain point when it goes back to an earlier part of the poem. For example, when it reaches "Ithola aring'o", the poem ricochets back to "Iringa ajaneko" (Line 3 of the response). This means that the poem can be recited infinitely. Two other versions of the rhyme are given below. The varying lines are highlighted.

(b) Nyako!

Call: Nyako
Response: Inyaka arabuon?
Ibuona atin?
Itinda aring'o?
Iringa ajaneko?
Inega agwendi?

Igwena achogo?
Ichoga aguogi?

Ikuoga arabolo?
Ibola ampira?
Ipira ajagopi?

Igowa ayie?
Iyieya anyako?

(b) Girl

Call: Girl!
Response: You yield me, am I potatoes?
You despise me, am I small?
You savour me, am I meat?
You avoid me, am I a lunatic?
You slaughter me, am I your chicken?
You scrape me, am I a bone?
You reprimand me, am I your dog?
You ripen me, am I bananas?
You throw me, am I a ball?
You ask me for a refund, am I your debtor?
You anchor me, am I a boat?
You accept me, am I a girl?

In version (b), the poem changes in line 10. To "*bolo*" can mean either to "wrap loosely around the body" or to "throw". The version takes the latter meaning. We notice also that the poem goes back to the first line by virtue of the last line ending in the word "nyako" which is the initial word that sets the chain going. Like the first version, it can be recited infinitely. In yet another version, the words of the first lines are the ones that vary from the first two examples given above.

(c) Nyako   **(c) Girl**

Call: *Nyako, ipong'!*   Call: Girl, you are so full (well-
                                            built)!
Response: Apong' an yawo?   Response: I am full, am I a well?
Iyawa athigo?   You open me, am I a door?
Ithiwa api?   You decant me, am I water?
Ipiya awinyo?   You perch me, am I a bird?
Iwiya athol?   You weave me, am I a rope?
Ithola aring'o   You roast me, am I meat?
Iringa ajaneko?   You avoid me, am I a lunatic?
Inega aguendi?   You slaughter me, am I your
                                            chicken?
Iguena achogo?   You scrape me, am I a bone?
Ichoga aguogi?   You reprimand me, am I your
                                            dog?
Ikuoga arabolo?   You ripen me, am I bananas?
Ibola asuka?   You wrap me, am I a sheet?
Isuka awich?   You plait me, am I hair?
Iwiya athol?   You weave me, am I a rope?

Rateng' Oyang'o Dhiang'   **Rateng' slaughtered a bull**

Rateng' oyang'o dhiang' wuod Odero.   Rateng' slaughtered a bull, son of Odero.
Dhiang' ne wayang'o nyaka juma.   We slaughtered the bull for a week.
Rang'ol ong'olo dhiang' wuod Odero.   The lame one cut the bull, son of Odero.
Dhiang' ne wang'olo nyaka orumo.   We cut the bull till it was finished.
Rabam obambo dhiang' wuod Odero.   "Rabam" splayed the bull, son of Odero.
Dhiang' ne wabambo nyaka orumo.   We splayed the bull till it was finished.
Racham ochamo dhiang' wuod Odero.   The left-handed ate the bull, son of
                                        Odero.
Dhiang' ne wachamo nyaka orumo.   We ate the bull till it was finished.
Rakuom okumo dhiang' wuod Odero.   The hunchback detained the bull, son
                                        of Odero.
Dhiang' ne wakumo nyaka juma.   We detained the bull for a week.
Rabondo oramo bura dhi Kisumo.   The bald-headed insists the case goes
                                        to Kisumo.
Bura ne wayalo nyaka Bondo.   We argued the case up to Bondo.
                                        The squint-eyed revived the bull, son of
Rachiero ochiero dhiang' wuod Odero. Odero.
Dhiang' ne wachiero nyaka owuotho.   We revived the bull till it walked.

103

This elocutionary poem talks about an imaginary party at which Rateng', literally "the black one" but used here as a praise name, has slaughtered a bull for his friends but complications arise which force them to revive the animal. The fantasy in the poem lies in the fact that the bull is revived after it has supposedly been eaten. Reading between the lines, the word "dhiang", which literally means a cow or a bull, also implies the abundance of the meat. Rateng' must have slaughtered enough bulls or cows to last a week.

Sung by adolescents as a pastime, the poem details some of the common disabilities and puns on the words using the roots to create new meanings. For example, "ng'ol" as a noun means lameness but to "ng'olo" means "to cut". The other correspondences are:

"Rabam" — he who limps, "bambo" — to splay.
"Racham" — the left-handed, "chamo" — to eat.
"Rakuom" — the hunch back, "kumo" to detain or deny access.
"Rabondo" - the bald-headed, Bondo — a place in Nyanza.
"Rachiero" — the squint-eyed, chiero — the squint (n), to revive (v)

The reference to Kisumu, the administrative headquarters of Nyanza Province, shows how serious Rabondo took the matter but the fact that the case only goes as far as Bondo is to indicate that it needed not go that far. The poem can be rendered solo or chorally.

Beer drinking songs (Wende kong'o)

Kong'o Ochwere

Chakore gi oonja.
Chakore gi oonja yawa yaye!
Chakore gi oonja.
Chakore gi oonja, yawa yaye.
Kong'o ochwere okan orum.
  Kong'o wamadho pile pile.
  Kong'o wamadho degi degi.
  Kong'o ochwere okan orum.

Madhore manade,
Madhore manade, yawa yaye!
Madhore manade,
Madhore manade, yawa yaye.
Kong'o ochwere okan orum.

Alcohol forever

Starting with "oonja".
Starting with "oonja", our people!
Starting with "oonja".
Starting with "oonja", our people.
Alcohol forever will never get finished.
  We drink alcohol day after day.
  We drink alcohol pots upon pots.
  Alcohol forever will never get finished.

What a drinking.
What a drinking, our people!
What a drinking.
What a drinking, our people.
Alcohol forever will never get finished.

Kong'o wamadho pile pile.	We drink alcohol day after day.
Kong'o wamadho degi degi.	We drink alcohol pots upon pots.
Kong'o ochwere okan orum.	Alcohol forever will never get finished.

"*Kong'o ochwere*" is a common song at beer drinking places. It expresses the fact that drinkers never seem to get sated with alcohol however frequently they drink it. But there is also the underlying realisation that brewers are continuing with their trade and so drinkers have to keep drinking. In the performance, a soloist sings the first five lines of each stanza and the chorus repeats, then goes to the lines of the refrain singing the first two, with the chorus joining in the last. The performance can be accompanied with foot thumping and hand-clapping and can be repeated several times and added onto as the mood dictates.

The word "oonja" refers to a swig given to the prospective buyer as an appetiser but it is also demanded by the buyer to detect the strength of the brew before buying.

Dhing' go jawajawa   The strainer goes "jawajawa"

Dhing' go jawajawa	The strainer goes "jawajawa"!
Jomadhee...	People have drunk it.
Dhing' go jawajawa	The strainer goes "jawajawa"!
Jomadhee joywe dhogi joling' ka	People have drunk, wiped their mouths
matuo.	and posed like the sick.

This song, performed at beer-drinking occasions, has some discreet criticism of the revellers. Like in "Kong'o ochwere", there is the feeling that drinkers never get satisfied, and therefore pose innocently like the sick so that they can get some more beer. The Luo strainer for making "*busaa*", a cereal beer made out of flour, is a sock-like woven instrument. The beer is poured into the strainer which is shaken and makes the sound "jawajawa" before it is squeezed to let the refined beer down into a pan.

Nyatiti songs

J. Oreng' *(by Lucas Odote)*   **J. Oreng'** (by Lucas Odote)

Awerie Joshua Oreng' wuod Asembo   Let me sing your praise, Joshua Oreng'
Ja Nyagoko Kamito   The son of Asembo, the man from
                                       Nyagoko Kamito.
Osiepna jayadha ubudha gi Obondo   My friend you entertained me with
koth lal   Obondo, the disappearing rain.
Ogare wuod Owino Obira   Ogare, son of Owino Obira.
Awerie bwana Oreng'   Let me sing your praise Mr Oreng',
Oreng' in Luo kajaluo ja Nyagoko ja Oreng' the Luo-man in Luo-land.
Kamito.   The man from Nyagoko and Kamito.

Jayadha wuod Asembo.   My good friend, son of Asembo,
Nene itera thum ka rech.   You took me to perform in the land of fish,
Idwara koda Otiya.   You bid me come with Otiya.
Rarieda tok ka jopuonj   In Rarieda behind the teacher's place
Odote nene awer ka jamwa.   Odote I sang in the land of foreigners.
Obare Demba jok moyudo obet kanyo.   Obare Demba are among those I found
                                       seated,
Jobet ni dwa budho ngolo.   Seated to listen to the music.
Abonyo odiero ja Uyoma.   Abonyo *odiero** from Uyoma,
Odiero be obet kanyo.   Odiero was also seated there,
Obet ni dwa budho ngolo.   Because he wanted to listen to the music.
Olulo ma ka Ochenya.   Olulo son of Ochenya,
Olulo be obet kanyo.   He was also seated there
Obet in dwa budho ngolo.   Seated to listen to the music.
Obondo koth lal.   Obondo, the disappearing rain
Wuod Asembo obet kanyo.   The son of Asembo was seated there
Obet ni dwa budho ngolo.   Seated to listen to the music,
Nora Opiyo nyar Gombe.   Nora Opiyo, daughter of Gombe,
Nora be obet kanyo.   Nora was seated there,
Obet ni dwa budho ngolo.   Seated to listen to the music.

Nene awer ka rech.   I sang in the land of fish
Jaodi nyar Asembo Kamito.   Your wife from Asembo Kamito
Ne oyang'o gweno rabet mawiye   Slaughtered a huge fowl.
otimo lulu.
Pilu pilu noyieyo kanyo.   She added *pilu pilu* (pepper)
Biringanya ne onganyo kanyo.   She added *biringanya* (egg plants)

**Odiero* means a whiteman. It is used as a laudatory for a gentleman.

Kamlar ne olaro kanyo.	She added kamlar (onions)
Kitungu ne ong'ado kanyo.	She cut onions.
Karat ne ong'ado kanyo.	She cut carrots
Ochop saa chiemo Odote.	When it came to meal time, Odote,
Pilu pilu pilo dhowa.	Pepper peperred our mouths.
To waluowe kuon aluowa.	But we just piled ugali on top.
Karat ne rado dhowa.	Carrot carroted our mouths
To waluowe kuon aluowa.	But we just piled ugali on top.
Biringanya nganyo dhowa.	Biringanya nganyad our mouths
To waluowe kuon aluowa.	But we just piled ugali on top.
Pilu pilu pilo dhowa.	Pepper peperred our mouths.
To waluowe kuon aluowa.	But we just piled ugali on top.
Ogare Demba Odote.	Ogare Demba Odote
Rawer ne waneno ka ja rech	I saw Rawer in the land of fish
Ayude be ka or Oreng'	I also encounteted Oreng's son-in-law
Wuod Asembo osiepna	The son of Asembo, my friend.
Oreng' nyasach mtoka	Oreng', the god of vehicles
Joshua jaluo ka jaluo	Joshua the Luo-man in Luo-land,
Ja Nyagoko ja Kamito	From Nyagoko and Kamito.
Oreng wuod Asembo jayadha	Oreng', my great friend son of Asembo.
Oreng' nyasach mtoka	Oreng', the god of vehicles.
Fundi maler Bwana Oreng'	The expert worker, Mr Oreng'
Gima omiyo aheri Joshua Oreng'	Why I respect you, Mr Oreng',
Oreng' nyasach mtoka	Oreng' the god of vehicles.
Muindi moro owuok Kampala	An Indian arrived from Kampala.
Owuok piny gi Amin Dada	He came from the domain of Amin Dada
Kech Bwana Amin oriembe	Because Mr Amin had expelled him.
To owuok to lori okethore	He left but his lorry broke down.
To muindi nwang'o Bwana Oreng'	An Indian found Mr Oreng'
Ni fundi ni Oreng' gony mtoka	"I say mechanic please overhaul this vehicle"
Oreng' twe mtoka	Oreng' dissembled and re-assembled the vehicle.
Siga singa gwe lori dhi	The Sikh kick-started the vehicle and set off
Gweyo ni wach Bwana Oreng'	Kick-started on account of Mr Oreng'
Oreng jaluo kajaluo x2	Oreng' the Luo-man in Luo-land
	Oreng' the Luo-man in Luo-land
Ja Nyagoko ja Kamito	From Nyagoko and Kamito.
Oreng wuod Asembo osiepna	Oreng', my friend, son of Asembo,
Ago ni thum ka pang	Let me play my lyre for you here in town

Ka boma bwore	In the city of Nairobi.
Wasungu budho Odote katwech	Europeans entertained Odote in the city of fashion.
Agonie thum Bwana Oreng'	Let me play my lyre for you, Mr Oreng',
Fundi maler ja Kamito	The expert mechanic from Kamito
Osiep Obondo wuon Oluga	The friend of Obondo son of Oluga.
Ago ni thum Bwana Oreng'	Let me play my lyre for you, Mr Oreng'
Oreng' nyasach mtoka	Oreng' the god of vehicles.
Jaduong' monyuom nyare ndiga	The old man who received a bicycle as his daughter's bride-price.
Wuod Asembo osiepna	The son of Asembo, my friend.
Oreng' jaduong' monyuom nyare ndiga	Oreng' the old man given a bicycle for bride-price.
Kod dhok ariyo	Along with two head of cattle:
Achiel dhiang' rapala	One a spotted cow
Achiel dhiang' dibuoro	The other a brown one.
Jaduong' riembo ndiga	The old man rides
Obuko pakore	And begins to praise himself:
Nyithiwa yande ichaya ga	Brethren, I used to be scorned
To duong'na okelo ohala	But my manhood has earned a profit.
Kijande yande nyiera ga	Young men used to laugh at me,
To duong'na okelo ohala	But my manhood has earned a profit.
Wahia yande siya ga	Children used to jeer me,
To duong'na okelo ohala	But my manhood has earned a profit.
Nyithindo yande thiraga	Children used to belittle me,
To duong'na okelo ohala	But my manhood has earned a profit.
Jodongo yande nyiera ga	Old men used to laugh at me,
To duong'na okelo ohala	But my manhood has earned a profit.
E nying Bwana Oreng'	In the name of Mr Oreng'
Oreng' jaluo kajaluo	Oreng' the Luo-man in Luo-land
Ja Nyagoko ja Kamito	From Nyagoko and Kamito
Oloso gari muindi gwe lori dhi	He repaired the vehicle The Indian kicked his lorry and set off
Oreng' wuod Asembo	Oreng' son of Asembo,
We wagonie thum Bwana Oreng'	Let me play the lyre for you, Mr Oreng'.
Ogero lelo	He has built extensively:
Bia ne wamadho e odi	We drank beer in your house
Soda ne wachamo e odi	We also "ate" soda in your house
Nyiri ne wabudho e odi	Girls entertained us in your house.
Ogwaheri wuod Asembo	Goodbye son of Asembo
Aluori nyasach mtoka	I respect you the god of vehicles

Hunde gonyo anuang'o ochido	I've seen today's mechanics rather dirty
Hunde ochido otar atara	The mechanics are dirty and unkempt
Oreng' bwana olou	Oreng' outshines you all
Hundi tosha ja Kamito	The sufficient mechanic from Kamito
Hundi maler	The smart mechanic
Aluori nyasach mtoka	I respect you the god of vehicles
Aweyi Bwana Oreng'	Let me leave you Mr Oreng'
Jalopo gi Odote	He who fishes with Odote
Koro aweyi Bwana Oreng'	Now I leave you Mr Oreng'
Ja Nyagoko ja Kamito.	The man from Nyagoko and Kamito.

(Panegyric *nyatiti* and box guitar recorded in vinyl disc: Mwenge Label 10B 1974).

This is a panegyric rendered in the song mode accompanied by the most famous Luo musical instrument, the *nyatiti* and a box guitar.

In the poem, the musician lauds a mechanic called Joshua Oreng'. In characteristic Luo poetic style, he refers to Oreng' in elaborate descriptions naming his geographical origin (Asembo Bay, referred to as "the land of fish" as it is a fishing bay) and anybody known to be his relative or friend. Thus when he names people among the audience at Oreng's home, the musician is first indicating in what kind of regard people hold Oreng' (if they did not, there would not be such a crowd) but he is also implying how much the people appreciated his music.

Very appreciable in this poem are the poet's diction and coinage of words. For instance, he refers to Oreng's magical abilities to repair vehicles. This is to say that Oreng' is a super mechanic. Indeed everything in Oreng's life seems to be grand as when the musician says that Oreng's wife "slaughtered" a fowl. In Luo phraseology, you can only slaughter a bull, cow, sheep or goat. To slaughter a fowl is to say that it was a giant chicken.

There is also the semantic improbability in "we ate soda" meant to imply the huge amounts of soda they drank that it could be considered a meal on its own.

Notice also the coinage in describing the codiments that went into the food (pepper, onions and egg plants). Out of the nouns *pilu pilu*, *biringanya* and *karot*, the poet coins verbs using the same sounds so as to get "pilo" (splits) from "pilu", "nganyo" (mixes) from "biringanya" and "rado" (crushes) from "karot".

All this praise is poured because of Oreng's epic repair of an Indian's car (a historical allusion to the 1971 expulsion of Indians from Uganda by Idi Amin), his ability to remain clean despite his type of job and the fact that he has built a good house and has lately been honoured by being given a bicycle as bride price for his daughter.

109

A bicycle might not be a very significant thing in today's world. But in days past when the contraption was introduced in Luoland, it was a very prestigious possession. The fact that a bicycle was one of the items in the bride price list means great hounour to Oreng'. This justifies his pride when he cheekily refers to his manhood having earned a profit, i.e., he fathered a daughter whose bride price yielded a prestigious item hitherto beyond his dreams.

Msonga Odhil (by Ogwang' Okoth)

Mano Odhil Msonga dak go tek

Oke Ochieng'
Machiegni wuod nyar Nenga
Ogare ja Alego, Ogwang' Lelo
nyakwar Owino
Thum chieng' oketh kara
Koro awacho gi Odhil Msonga
Ka Msonga
Odhil dakgo tek
Andule nyakwar Owino
Iluonge Msonga Chacha wuod Owinga

Kichake koda laki
To ochaki kod huoke
To koro ti unubed nadi?
Msonga ma omin Owino
Momo dwaro kendo momo bin okwak
nyamin
To tere e tiend baba
Momo nopim timbe
Eka wuon bende ng'eyo
Ni mhiani kare dwaro oromo bet kod
ng'ato
Msonga wuod Okech
Msonga omin Ojudi
Ojudi ng'ato ochodo wuon kong'o
Mbu kong'o nene owene
Gi kube pep tendeng'
Glas bende omiye

Msonga Odhil by Ogwang' Okoth

Now that's Odhil with whom staying is difficult.
Nephew of Ochieng',
Welcome son of the daughter of Nenga.
Ogare from Alego, Ogwang' Lelo, the grandson of Owino,
Music might eventually ruin me
Now I speak with Odhil Msonga, the son of Msonga.
It is difficult to stay with Odhil,
Andule the grandson of Owino.
He is called Msonga Chacha son of Owinga.

If you charge at him with your teeth,
He sets on you with his toothless gum.
So how would you compromise?
Msonga the brother of Owino,
A mute who wants to marry fondles his sister
And takes her to his father's feet.
The mute mimes the act,
Then his father realises
The child is old enough to live with someone.
Msonga son of Okech,
Msonga, the brother of Ojudi.
Ojudi, someone seduced the beer seller
All the drinks were left to him:
The jerrycan
And the glass

110

Chupa be omiye	Even the bottle, he was given.
Inyise ni in meth magi gin meki	You drink, all these are yours
Ng'ama ihero to wamiyo	We will only give to him whom you choose.
Msonga awacho gi Ogunyo ka Andere	Msonga I speak with Ogunyo son of Andere.
Ogunyo miluma kia ng'at modhier	Ogunyo, appetite doesn't recognise a pauper.
Kata idhier sana	However poor you are
To ionge kod wuoche	You have no shoes
To ionge kod sati	You have no shirt
To ionge kod onyasa	You have no shorts
Kendo iwuok idhi e chiro	But when you leave for the market with
To in kod pesa	money.
Pesa ma dinyiew go law	Money you can use to buy clothing
Gima jonyie kendo mbuta ema ineno	What shocks is that "mbuta"* fish is all you see.
Ineno mbuta mowang'	When you see the fried "mbuta",
Kendo ema inyiewo	That is what you buy.
Bin ikel eot	Then you bring it home
Mbu inichodh go kuon	And you consume it with ugali.
To onget pok inyiewo	But you have not bought a blanket!
Ajei wuod Owino osiepna	Ajei the son of Owino my pal.
Nyakwar Owino	The grandson of Owino,
Msonga omin Oloo	Msonga the brother of Oloo.
Oloo gik moko mit duge	Oloo everything is tasty when naked.
Ma kata odog njugu	Even if it is groundnuts,
Nyaka bin iduny njugu	You must first un-shell the nuts.
Eka nimuod iye	That is when you crush the nuts.
To kata odog bando	Even if it is maize,
Nyaka inipok bando	You must first strip the cob.
Kata odog niang'	Even if it were sugar cane,
Niang' bin ipil tendeng'	You must first peel it all up.
Msonga nyakwar Owino	Msonga the grandson of Owino.
Ajei en owadwa	Ajei is my brother.
Odhil wuod Oloo	Odhil, the father of Oloo.
Msonga okew gi Owuor	Msonga, the nephew of Owuor.
Owuor ka Msonga	Owuor, son of Msonga.
Majawa ka Msonga	Majawa, son of Msonga.
Mdhodho Ka Msonga	Mdhodho, son of Msonga.
Odido nyar Alego	Odido the daughter of Alego.
Odhil dak go tek	Odhil with whom it is difficult to stay.

*Nile perch.

111

Msonga en omera	Msonga is my brother,
To en omera diriyo	He is my brother twice.
Ng'at ma ariwo go wat	The one with whom we share relations
Agoro en owadwa	In Agoro, he is my brother.
Kamlar en owadwa	And in Kamlar he is my brother.
Kwadhie kaneyi Kamlar man pinje	If we go to your maternal uncle's in Kamlar,
Owuor ka Msonga	Owuor son of Msonga,
Gi Mdhodho ka Msonga	And Mdhodho son of Msonga,
Majawa ka Msonga	Majawa the son of Msonga,
Kamlar man ka Luo	Kamlar who reside in Kaluo.
Ka wadhi mwalowa	If we go to our lower lands,
Oliech wuon Neko	Oliech the son of Neko,
Oliech maka Neko	Oliech the son of Neko,
Oliech maka Neko ka Nyawiri wuod Ong'udo	Oliech the son of Neko of Nyawiri son of Ong'udo,
Kamlar man mwalo	Kamlar of the lowlands.
Ajei wuod Oloo oomo Ogwang' Lelo	Ajei son of Oloo invited Ogwang' Lelo
Ogwang' mosiep Oonga	Ogwang' the friend of Oonga.
Oonga nyar kanisa oneno kuon kod gweno	Oonga, a woman of the church sees ugali and chicken.
Lemo ne rure piyo	Her prayers are hurried
We odok gi alot	But let it be vegetables
We odok gi alot	Just let it be vegetables.
Nyani eno dend Yesu	This lass will implore Jesus,
Nyasaye mungu ruoth yie ikonya	Oh God almighty bless me please.
Gigi gin boke	These are leaves (weeds)
Gigi gin boke koth gigi ok wang'eyo	These are leaves whose origins we know not
Iyie ikony wae	Please bless us
Kod nying wuodi Kristo to wakawe	In the name of your son Christ we take it.
Ajei wuod Oloo ka Olua	Ajei, son of Oloo the son of Olua.
Odhil dak go tek	Odhil with whom it is difficult to live.
Oriti wuod Oloo ralweny	Farewell son of Oloo, the bellicose.
Msonga nyakwar Owino.	Msonga the grandson of Owino.

(Nyatiti recorded on vinyl disc Label: NJAGA 3B)

In this poem, Ogwang' Okoth, arguably the most accomplished Luo "nyatiti" player, is at his best with wry humour as he makes a commentary on various aspects of life — about the choices people have to make and the contradictions such choices lead to. He sets the tone of such contradictions right from the beginning when he says that music might very well ruin him. This alludes to a general attitude among the Luo that only wayward people become musicians. Yet the musician seems to be stating that this is his choice in life and if it is going to ruin him, then so be it.

Soon after this, he presents a very graphic situation while describing the subject of his praise, a man called Msonga. The musician sings about Msonga's prowess, that if you charge at him with bared teeth, he replies with his toothless gums. In which case, you are not on level playing ground. But this is not because you have teeth and will therefore scare off Msonga. Rather, it is to say that Msonga's contemporary for your teeth are toothless gums. Imagine then that he has to make use of teeth also! It also implies that Msonga is not one to take an affront lying down.

The musician then moves into a series of humorous anecdotes. The first is his talk about the mute who wants to marry but who, lacking verbal abilities, can only mime his intention, and embarrassingly, by using his sister. If Ogwang' seems to be poking fun at the mute, he might also be satirising the lack of sensitivity in the mute's parents, who have failed to notice the maturity of their son.

Secondly, the poet tells us about this woman who is selling beer and who has forgotten the commercial intention and handed over all the beer to her new-found lover. Love has turned her head as it often does to many people. Could the poet be saying that emotions often overcome reason?

Then Ogwang' looks at the appetite which cares not whether you are poor or rich. This is a common truism but it takes the poet's voice to articulate it. Using this fact, the poet shows how setting priorities can be difficult and how people tend to acquire things on impulse. One would logically think the pauper needs to spend some money on clothing. But he is overwhelmed by the appetising sight of fried fish and this is what he buys. If this might look like despicable behaviour, on hindsight, the pauper might be right after all: that it is better to be full rather than to be well dressed and hungry.

The fourth point of humour and cheeky insinuation is when the poet talks of things being tasty when naked. He mentions that before anything is consumed, it has to be kind of undressed. He leaves unsaid, perhaps, what he is intending to say about sexual intercourse.

Finally, the poet pokes fun at the Christian woman who, when a good meal is set, is in a hurry to finish her prayer but not otherwise. As it were, chicken is a delicacy among the Luo but not so vegetables, hence the woman will take ages reeling God's praise names as if to delay the agony of going through an undesirable meal. The woman's derisive attitude is revealed in her reference to the vegetables as wild leaves.

113

War songs

Lwanda Magere	**Lwanda Magere**
Gwari wuod Were	Gwari son of Were
Ouko nyang' jawuoro (x5)	Ouko, the greedy crocodile (x5)
Magere wuod Atiga	Magere son of Atiga.
Koro nyang' jawuoro	Now the crocodile is greedy.
Magere wuod Asande	Magere son of Asande
Ogweno min jobilo	Ogweno the mother of magicians.
Magere wuod Apoda	Magere son of Apoda
Koro nyang' jawuoro x2	Now the crocodile is greedy.
Onjelo oloko mare	He has overwhelmed "onjelo".
Koro nyang' jawuoro	Now the crocodile is greedy.
Onjelo obuogo ringo	He has scared "onjelo" into flight
Koro nyang' jawuoro	Now the crocodile is greedy.

(Source: Oby Obyerodhyambo).

This is a song celebrating the martial might of the greatest historical Luo warrior, Lwanda Magere. The warrior is metaphorically referred to as a crocodile who goes on the rampage, greedy for his opponent or perceived enemy. This greed is made even more ominous, according to this poem, by the magical nature of the warrior as captured in the praise of Magere as the mother of all magicians. As is typical with Luo poetry and elocutionary speech, the warrior is lauded as the son of so many people.

The word "onjelo" is an abbreviation to refer to the Nandi people who border Luo country and who frequently fought with them. In fact, the word is a corruption of the name "Kalenjin", the composite of ethnic groups among whom are the Nandi.

114

Love songs (Oigo)*

Nyagwenda Ywagore Tok Dala

My chick its life in the tree behind our home,
Crying *chiyo*;
The kite has carried away my chick,
The little cock lamented its life.
So would I shout in distress,
Would flap my hands mournfully,
Flapping in imitation.
My chick laments in the tree behind our home,
Crying *chiyo*;
The kite has carried away my chick,
The little cock lamented its life.
So would I howl inconsolably,
Yes, stumble with sorrow,
Stumbling in invitation.
My chick laments its life in the tree behind our home,
Crying *chiyo*;
The kite has carried away my chick,
The little cock lamented its life.

Yala ere Yala

Yala, O sing the *ree* for Yala,
Sing the *ree ree yo*,
These coming days the clerks will be writing,
The skirt of Adore, the daughter of Isa,
Is printed with boards on one side,
Plain cloth on the other;
Amara's mother cannot afford a bicycle
She travels on foot,
But the Kamnara gambol on wheels;
Even Oloo the musician of Nyabondo Village
Has forsworn travelling by train;
How can a mere musician fly in an aeroplane?
So Yala, I sing the *ree* for Yala,
Sing the *ree ree yo*,
These coming days, the clerks will be writing.

---

*Poems and notes are quoted verbatim from a series presented by Henry Owuor Anyumba
and Gerald Moore in *Introduction to African Literature* edited by Ulli Beier.

The *oigo* are love songs which were sung by girls of marriageable age when they went to visit the young men with whom they were courting. This was often called "visiting the *simba*". The *simba* was the hut in which young men slept and entertained their guests. The visit was usually carefully organised at or near full moon. As the girls walked to their destination, they sang the *oigos* either individually or as a group, maintainng the performance all the way by singing in turns. There was no formal order of singing; the more musically gifted girls or the more effusive took the lead parts according to their mood.

Meanwhile the young men were waiting and listening until the first faint *oigo* melody reached their ears. Then one of them stood on a raised piece of ground just outside the gate of the homestead and announced at the top of his voice: *Ogoree, omolo* (The landing has taken place, they have arrived).

At the gate the girls stopped moving but continued singing the *oigos* until a grandmother of the compound, who had placed herself nearby, offered them gifts: metal ornaments, beads or rings. As part of the evening's entertainment, the young men smoked a gourd-pipe of opium or played enthusiastically on a *ree* flute while the girls sang the *oigos*. Often the hosts would have invited a lyre player as well.

The *oigos* were also sung while girls collected firewood or were going to draw water, but this was regarded as a kind of rehearsal. Girls who were close friends were often known by their favourite *oigos*. Late in the evening, while travelling to a gathering at a lyre performance, they would decide to follow different paths (the longer and more tortuous the better) shouting the *oigos* at each other. The girls also used the *oigos* to introduce themselves to the lyre player before addressing him. This beautiful custom has unfortunately died out completely ... and the *oigos* translated here were recorded by elderly women who remembered them from their youth.

The style of the *oigo* singing is extremely distinctive. The singer trills in a bird-like voice and conveys an impression of being possessed by the stream of song within her, breathless and helpless. The emotions expressed are often sorrowful and almost hysterical, yet the singer exults in her ability to sing endlessly like a bird.

Her accomplishment will be jugded by her skill and power in this *redo* style, refrains such as *doree ree yo* being much more repetetive than can be covered in these translations .... *Nyagwenda Ywagore Tok Dala* stresses the sorrow of the *oigo* singer ... while *Yala ere Yala* is a modern song in the *oigo* style, in which the singer mocks at the new-fangled fashions introduced by the shops. Yala is a small trading centre in Luo country, and this song probably dates from the time when the first overseas goods were being offered for sale there. Her satire plays over the young clerks, the bicycle owners and the new printed cloth.

The word *oigo* seems to mean slightly different things in different localities, and so a true evaluation of the songs would have to take these into account. Nevertheles, the following conclusions can be based on the songs printed here.

The girl in the *oigo* songs is a type representing only certain characteristics of girlhood, as expressed within the special culture of her tribe. She lives in a dreamland, though much tempered by the idealised role she longs to play in the community. By implication, singing is regarded as a good thing, especially when it is powerful — so that everybody can hear it — and is persistent. As with a bird, singing appears to be the natural outpouring of the life force itself.

The prestige of clan and family depended not only on the prowess of its young men but also on the zealous way in which its women represented its interests in song and dance. For a group of girls, the *oigo* was a means of announcing their presence and of differentiating themselves from the older married women; for an individual, a way of expressing her idiosyncrasies. Educationally, the *oigos* were an amusing way of criticising flagrant breaches of conduct. The *oigos* are, howerer more reflective and less excited than the insistent *ree* theme would suggest; they are simple, rather repetetive but nevertheless delightful.

Wende tho kod kuyo (Dirges)

Ywago Owiti Odero	Mourning Owiti Odero
Ochamo ka Nyakiti ma ji oluoro.	(They) have consumed of Nyakiti whom people fear.
Dede ochamo ka Nyakiti ma ji oluoro.	Grasshoppers have eaten of Nyakiti whom people fear.
Ere!?	Where!?
Ochamo ka Nyakiti ma yande riek.	(They) have consumed of Nyakiti who was clever.
Bonyo ochamo ka Nyakiti ma yande riek.	Locusts have eaten of Nyakiti who was clever.
Ere!?	Where!?
Par Odero odong' nono ma wuon bilo.	Odero's home is deserted, owner of charms.

117

Owiti Odero ma ranyona ma wuon		Owiti Odero the great, the owner of	
bilo.		charms.	
Ere!?		Where!?	

This solo dirge, performed by a man, was collected by Reuben Nango at a funeral in Karachuonyo, South Nyanza. It is chanted and accompanied with "goyo sira" which is an aggressive run by the mourner simulating a fight with death. In doing the "sira", the mourner usually carries in his/her hand whatever item is readily available, mostly a club, spear or a branch. In this dirge, the mourner compares the death of Owiti to a locust invasion. He first of all refers to grasshoppers in general before identifying locusts specifically. In Dholuo, the word "dede" refers to the whole grasshopper progeny with specific names for different types, e.g. "det bonyo" means "locusts", "det lang'o" means the "variegated hopper", etc. The idea of desertion is meant to emphasise the loss of the dead person as the principal personality in the home.

"Ere" is both mnemonic and semantic in expressing the sense of loss. Nominally, "ere" means "where"?

Loo		**Earth**	
Solo:	*Loo, loo nyonuru loo.*	Solo:	Earth! Earth! Trample the earth
Chorus:	*Loo*	Chorus:	Earth.
Solo:	*To dak unyone?*	Solo:	Why not trample it?
Chorus:	*Lo jajuok.*	Chorus:	The evil earth.
Solo:	*Loo otero Agwingi ma woud oremo.*	Solo:	Earth swept away Argwings of Gem.
Chorus:	*Loo*	Chorus:	Earth
Solo:	*To dak unyone?*	Solo:	Why not trample it?
Chorus:	*Loo jajuok.*	Chorus:	The evil earth.
Solo:	*Loo otero Mbuya ma ja Rusinga.*	Solo:	Earth swept away Mbuya of Rusinga.
Chorus:	*Loo.*	Chorus:	Earth
Solo:	*To dak unyone?*	Solo:	Why not trample it?
Chorus:	*Loo jajuok.*	Chorus:	The evil earth.

A universal dirge among the Luo, "Loo" can be adapted to mourn anybody. In which case, the names are substituted to suit the occassion. But names of great Luo sons (such as Tom Mboya and Argwings Kodhek alluded to in the poem) who have died are usually included as an emphasis that the earth is determined to finish people. The dirge calls upon the mourners to trample the earth as a protest against the interminability of death. It can also be interpreted as a call to the remaining to be steadfast while still alive because eventually, the earth will consume them.

Chapter 5

NARRATIVES

Introduction

Among the Luo, story-telling brings together members of a family, nuclear or extended, to share in the creativity of the community. Traditionally, stories are narrated in the evening after the last meal of the day just before sleeping. Many times, stories are told as an overture to sleep. A mother in her hut can tell a variety of stories to her children out of her own volition or after being requested. In turn, the children also tell stories to the gathered members of the family. Older family members are at hand to rectify any mistakes in the plot as the young ones get to grips with the twists and turns of the stories.

Performance

Setting

Stories are told in the *siwindhe*, the hut of "Pim", an old woman who is essentially a grandmother to the boys and girls of the village. She commands a lot of respect but is very intimate and liberal with the children. Her hut is the sleeping quarters for the girls of the homestead and those from the neighbouring homesteads. Pre-adolescent boys also sleep at her hut. The grandmother sleeps in her bed called *"uriri"*, located apart from the youth. It is from there that she controls all proceedings in the *siwindhe*.

Sleeping in the *siwindhe* is compulsory for the females and for the young boys as the hut is a formative institution where the basic norms and mores of the society are imparted to the youth. Particularly for the females, *siwindhe* is an indispensable educational centre where they are instructed on how to take care of themselves as women, how to relate to the males and what aspects of behaviour are acceptable. Matters of the *siwindhe* are top secret and must not be divulged to those outside the circle of its membership.

Boys sleeping in the *siwindhe* move out when they reach puberty and sleep in the boys' hut, called *simba*. It is situated at the gate of the homestead. *Simba* is a bachelor's hut, built by the son in that homestead.

In the *simba*, the teenagers can continue telling the same stories learnt in the *siwindhe*. However, they tend to recount tales of a historical nature discussed in the men-only hut called *duol*. This is the private hut for the male head of the family or homestead and where he meets his contemporaries, guests and the male fraternity of the homestead.

All the males in the homestead have their meals at the *duol* except the very young ones. Here, they learn of the exploits of the past society and the historical foundations of the community. The discussions in *duol* concentrate on heroes, wars, bravery, hunting expeditions, herding, etc. Such are the matters that pervade the *simba* discussions when the boys are alone, apart from matters concerning relationships with the opposite sex and social adventure.

In both *simba* and *siwindhe*, the teenagers share sleeping facilities — notably the mat and available covers for the body. As they gather, the youth talk about matters that interest them as they prepare the sleeping quarters and each takes his or her usual position.

With changes in social set-ups and with family structures becoming more and more nuclear and separatist, the institutions of *simba* and *siwindhe* are diminishing, the latter especially. But they are still evidently extant in many rural settings in Luoland and still largely serve the same purposes.

Narrative overture

As the youth gather in the huts, their conversation eventually develops into riddling which in turn gives way to narration. In the *siwindhe*, when the grandmother is satisfied that everyone has come, she calls the house to silence by saying:

Ot mondo odhi kwath
Ot mondo odhi tung'
Ot mondo oduog diere
Ot mondo oling' thi.

(Let the house go grazing
Let the house go to the end
Let the house come to the centre
Let the house be dead silent.)

After this, everyone is aware that the narrative session has begun. It is usually the grandmother who tells the first story or asks for a volunteer. Whoever starts sets off by asking:

Agannue?
May I narrate to you a story?

The others reply:
Gannua.
Narrate to us.

Narration

After receiving the assent, the narrator starts off. There is no specific word or phrase to start each story, but there are a number of stock expressions which are used to begin stories. They include: *"Chon gilala* (A long time ago ...), *"Ndalo machon ne nitie"* ... (In the past there was ...), etc. At times, the narrator starts off with the names of the main characters of the story such as *"Otieng' gi Apuoyo ne gin osiepe ma ngita gi del ..."* (Spider and Hare were very great friends ...), or by naming the place where the story purportedly took place.

The story then continues, transporting everyone into the world of the make-believe, the world of suspense, the world of sorrow and joy, the world of satire and allegory and the world of long and short adventures.

In the course of the narration, the audience pays keen attention and instinctively reinforces the process by giggling at a funny point, exclaiming in surprise, clicking in disgust, lamenting in awe at the suffering of the hero(ine) or doing whatever relates to the changing mood of the story, so long as it is not adverse to the flow of the narration or the concentration of everyone else.

Story endings

At the end of each story, the narrator says:

Thu Tinda, adong arom gi bao ma kanera.
The end, may I grow as tall as the tree at my uncle's homestead.

The ending formula signals the next narrator to start off with the signal *"Agannue?"*. For purposes of order, the narration starts from one end of the room and progresses to the other end. Should the majority of people in the hut fall asleep before everyone has had a chance, the process continues the next night from where it stopped.

Everyone must tell a story, but there is no coercion. He who does not have a story to tell, either because of a memory lapse or because the intended story has been told by an earlier narrator, excuses himself or herself by saying:

> *Hasigro jaleny thee*
> The potsherd frizzles "thee".

This is to mean that the story has evaporated from the head like the ghee melts and eventually evaporates when put on a hot potsherd. However, it is considered shameful for one to always excuse himself/herself.

When everyone has had a chance to tell a story or when the grandmother feels that it is time to sleep, she brings the whole narration session to an end with the words:

> *Sigana go tielo*
> *Sigana go dhoot*
> *Sigana go tielo*
> *Sigana go widhi.*

> (Tale hit the bedroom
> Tale hit the door
> Tale hit the bedroom
> Tale hit the ledge.)

Conventions of performance

The beginning and ending formulas of narrative sessions mark the boundaries between the fictional world and the real. They establish "embassies" where whatever one says is protected by the immunity engendered. No offence is to be taken even if one feels that a particular story has been narrated to disparage him/her. This function is also achieved through setting the stories in the past. This then creates a freedom that enables the narrator to condemn and to praise through the stories.

The opening formula, *"Agannue"*, defines the role the narrator is going to play. The assent received from the audience establishes a contract with the narrator that as long as the story lasts, one is going to tell the narrative and the others will listen. The formula asks for permission to proceed but, the fact is that no one is ever denied the chance to tell a story. The apparent request is, therefore, a matter of formality, a question of etiquette and phatic communion.

Perhaps the most sacredly observed convention is the closing formula and the accompanying wish that one should grow as tall as the tree at the uncle's home. Implicit in this is the fact that the Luo admire height, especially in the males.

123

Being tall is seen as a mark of beauty. Stunted growth is shunned. Height is used as an incentive during story-telling when the narrator ends the tale by making an invocation that he grows tall. There is a belief that those who tell stories during the day stop growing.

However, children are known to tell stories when carrying out communal chores like fetching water, collecting firewood or baby-sitting during the day. The belief about not telling stories during the day has even been overtaken in the formal school set-up, where story-telling has moved from the *siwindhe* to the classroom. The sense of the belief, therefore, is that the activity of storytelling is so engaging and entertaining that it is better carried out at its own time when there is no distraction or hurry.

The reference to uncles needs to be understood in context. First, it is necessary to note that the word *"nera"* for "uncle" refers strictly to the maternal uncle. Paternal uncles are called "fathers", if we were to translate the Dholuo concept into English. In the Luo community, a maternal uncle is a child's closest relative outside the nuclear family. This is because the Luo are a patriachal society, and one can never have property disputes with maternal relatives.

The child who visits an uncle is pampered and given a lot of presents to take back home. Because the uncle is taken to be so benign, it is said that one who gets caned/slapped by an uncle becomes deaf. The point in this is that an uncle is so tolerant that it would take a lot of provocation for him to take such a measure against a nephew or niece. The child who necessitates such action is to blame. This then, is the kind of intimacy the wish seems to capture and elaborate.

Style in the performance of the Luo story

Drama

Since narration takes place in the dim light when virtually everyone is on the sleeping mat, there is very little physical dramatisation of the tale. There are hardly any elaborate movements and gestures. The drama is carried in the voice.

It is through the voice that the narrator creates the mood and even the characters. For example, the narrator shows the melancholy of a girl going to be sacrificed through the timbre of voice as she sings walking to the sacrificial place; the different sizes of Hare and Elephant are portrayed in the pitch of their voices as simulated by the narrator; idiosyncrasies of movement are depicted through ideophones while distance, height, depth or width are expressed through elongated words, if not repeated ones.

Song

One major characteristic of Luo stories is song. Not all narratives have songs, but many do. Such songs reinforce theme, create suspense, enhance plot development and divide episodes. They also summarise the tales, offer dramatic relief and involve the audience and the narrator in the performance, besides serving many other uses.

Regeneration

Song is used to string together the plot in what may be called "regeneration". Various episodes that exist as autonomous stories are strung into a single tale. Regeneration enables the expert narrator to give as much "good" narration to the audience as possible. But it also depicts the Luo perception of the world of narratives, which is that life can be seen as one whole consisting of elemental parts or that it starts with the parts that then constitute the whole. A narrator who reaches such a level of mastery sets the standards to which everyone else aspires.

It is, in fact, an ingenious way of killing two birds with one stone: whetting the audience's appetite as it looks forward to the climax of the next story and getting more than one's otherwise legitimate time but without causing offence.

Related to this idea is the existence of various versions of the same tale in the larger Luo community and even in neighbouring villages. The versions tend to be more divergent as one moves away from what may be considered the centre or origin. This is in terms of characters' names, settings and even the songs used. But still, it is easy to discern the common plot and themes. One may advance the theory that there once was a prototype narrative from which all subsequent versions sprung.

Characters and fantasy

Characters in Luo narratives can be human beings, animals, inanimate objects or fantastic creatures with or without physical manifestation. Among these are certain stock characters.

Among the human is the boy, Obong'o, and the girls, Awuor Awuor, Apiyo and Adongo. Obong'o is a name given to an only son while Awuor is the name to a girl born at dawn. Apiyo and Adongo are names for twin girls: Apiyo for she who emerged first and Adongo for the last.

The stock animal characters include Hare (called by several nicknames such as Nyagthin, Ogila Nyakarondo, etc), Hyena, Lion, Elephant and Hippo. The most remarkable among the fantastic characters is the ogre, commonly called Apul or Opul, although the latter name is mainly used in reference to the chief ogre. However, other creatures referred to in specific stories as hyenas or baboons, for example, are actually ogres when one considers that they display such characteristics as cannibalism and physical transmutation.

The characters are vehicles of fantasy and allegory. The fantasy in the narratives, however, goes beyond the characters and pervades the whole narrative realm. Manifestations of this fantasy are in:

(i)   the ability of animals to speak not only among themselves but even communicate intelligibly with people.
(ii) the immense energy in animals such as Hare who is so puny yet easily undertakes such herculean tasks as carrying the carcass of a whole Zebra as occurs in the story "Forest full of meat".
(iv) transformation of characters from one form to another, e.g., a human being becomes rock; a corpse changes into a speck; Hare falls down from heaven and becomes a chunk of meat and is able to consolidate again into a live animal after being cooked; Hare gets swallowed while inside a pumpkin into the elephant's stomach but is not digested and is even able to play a drum inside the bigger animal's stomach, etc.
(4)   chance occurrences such as the appearance of a dove just at the time when the ogre is cutting the tree trunk in order to kill the boy who cut its tail; or that of a barren woman at the scene where a mother chasing a prize from her husband has dumped her twin daughter and taken home the boy.

Numerous other fantasies may be identified in the narratives. They all enhance the fictional quality of the narratives and thus makes them true works of art.

Social functions

Through the narrative, called *sigana*, the Luo community conveys its wisdom, beliefs, traditions, customs, norms and a penal code of sorts to the young. The stories indirectly discuss normative and ethical issues. By analysing them, one is able to discern the moral code that regulates the community's life.

Kinship, for instance, forms a kind of social vortex into which the whole of society is sucked. In this book, the narratives "The bead of migration" and "Friendship ends but kinship remains" exemplify the centrality and permanence of kinship in different ways. In the former, the family of Ramogi splits because the brothers are engaged in sadistic antagonism not befitting siblings. Tragedy is the result. However, it is also implied in the story that independence and personal initiative is necessary especially where personality conflicts are likely to arise. In the latter, the tenacity of kinship is celebrated in the fact that only the brothers defy the stench of death and enter the hut when everyone else is repulsed.

The kinship fraternity is of course replenished through producing children. As with many communities the world over, the Luo regard children as a great asset, especially as perpetuators of lineage.

The Luo are patrilineal, hence the male children assume a special position in each family. Female children are considered as sojourners in the parents' homesteads because they are married and so technically become members of other clans. The girls are accordingly referred to metaphorically as "ogwang" (wild cat) or "nyaguok" (a puppy), the one belonging to the wilderness and the other often given out to a friend. These nominally derogatory references emphasise the temporary nature of the girls' residence in the parents' home and embody attitudes which are obviously changing as gender relations evolve.

This assumed transience gives the girls secondary significance in family affairs. The most senior sibling in a family is the first son who becomes the heir even if he is younger than all the girls. A man whose wife only has daughters is, therefore, ill at ease and would do everything to ensure that he gets a male heir. However, children are not taken for granted.

The girl is viewed as a potential source of bridewealth, paid when she is married. Signs of maturing, like the appearance of breasts, is taken as an indication of feminine normalcy. If such signs fail to appear, the family is concerned, such as in the story, "A problem of breasts". In this story, the parents go to great lengths to ensure that the anomaly is redressed.

All in all, children whether girls or boys, are still desired by all, an attitude which forms the foundation of the ideology which regards childlessness as a great personal tragedy. In folklore, the childless woman (called "*migumba*") is a tragic figure. She is, however, endowed with magical powers, as if to compensate for her "inadequacy". *Migumba* is usually the one with the luck and heart to adopt children abandoned by their parents for one reason or another. She becomes the surrogate mother to children begotten in unusual circumstances. For instance, in "The Mother of Twins", the barren woman takes the female twin who has been abandoned by her mother and nurtures her back to health.

Through such stories, the community shows its sympathy for *migumba* whose house cannot flourish like those of others because she has no offspring but embodies all that is motherly. The society thus ensures that an otherwise negative view that might be held against such women is dispelled if not neutralised. It is an attempt to demystify these women who usually live alone and run the risk of being branded sorcerers, witches or practitioners of evil arts. The stories stress that the women are important members of the society despite their childlessness, a factor they have no control over.

Just like *migumba*, orphans have a special position in the society, which insists that they be treated well. However, orphans invariably remain lonely as told in "Orphans" and "Cutting a middle finger". This underlines the fact that the presence of other relatives cannot fully replace that of the dead parents. In "Kijenje's best friend", the orphaned boy faces quite overt hostility and can only get solace from the magic calf.

Though orphans are alone and open to hostility, they have some uncanny luck and magic that makes their lives easier. In "Orphans", Awuor simply asks her dead brother's corpse to shrink and it happens. Kijenje also has a protector in the incredible cow and when he commits suicide to protest against its slaughter, everyone who eats it dies. In stories about the jealous step-mother, the orphans escape death, driving home the message that they should not be mistreated.

Jealousy, in practically every story in which it occurs, is condemned, usually with the jealous party inflicting harm to self. In "Apiyo and Adongo", for instance, the mother ends up killing her own child.

The Luo seem to consider jealousy as a trait that only exists among womenfolk. Apparently, men are not expected to be jealous. Thus, all the stories we have about jealousy have women as their main characters. This concept is entrenched even in the institution of polygamy where the co-wives refer to one another as "*nyieka*" a reference derived from "*nyiego*", meaning "jealousy". It is assumed that where women share a husband, jealousy is bound to thrive with the co-wife as its direct object. The stories of jealous and evil step-mothers hence fit into this worldview. While the jealous are condemned, the children listening to the story are sensitised to the existence of such realities, and they are challenged to be wary of such parents.

There is a tacit regulation that a wife does not beat up her husband although there are women who do so under the eaves of their houses. Even when this happens, the woman would never publicly celebrate the feat. In "Rading's wife meets her match", the wife flees in apparent search for sanctuary when she is the one who has beaten her husband. Humourous though this is, the significant point is that the woman does not want to expose the fact that she is capable of beating her husband but would rather give the impression that the accepted male domination is still intact. In effect, this is a protection for the male ego.

But by presenting the case of Rading' and his wife, the story questions the very basis of assumed male power. Physical assertion is usually the last bastion of male power or chauvinism. Here, the myth is shattered when Rading's wife fells him thrice without reply. The ironical twist comes, however, when she is also overpowered by her brother-in-law's wife.

The moral code that guides gender relations similarly regulates what food parts each gender can consume. For example, the Luo woman is not supposed to eat "*agoko*" (chest-meat). In strict Luo tradition, this is reserved for an elder who would invite his peers to feast on the roast meat served with plenty of chillies. The misfortune that befalls the woman in "A disobedient wife" results not only from her eating of the meat but also from her assumption of the male role. She has compromised authority in the home and usurped his privileges as a husband. Shorn of this position, the man cannot survive. When the woman wishes him death, she is actually only facilitating the imminent which comes to pass in the subsequent battle. The calamity lends strength to the proverb, "*Dhok e juok*" (Word of mouth is as good as sorcery). The story could thus be seen as a warning against talking loosely.

Of major importance in the Luo thought system is the grievous calamity known as "*chira*". This is a psycho-somatic affliction whose symptoms include reduction of body weight eventually leading to death. "Chira" befalls one who has committed a moral offence such as Obong'o's incest in "A heinous offence". Incest is one of the greatest offences one could ever commit. The punishment Obong'o gets is total extraction from the society symbolised by his incineration. Anthropologically speaking, this punishment seems to contradict the traditional Luo penal code which would have such an offender secluded or banished, not killed (Paul Mbuya, 1938). If the story, therefore, appears to exaggerate the punishment, it is probably to deter the young from even thinking of committing such moral offences.

There is also the concept of "*kwer*" (sanctions). For example, there are animals which hunters are forbidden to kill or even throw their weapons at. "*Arum tidi*" (the marabou stork) is such an animal. Kibwon in "Arum tidi" goes against the "*kwer*" and consequently pays for it in the dramatic encounter with the buffalo. Kibwon, as fate would have it, faces the full wrath of the animal and acts as an example to those who ignore the social and moral principles binding the society.

While presenting the community's moral code, narratives also exhort against personal weaknesses such as dishonesty, hastiness, vanity, arrogance and disrespect or spite for the disabled or the infirm. Such vices are often embodied in animal characters and warned against in narratives.

For example, there are many narratives about the hare and how he deceives his colleagues. His trickery is not celebrated but is used as a source of warning. When he maims and kills many of his friends in "Forest full of meat", the personality presented is that of an unreliable and sadistic friend. In other stories, he flees and keeps eluding other animals. Although the hare is a very popular figure in Luo oral literature, his portrayal is meant to discourage others from using his methods. In some cases, however, he is portrayed positively in juxtaposition with the greed of the hyena.

Vanity (*sunga*) is also condemned but ceremoniousness (*nyadhi*) is seen as a positive attribute. Flamboyance and poise are seen as signs of good breeding although the society still expects one to recognise the limits of these. Thus, Hare in "On the art of friendship" is fine as long as he poses that he can outdo his friends in every endeavour. Misfortune occurs, however, when he fails to achieve simply because he has over-estimated his abilities.

While the disability of such a charlatan is criticised, natural disability is treated with a lot of empathy. Consequently, children are discouraged from laughing at a disabled person. In "Awuor Awuor and the suitors", the girl's mother's disability is the ultimate test for the suitors. Those who laugh at the disability of Awuor's mother disqualify themselves by their lack of empathy and self-restraint. In "The four sons" and "The man-eater", the disabled dogs are ignored when they announce that they have heard their master's voice. The question the story raises is why it is that the disabled hear the voice before the "normal" dogs. The point is that the impaired have their own special abilities and are in fact as good members of the society as the able-bodied.

A collection of Luo narratives

The bead

The first parents of the Luo were Nyipir and Ramogi. Their first child, a son, was called Podho, and the second son, Arua. These were followed by many daughters and other sons.

When these children grew up, Nyakalaga Obong'o (God) provided them with wives and husbands respectively. In time, they multiplied and increased in number, until the population grew large enough to form a chiefdom. Ramogi became their first chief and ruled justly for many years.

When Ramogi died of old age, Podho took over the chiefdom and like his father, was a fair ruler. Arua, his brother, enjoyed hunting and looking after the animals. He was an outdoor man. There was no rivalry between them.

Then one day a big elephant came wandering into the compound which housed many members of the chieftain. Arua happened to be nearby. He was agile and swift of foot. He rushed to the little enclosure in which there was a shrine and a pot of *bilo* (magic herb). He picked up the sacred spear and took good aim at the animal. He wounded it, but not fatally. The animal escaped into the jungle with the spear stuck in its hide.

When word of what had happened reached Podho, he was outraged and insisted that Arua bring back the leadership spear. Arua had to go and look for the spear in the jungle. Everybody pleaded with Podho to excuse his brother from undertaking such a dangerous journey, but the chief would not change his mind.

"He did it out of spite and he must suffer the consequences," Podho said adamantly.

"Prepare *kuon anang'a* (ugali cooked in milk), some grilled meat and sweet potatoes for me. Make ready one or two gourds of *uji* as well. I shall leave for the jungle tomorrow," Arua instructed his wife. Her heart was heavy. She imagined the dangers that her husband would encounter in the unknown mysterious jungle, and was afraid. However, she did exactly as she was instructed. The following morning, at the first cock-crow, Arua set off, carrying his own spear and shield, together with the food his wife had prepared for him.

He was sad, but determined. He did not know which way to go at first, but eventually he decided to follow the sun. After travelling to the west for some days, he left behind the land of human beings — *ochung tir"* (upward ones) and entered the kingdom of the animals. Then he changed his course and travelled to the south-west. After roaming around the jungle for a long time, all his provisions ran out.

One day, he was feeling exhausted, hopeless and miserable. He lay under a tree to rest and gather some strength before he could go on. When he woke up at sunset, Arua found an old woman standing close to him, watching him. He felt frightened because all his life, he had never seen such a peculiar person.

The woman was ancient, withered of body and battered all over. But when she spoke to him, her voice was sweet, lovely and pleasant to listen to.

She was kind and sympathetic. She led Arua into a *kiru*, a small hut, and gave him some food. Then she made him tell her his business in the jungle, so far from the home of the upward ones. When he had told her the story of the spear, the woman asked him to stay the night and take a rest. He agreed.

The following day, the woman directed him to a larger *kiru* in which there were spears of all types. Some of the spears were large, some small, some short. Some had narrow blades, others thick ones and so on. Their sight alone alarmed and overwhelmed Arua. The old woman had told him that he would find the sacred spear among the collection.

For three days, he looked for the *bilo* spear and for three days, he was unable to find it. He grew frustrated and was on the verge of despair. But he tried again and fortunately, on the fifth day, when he was almost giving up, he found the spear. He took it out carefully, and ceremoniously brought it into the old woman's hut. They rejoiced together and Arua spent many joyful days with the old woman recovering from his fatigue.

Before Arua set off on his journey back home, the old woman gave him some beads which were very unique in colour, appearance and pattern. He was grateful for all that she had done for him. After carrying what provisions she had prepared for him, he hurried away with a lighter heart and a more cheerful mood towards his brother's chiefdom. He was full of hope and expectation. When he had gone a few yards, he looked back, but neither the old woman nor her *kiru* were in sight. They had vanished! He could not understand.

131

The journey back proved gruesome. He met many fierce wild creatures of the deep jungle. What saved him from being attacked was the fact that he had then grown hairy and had also taken on the smell of the jungle. As a result, wild animals did not bother much about him. He had become just like one of them. In addition to this, and obviously more important, he carried the sacred spear and beads which had protective powers.

When eventually he arrived home, he was sick with exhaustion. Nevertheless, he called a big meeting at which he handed the spear to his brother. There was much uneasiness in the village, and also between the two families which would only wear off with time.

Many seasons came and went and people were already beginning to forget what had happened between their chief and his brother. Then one day something else happened that opened the wound that had already began to close up.

One of Podho's children swallowed a bead from the set the old woman had given Arua in the jungle. Arua was furious! He beat up all the members of his household for exposing his beads to outsiders. Then he went to his brother and demanded the bead back. Nyipir, his mother, who was still alive, pleaded with him to contend with any type of bead his brother could find, but he would accept no plea. He argued that since they did not intercede when he lost the spear, people should not interfere in this.

"I want my bead, not an imitation," he said.

As a result, Podho got fed up and in rage took a knife and cut open his daughter's stomach to get out the bead. He found it in the child's intestine. But of course, the child died.

The whole family had been defiled. No amount of libation could cleanse the chief and his people. The best thing that the sons of Ramogi could do was to part company and break up the home and all that their father and mother had built up. It was a sad incident and a very explosive situation.

Civil war could break out at any time in the chiefdom. The atmosphere was charged with tension which mounted daily. In the end a decision was made. Those who supported either of the brothers rallied behind him while they levelled bitter accusations against one another. The worst split had occurred and the two brothers were responsible for it.

Those who supported Arua went east, crossed the River Nile and are settled in Uganda and Kenya. They are the present Acholi, Padhola, Lang'o and Alur of Uganda and the Southern Luo of Kenya and so on. Supporters of Podho followed him to the west and scattered all over in different countries of Africa. It is said some of them are to be found in Nigeria, the Congo and Central Africa.

Tinda.

(Source: Odaga, A.B. *Thu Tinda*, Lake Publishers and Enterprises Ltd: Kisumu, 1980).

132

Nyamgondho son of Ombare

At Gwasi in Luo-land, there lived a poor bachelor called Nyamgondho, son of Ombare. He had inherited nothing from his father and was a fisherman of no repute.

Each evening, unable to sell any part of his catch, he ate it all himself, in this way staving off hunger until the next day when, once more, he would go down to the lake and set his traps.

One afternoon, he went down to the lake and found all his traps empty. They had not caught a single fish. Nyamgondho was sad: empty traps meant an empty stomach. He reflected on his poverty, despair creeping slowly into his heart.

Then he prayed to God. "Chief of creation, chief of water," he cried, "you know I'm a poor man. Help me to catch some fish. God, you never spurn your children. Look on me with kindness. I set my traps last night but caught nothing. Please help me!" Standing on the shore, he prayed earnestly, his eyes fixed on the sun.

When he came to inspect his traps next day, he was disgusted to find, not a rich harvest of fish, but a shrivelled old hag. The very sight of her revolted him and he turned to run. But the woman stopped him, saying in a quiet voice, "Please don't leave me. I'm human just like yourself."

These gentle words moved Nyamgondho and set him wondering. He decided at last to free the hag and take her home. There, he built a hut for her, and this ugly guest from the lake soon became his wife.

On the morning after his marriage, Nyamgondho awoke to an astonishing sight. The poor fisherman found his house astir with vast numbers of cattle, sheep, goats, ducks, and barn-door fowl. This was the woman's wealth, mysteriously treasured up in the unknown depths of the lake. Nyamgondho was now a rich man at whose house crowds flocked to eat, an *okebe* of rare succulence; a man whose cows one person could not milk in a whole day. So great was his wealth that as time went by, he married more wives.

Now in those days, the elders and the rich used to meet for beer parties. Since Nyamgondho, as the Luo say, had swollen his poverty and burst forth a rich man, he was eligible now to sit and drink with the elders. He was invited one day to a feast where *hwachra*, the new harvest beer, would be drunk. This being a festive occasion for the people, the elders drank so heavily that it seemed they would never go home as old people are required to do after an important feast. But since a man should not dry himself where he has bathed, they eventually left and went staggering off into the night.

When Nyamgondho arrived home, tired and tipsy, he found his gate securely locked. He called loudly, but no one replied. The woman of the lake and his younger wives were fast asleep. He called them each in turn, but none heard his voice.

133

Nyamgondho called and his home kept silent. His cattle moved about silently swinging their tails and huffing and puffing in the dark.

"People of my home, open this gate!" he roared. But no one heard. He shouted again, calling and calling till his throat was dry and his voice hoarse. Only the chirring beetles seemed to listen. It was a cold night. A thousand stars and fireflies lit the sky. The world was still.

And now, his patience exhausted, Nyamgondho grew angry.

He began heaping abuse on his elderly wife, "Since when have slaves refused to obey their masters? Even a hag I pulled from the lake won't hear me!" he cried. "Me, the son of Ombare, a kind fellow."

Alas, the woman of the lake now awoke and heard his insults clearly. She came to the gate in an angry mood, saying bitterly, "Rail at your younger wives, not at me. I am your mother. I am the eyes you see with."

These were harrowing words for Nyamgondho. "What? You, my mother!" he retorted. "A helpless wretch I fished from the lake! A slave! A helpless slave!" His taunts pierced the old woman's heart like thorns.

"Nyamgondho son of Ombare," she said, "I see you are proud and ungrateful. Our marriage is now at an end. Today, I am leaving you. Again you will be poor, rolling about the world like a stone. You will cry after me, but in vain."

"How can my wealth disappear?" Nyamgondho asked. "What did you bring, you picked-up-thing that I bred in my home?" And he stormed off to his *duol*.

At dawn the old woman arose. She prepared to return to the depths of the lake where once she had dwelt in wealth and glory. When she left, all the domestic animals left too. Those tied to pegs broke ropes and followed her; the goats, the hens, the cocks and pullets, the short ducks and the silly sheep, they all thronged after her. She led the way and her wealth followed behind. Soon, waking from his drunken sleep, Nyamgondho also followed. But it was too late. With her animals faithfully following, the old woman walked down the shore into the depths of the lake. Even the granaries and their contents rolled after her and soon, the smooth waters of the lake had covered them all. There was nothing left.

On the shore, Nyamgondho gazed on the lake, speechless, his chin resting on his walking staff. So profound was his grief that he died there alone by the shore.

Even to this day, you can see the tell-tale footprints of the cattle and birds this man once owned. What is more, when Nyamgondho died, he grew into a tree, which can still be seen on the shore at Gwasi.

Songs are the best way of expressing our happiness or sorrow, our success or failure. Here is one to remind you of the son of Ombare:

Chon nene nitie ng'at moro
Nyamgondho wuod Ombare
Jalni nodak but nam, Gwasi!

Nohero dhi lupo
Hero lupo
Lupo nam Gwasi
Chieng' moronodhi limo huira
Noyudo huira nono
Aye bang'e nochako yuak niya:
"Yaa Nyasaye Nyasaye
Dak ikonya Ikonya
Ayud rech."
Kinyne kane odhi limo huira
Noyudo dhako moti
Dhakono ne okone niya:
"Nyamgondho wuod Ombare
Dak ikawa mondo itera pacho...?

(Long, long ago there was a man,
Nyamgondho son of Ombare.
He lived by the lake at Gwasi.
He loved to go fishing.
He loved to go fishing.
Fishing in the lake at Gwasi.
One day he went a trap to check.
But found the trap was empty.
Later the following prayer he moaned;
"Yaa! O God why don't you help me
Help me get some fish!"
When next he went to check his trap
He found an old woman who begged him
thus:
Nyamgondho Son of Ombare
Why don't you take me home ....?)
Tinda

(Source: Onyango-Ogutu, B. and Rosco, A.A. *Keep My words*, EAEP, 1974).

The voice

A long long time ago, before our great grandfathers were born, there was a girl called Julu, who was an only child. Then one day, there was a disaster. All her parents and all her relatives died leaving her all alone in the big homestead.

She cried and cried, but they did not come back to her. She did not know what to do in this home, all by herself.

One day she took her father's stool, placed it right in the middle of the round compound, fenced by a high euphorbia hedge, and sat on it. She just sat and kept

135

quiet, lost in thought, thinking of how she was going to manage all alone in a lonely place, with no one to support her, talk to her and keep her company. When she had been sitting for some time, she thought she heard a voice calling her. She listened more intently, but for some time nothing happened.

"Mmm, who can be calling me seeing I am so much alone in the world?" she said to herself. Then she heard the voice again, this time very distinctly.

"Julu, what is wrong with you? Why do you keep quiet when I am calling you?" the voice asked. She felt puzzled and even frightened. She did not know what to say, so she just kept quiet. Again she heard the voice calling her name. "Julu", and this time she answered in a moanful song:

> Julu, ee, Julu, who is calling me?
> Julu, who is calling me? Julu, who is calling me?
> Julu, who is calling me? Julu,
> I have killed everybody eee, eee, Julu,
> My grandfather is haunting me, Julu.
> My grandfather is haunting me, Julu.
> Julu, ee, Julu who is calling me?
> Julu, who is calling me?
> Julu who is calling me, Julu?
> I have killed everybody Julu.
> My mother is haunting me, Julu, ee Julu.
> My grandfather is haunting me, Julu.
> My father is haunting me, Julu, ee Julu.

All this time, a strange thing was happening. While she had been singing, the stool on which she was sitting had been sinking slowly into the ground. The legs of the stool were all in the ground. She stopped to rest a little, but she did not rest for long, because she heard a voice calling her once more. And she replied, once again in a song:

> Julu ee, Julu, who is calling me, Julu?
> Julu ee, Julu,
> My grandmother is haunting me, Julu, Julu.
> My grandmother is haunting me, Julu.
> My father is haunting me, Julu.
> I have killed everyone, Julu, ee, Julu.
> My grandmother is haunting me, ee, Julu.

The stool continued to sink and Julu with it. She had now sank up to the chest, below her breasts. She kept quiet, she did not know what to do and still did not know who was calling her and why. She once again heard her name being called and, once again, she responded immediately:

136

Julu, ee, Julu, who is calling me, Julu, ee,
I have killed everybody, Julu.
Is it my grandmother who is haunting me?
Julu, ee, Julu.
Is it my grandfather who is haunting me?
Julu, ee, Julu.
Is it my mother who is haunting me?
Julu, ee, Julu.

She paused again. She had continued to sink and the soil was almost covering her neck. She could hardly breathe. Again she heard the voice calling her, but she could only answer quietly. Then she tried to turn but she could hardly see a thing; and once again she began to sing, but with a lot of difficulty this time.

Julu, ee, Julu who is calling me, Julu?
Julu who is calling me, Julu?
Julu, ee, Julu

By then the earth had covered her up completely. She had been buried alive. Then she heard one more voice, but she could not respond to the call. The earth swallowed her and she disappeared in the ground, leaving no trace.
Thu Tinda.

(Source: Odaga, A.B., *Thu Tinda*, Lake Publishers and Enterprises Ltd: Kisumu, 1980).

Kijenje's best friend

Kijenje was an orphan who lived with his uncle. He spent his days with the other boys in his group tending cattle in the countryside. Now feeling bored with their task one day, the boys began to wrestle with one another, chasing each other through the grass and flinging mud-balls about. It was the happiest afternoon of their lives. But when the sun began to sink low in the sky and the hour came to return home, there was no sign of their cattle.

Afraid to face their parents without the animals, the boys decided to run away.
"I'm going to my aunt's," said one.
"I'm off to my uncle's," said another.
"I'll make for granny's," said a third.
Almost alone in the world, with no relative except his uncle, Kijenje had nowhere to go. He turned the problem over in his mind, and then, swearing by his ancestors, declared: "I'll search for those cattle till I find them!" And with these bold words, he struck out across the countryside. Happily, he soon discovered the animals' trail from hoof-prints in the soft earth.

But by then the cattle were far away. Lang'o thieves had stolen them and were herding them across the countryside at a furious speed. Before he finally caught up with them, Kijenje had run, walked and rested innumerable times. And now he found himself in the heartland of the Lang'o. The cattle had been driven to a village and when Kijenje crept stealthily up to a small hut, he was overjoyed to find his own pet cow inside. He approached the animal with his heart fluttering and the creature responded by wagging her tail and licking his hands.

Meanwhile, the Lang'o warriors had seen him and rushed at him brandishing spears clearly determined to kill him. But an elder restrained them.

"He's only a child," he said. "There's no reason for him to die. Let's just say we've found ourselves another cattle boy."

The warriors were, however, unhappy. Who was this boy? Where was he from? What did he know about the stolen cattle?

They had noticed that one cow seemed to know him well. Kijenje answered boldly, swearing he was an orphan without home or family, roaming the land quite aimlessly, "I know nothing about your cattle," he added, "and as for the cow you mention, I've never set eyes on it before." Finally, he offered himself as a cattle boy and promised to work conscientiously.

Impressed by his frankness, a Lang'o warrior took him to his home where he was given food and lodgings. The next day, he went out early to herd cattle with some Lang'o children. The weeks passed by and soon any suspicions which these children might have harboured against Kijenje melted away. But among the Lang'o adults, it was different. With the dawning of each day, they grew more certain that Kijenje was a spy.

"This child has come to find the Luo cattle," they said. And they decided to poison him forthwith.

Driving the cattle home one evening, Kijenje was told by his pet cow how matters stood between him and the Lang'o; and on their arrival at the house gate, the cow grew uneasy, warning him that poison had been put down. To go through the gate would mean certain death:

Buuu, Kijenje!
Buu, Kijenje!
Kiri luw rangach, Kijenje!
Mwom mana chiel, Kijenje!
Rangach oyieye yath, Kijenje!
Buuu, Kijenje!

(Buu, Kijenje!
Don't go through the gate, Kijenje!
Go in through the fence, Kijenje!
Poison is by the gate, Kijenje!)

138

Heeding this advice, Kijenje climbed through the euphorbia hedge. Once indoors, he was treated as though nothing was amiss and served with food and drink that was not poisoned.

Time passed. The Lang'o seemed content to leave Kijenje alone. They were happy to see him stroll out each day to herd their cattle over the plains. But Kijenje himself was always worried. He feared for his life, yearned for home, and longed to escape. Years passed since that merry afternoon in Luo-land.

Then one day, at dawn, his cow told him bluntly: "Today they're going to slay you."

An old woman gave him the same warning: "My people are plotting to kill you," she said. "Don't come home tonight. Escape now, while you can." She was a kindly woman whose blind wet eyes, scum-covered and bloodshot, Kijenje had bathed till her sight returned. Her warning was a measure of her gratitude, and now she helped Kijenje untie the cattle and set off in the early morning light, singing and whistling as he went.

He sang and whistled his way over the plains, driving the cattle before him until he was far away from the homes of the Lang'o:

Ng'at mawuogi badhina kanera kanera
kanera
Ng'at mawuogi badhina kababa kababa
kababa
Ng'at mawuogi badhina kawaya kawaya
kawaya
Kawaya kawaya acham chira yawuoyi
Kawaya acham chira yawuoyi
Pino k'Odolo
Kich k'Odolo
Oganje oyaye

(One leaves saying: To my uncle's uncle's
uncle's
One leaves saying: To my father's father's
One leaves saying: To my auntie's
auntie's
At my aunt's at my aunt's I daunt boys'
courage
At my aunt's I daunt boys' courage
Wasps k'Odolo
Bees k'Odolo
Oganje oyaye)

In a remote part of the country, Kijenje chanced on some Lang'o warriors, also herding cattle. They ran towards him with spears raised; but from his pet cow's ear flew bees and wasps which put the warriors to flight. The cow herself had prepared this: she knew the dangers facing a single boy herding cattle in a strange land.

In their rush to escape, the Lang'o deserted their cattle, which now joined Kijenje's. Curiously, a similar incident occurred later in the day. Once more the Lang'o fled, dropping their spears and leaving their cattle.

And now, driving an enormous herd ahead of him, Kijenje moved across the land, singing gaily as he went: "*Ng'at mawuogi badhina kanera kanera ....*"

Eventually he found himself in a country familiar to him. He was approaching the village he had left so long ago.

A woman throwing refuse beyond her gate thought she herd the sound of a familiar voice piercing the air in song. The music was faint, borne to her ears on waves of the wind, then fading with the breeze: "*Ng'at mawuogi ... Kawaya ... Oganje ...*"

She hurried back to her compound, shouting excitedly: "Someone's singing like Kijenje! Someone's singing like Kijenje! Can you hear it?" But an elder rebuked her, insisting that she was drunk.

Do you usually drink beer in the morning?" he asked. "Kijenje indeed! He died years ago — many years ago, and you know it. Is this the time to be dreaming about him?"

The good woman found a seat and held her peace. But again, she heard the singing and now she insisted more firmly, "Someone really is singing like Kijenje". And as she spoke, the song came floating through the compound loud and clear: "*Ng'at mawuogi badhina kanera kanera kanera ....*" And the people were amazed.

Kijenje reached the gate and stood there, smiling and singing merrily.

"The child has indeed returned!" his uncle cried, and welcomed him into the house. He ordered a bull to be slaughtered in the boy's honour. The people were filled with joy, and happiness spread through the compounds.

Several months later, however, Kijenje's uncle took a wife and, granting her the privilege of all new brides, let her choose a beast for slaughter. Alas, the wretched woman chose Kijenje's cow, and her husband agreed to kill it at once. "Now you've chosen it we must kill it," he said, "even though it's my nephew's pet."

An old woman hotly protested, saying, "You can't do this. Kijenje's father left him the animal, and it's helped him during his stay among the Lang'o." But her plea failed to move him. He was a stubborn fellow.

Without delay, he gathered some friends, caught the cow, and in the twinkling of an eye had cut its throat. With equal dispatch, the poor beast was skinned, quartered, and roasted.

When Kijenje returned from a walk and asked after his pet, he was shown a pathetic heap of bloody skin and bone. Demanding to know who had done the deed, Kijenje was interrupted by his "lesser father". "I slaughtered the cow and I have eaten it!" he cried. "Remember, this is my home. When your father died, his home died with him." These cruel words cut deep into Kijenje's heart. Sadly, he begged leave to have at least the cow's head. "Take it!" sneered his uncle. "There it is thrown by the fence!"

Burdened with grief, Kijenje moved away and took the blood-stained head. Then digging a hole in the earth, he buried the head, and himself also.

And it happened that all who ate the cow's meat at his uncle's home that day, including the new wife and the wedding guests, died a quick and painful death.

Tinda.

(Source: Onyango-Ogutu, B. and Rosco, A.A. *Keep My words*, EAEP, 1974).

The girl who pierced the mother's eyes

Once upon a time, there was a big, big drought on earth. Hearsay had it that the crocodile had swallowed the pot of rain. The elders, therefore, met to discuss how the problem could be solved. They decided to consult the village medicineman, who told them that the crocodile wanted to be given a girl to eat before he could release the pot.

The elders searched throughout the community for suitable sacrifice and finally settled on a maiden called Oganda. She was also the most beautiful girl in the whole village. When Oganda's father was informed about the decision to sacrifice his daughter, he did not think twice about it. If it was the only solution to the community's problem, he reasoned, he had no objection. "Let her go so that we can get rain," he said.

Oganda was then taken by a team of elders and the journey begun to the lake where the crocodile lived.

On the way, she met her aunt who asked: "Where are you going, my niece Oganda? And why are you crying?"

Oganda replied in song:

My fathers have conspired with the vultures, oh.
My aunts have conspired with the vultures, oh.
My in-laws have conspired with the vultures, oh.
It is Oganda who must die.

But this song did not move Oganda's aunt into doing anything to help her. Instead, she said: "Just go so that we can get rain."

Next, Oganda met her uncle who also asked, "Where are you going, my niece Oganda? And why are you crying?"

Oganda replied with the same song:

> My fathers have conspired with the vultures, oh.
> My aunts have conspired with the vultures, oh.
> My in-laws have conspired with the vultures, oh.
> It is Oganda who must die.

As they walked on, the next person they met was Oganda's adoring lover. When he asked where she was going and she replied with song, crying, he told her and the company escorting the girl to wait for him as he went to collect a spear, club and machete. Then he told Oganda to sing after he returned to accompany her on the journey.

> My fathers have conspired with the vultures, oh.
> My aunts have conspired with the vultures, oh.
> My in-laws have conspired with the vultures, oh.
> It is Oganda who must die.

As they approached the lake, he told her to sing even louder.

> My fathers have conspired with the vultures, oh.
> My aunts have conspired with the vultures, oh.
> My in-laws have conspired with the vultures, oh.
> It is Oganda who must die.

As soon as Crocodile heard the song and knew that its food was on the way, he vomitted the pot of rain and it started pouring immediately. Crocodile opened its mouth very wide waiting to swallow the girl.

Oganda and the team found him in this state, with the mouth wide open and the eyes closed in anticipation. The elders stopped a distance away and urged Oganda to go and be eaten. Although she was afraid, she just walked on because her lover was ready to die with her. When they reached Crocodile, her lover took out his spear and impaled the animal on it. When the elders saw how the animal dashed out of the water towards the two, they all scattered and returned home believing that Oganda and her lover had been killed. However, Oganda's lover managed to kill the crocodile. He then took Oganda as his wife and made a new home for her, far away.

One day, a certain woman from Oganda's former village was passing by her new home. She saw Oganda busy pounding outside her house. When the woman went back to her village, she reported to Oganda's parents that the girl was still alive.

But they did not believe her. "This woman is mad," they said. "How can she talk about Oganda who died a long time ago? The woman tried to prove her report but no one paid her any attention.

One time, however, Oganda's mother was also passing by her daughter's new home when she stepped on a thorn. She sat down and tried to remove it in vain. Then she peeped into the homestead and called the woman she saw to go and remove the thorn from the sole of her feet. When Oganda went and found that it was her mother who had let her be taken away to be fed to the crocodile, she took a sharp thorn and, instead of using it to remove the other thorn, pierced her mother's eyes. Her mother became blind for the rest of her life.

Tinda.

(Collected from Susan Awuor Miruka at Asembo Bay, 1984)

Sigand Oganda

(The girl who pierced her mother's eyes)

Ndalo moko piny notuo ahinya. Ne iwacho ni nyan'g omuonyo aguch koth. Jodongo nochoko bura moyalo gima ditim. Nyang'ne owacho ni odwaro nyako eka ong'ulo agulu. Ji ne ong'icho moyiero nyako miluongo ni Oganda nikech en ema nober malombo wang'. Kane owachne wuon to oko ni odhi adhiya koth ochwe. Ne okaw Oganda ka itero kanyang' kendo e yo ne oywak aywaka. Ne oromo gi waygi. "Oganda nyathiwa idhi kanye miywak aywaka ni?" Oganda nochako wer :

Ka-baba duto winjo gi arumbe yo
Ka-weyena duto winjo gi arumbe yo
Ka-yuocha duto winjo gi arumbe yo
Oganda ema nyaka tho

Waygi to noduoke ni "Dhi adhiya piny otwo rwok". Ne oromo gi nergi "Oganda nyakewa idhi kanye ma iywak aywaka ni?"

Ka- baba duto winjo gi arumbe yo
Ka-weyena duto winjo gi arumbe yo
Kayuocha duto winjo gi arumbe yo
Oganda ema nyaka tho

Kaye ne oromo gi osiepne mohere kabisa. Kane ochako wer to osiepne oko ni, "Ritauru kanyo". Ne odhi oomo tong', arungu gi opanga kaye ochako wer ka gidhi. Nyang' ka ne owinjo wend Oganda no to ne ong'ulo agulu kong'eyo ni nyako biro, kendo nong'amo dhoge maduong' koikre chame. Sama ne ong'ule agulu no to koth ochako chwe. Oganda gi osiepne ne oyudo ka nyang' ong'amo dhoge ma kata wang'e ok nen. Ne ochwoyo duond nyang' gi tong ma otho. Ne okawo Oganda ma okende.

*Chieng' moro dhako moro ne onene ma odhi onyiso wuongi to wuongi
nokoneni,"Dhakoni janeko! Oganda mane otho cha!?" Kata dhakono ne otemo wacho ni
adier ne oneno Oganda to ok ne gidewe.*

*Katakamano mingi chieng' moro ne kadho but dalagi monene. Ne oyudo kudho ochuoye mit
oluonge ni okolne kudhono. Oganda ne odhi gi kudho ma ochwoyo wang' mingi ma mingi
olokre muofu.*

Tinda.

Apiyo and Adongo

Once upon a time, there were two girls. One was called Apiyo and the other Adongo.
The two girls had one father, but different mothers. Adongo lost her mother when
she was an infant, and was then brought up by Apiyo's mother.

Adongo's stepmother disliked her for various reasons one of which was that
she was more beautiful than Apiyo. Apiyo had all the good things one can imagine
while poor Adongo went around in rags, with an empty stomach most of the time.
Her father was well aware of his daughter's plight, but he was unable to intervene.
He kept on consoling her, telling her to persevere and be an obedient girl. She tried
very hard to obey her father.

One day, Apiyo and Adongo went to the bush to gather firewood. Adongo picked
up a beautiful necklace and was very pleased with her find. When they arrived
back home in the evening, Apiyo's mother ordered Adongo to hand over the necklace
to Apiyo.

Naturally, Adongo didn't want to part with her necklace, but her step-mother
insisted that she give it to her daughter. She snatched it from her and handed it to
Apiyo, her own daughter. The woman's cruel actions had become unbearable to
the young motherless girl. She wept and went to bed without eating the dregs and
remnants of Apiyo's supper, which often formed her meals.

Sleep did not visit her eyes that night. She stayed awake, thinking and perfecting
her escape plans. She wanted to escape from Apiyo and her mother.

She must go to her maternal uncle, the only one she knew. She would live with
him and never return to her father's home.

She had never visited her maternal uncle before, but she knew the village in
which the home was. She left her home very early in the morning, before the buck
was up to urinate.

On her way to her uncle's home the first person she met was an old man. He
spoke kindly to her and asked where she was going and why she was crying and
feeling so sorry for herself.

When she narrated her story to him, the old man told her, "Do not cry, your troubles will soon come to an end. Just walk on, follow the same path, it will lead you to your uncle's homestead."

She walked on and on, along the path that she had been shown by the old man. Then she came across a most unusual thing. At the side of the road, there was a grinding stone full of millet. She made as if to pass it, but the grinding stone spoke to her and said:

"Please, grind the millet that is on my back, I beg you," it croaked in a frightening strange voice.

"All right I'll do it," Adongo said and ground everything to the last grain.

The grinding stone was grateful and told her, "You are going to your uncle's home, so walk on. But when you reach the crossroads, take the narrow path, not the wide one."

"Thank you," Adongo said and walked on, very much alert so as not to miss the crossroads she had been instructed to look out for. Soon, she came upon a small river, with only one tree plank for a bridge. Nearby, close to that bridge, she spotted an old woman who was bathing. Her face lit up when she noticed that Adongo was looking at her with some interest.

"Come and rub my back for me. My arms are all knotted up by old age. I can hardly reach some parts of my body," she called Adongo.

"Yes, I shall be glad to be of some help to you," she replied and eagerly gave the woman's back a thorough rubbing. She also cleaned other parts the woman could not reach easily.

The woman thanked Adongo and asked her why she was going to her uncle's home so early in the morning. Adongo told her what had been her plight in her father's home, and the cruelty her step-mother and step-sister had meted out to her. The old woman expressed her sympathy and told her not to worry, that her troubles would soon come to an end.

Then she added: "When you reach the crossroads, take the narrow path, not the wide one." She repeated the same instructions the grinding stone had given her.

"Thank you very much," Adongo replied as she walked away hurriedly. When she came to the crossroads, she remembered to take the narrow path as she had been instructed.

Later that afternoon, Adongo arrived at her uncle's home. Everyone was pleased to see her. Before she had even rested, her uncle had given her some work to do. And although she was hungry and tired, she willingly listened to his instructions.

"Go into the kitchen, which is situated in the outer room of that main house," her uncle began and continued, "On the far side of the room, you will see a gourd full of sour milk. I want you to churn it until I come along to check if you have churned out some butter, and whether it has separated from the milk. Don't open the stopper to find out on your own. Just go on shaking it and wait for me. Do you understand?" he asked, looking intently at her.

"Yes uncle," she replied

"There is also a quail grilling at the fireplace," her uncle said. "It smells good and very appetising and I realise you must be very hungry, but don't eat it. Don't touch it. Go and do as I have told you."

"Yes uncle," Adongo answered looking keenly around her. She felt weak as she walked towards the main house to carry out her uncle's instructions. For a long time, Adongo shook the gourd while she sang and kept time with the sound of the milk inside the gourd. The quail was hanging on the fireplace, and there were just enough glowing embers of the fire to allow it to brown slowly. She watched it and salivated continually, but she resisted the temptation to touch it.

When at last her uncle came into the kitchen to find out how she had performed the task, he was pleased to see that Adongo had obeyed his instructions and had done everything very carefully.

"Well done, Adongo. You may now take that large earthenware bowl and pour the milk from the gourd into it. Let's see if enough fat has collected at the top," her uncle said in a pleasant voice with a twinkle in his eyes.

Adongo once again did as she had been told. And to her dismay, instead of fat and milk, many necklaces like the one she had lost to Apiyo, gushed out. These were followed by several other ornaments, clothes, waist tassels and all the other things that she had longed for but had been denied her by her cruel step-mother and her equally cruel step-sister.

Special waist beads of assorted colours: red, black, white, yellow, blue, as well as earrings, special skin garments, and many other things just kept dropping and pouring from the gourd. They lay on the ground in a heap between her legs. They were all hers to pick and keep, to own and wear as her very own! It was incredible. Adongo could not believe this was really happening to her. She felt as if in a dream.

She was extremely happy and spent many days with her uncle's family. She did not want to return to her father's home, but her uncle insisted on it.

"Just go back to your home because nobody, neither your step-mother nor her daughter nor anyone else, will extort anything from you. They won't have the desire to do it. These are all yours. They will only admire them. Neither will anyone maltreat you any more. For the fist time, you are going to know new happiness and love in your home," her uncle said.

"Uncle, if you say so, I shall have to return because I trust you, but these two, my step-mother and her daughter, have made life very difficult for me," Adongo replied.

In a way, she was glad to go back home, if only so that she could show off her newly acquired possessions to Apiyo and her mother.

At home, Apiyo couldn't believe that the things really belonged to Adongo; and when she told her mother about them, she became extremely jealous. She rushed out and touched them and admired them, one by one. But she could not take them from her, she had no desire to do so.

"You also must run to my brother's home. He will give you many things, far better than Adongo's. Her uncle is only a simple elder in his clan while my brother is a chief over several clans, and very rich too. My brother's cattle are uncountable," the woman told her daughter, while her heart was full of envy and hatred for Adongo.

Early the next day, Apiyo set off for her uncle's home. The first person she met on the way was that old man Adongo had met when she was going to her uncle's home, escaping from Apiyo and her mother.

The old man asked her eagerly, "Where are you going so early in the morning,"? Apiyo's answer was prompt and short. "It is not your business to know where I am going."

The old man blinked, his grey eyebrows quivering with displeasure, but he said nothing further to Apiyo as she walked off.

After some time, she came across a grinding stone by the roadside. It was full of millet. And just as it had asked Adongo, it spoke out and requested Apiyo to grind the millet on its back.

"Who, me? Grind what? Even at home I don't do that sort of work. That is Adongo's job. So I shan't *"ridha"* the millet for you, and you dare ...." she sputtered out, looking scornfully at the grinding stone.

"It is all right, continue along the same path but when you reach the crossroads, please take the narrow road and not the wide one," the grinding stone told Apiyo, who did not stop even for a second to get the instructions properly, nor to thank the grinding stone as Adongo had done.

She ran most of the way and soon came to the same river, where Adongo had met the old woman. Once again the old woman was there. She spoke to Apiyo and asked her to rub her back for her. Just as she had been rude to the old man and the grinding stone, she spoke rudely to the old woman and shouted: "Mmmmm, me! I can't touch you and I shan't '*guoka*' your back for you. You are the most nauseating person I have ever seen. You are worse than a dog." She pouted rudely at the woman who sat grinning pleasantly at her as she spoke.

"Fine enough, cross the river and walk on," the woman told her and added, "When you reach the crossroads, follow the narrow road, not the wide one," the old woman said with a gleam of mischief in her eyes. She remained chuckling to herself as Apiyo crossed the one-poled bridge onto the other side.

At the crossroads, she took the wide road instead of the narrow one and as a result, went round and round in circles, eventually reaching her uncle's home very late in the evening, tired, hungry and angry.

147

Apiyo's uncle gave her the tasks similar to those which Adongo's uncle had allocated Adongo. Apiyo said nothing but kept on uttering rude remarks as her uncle gave her the instructions. She didn't want to do any work and so she walked away from her uncle showing much displeasure. He remained standing, shaking his head in disappointment at his niece's rudeness.

Once alone in her uncle's kitchen, Apiyo shook the gourd of milk only a couple of times, then she put it down. She moved close to the fireplace and lowered the quail, so that it could grill faster. As she did this, she pinched the bird's breast and shoved it into her mouth. As soon as she did this, a cock that was pecking at some grains near the entrance of the room began to crow.

"She has eaten the quail," the cock crowed.

In her rage, Apiyo jumped at it, caught it by its neck and wrung its neck. She left it jumping up and down, upsetting utensils in the kitchen. Her uncle rushed into the room to find out what had caused the disturbance. It was his favourite magic cock. His niece had killed it and he was outraged by her impertinence.

"Is this the best you are capable of doing?" he asked her, his eyes flaming with anger. Apiyo kept quiet, looking unmoved.

"All right, take that big bowl and pour the milk from the gourd into it and see if enough fat has formed on the milk."

As Apiyo emptied the milk from the gourd onto the bowl, lots of rats and snakes rushed out and snuggled between her legs. She ran out of the house, yelling, calling her parents to come to her rescue.

Snakes of all types and rats of all kinds and sizes rushed out of the gourd and followed close behind her. They chased her all over the home, and her uncle had to do something to stop them from driving her mad.

She returned home to her mother empty-handed, with no presents from her uncle. From that day, mother and daughter changed their attitude towards Adongo. In fact, Adongo and Apiyo became good friends and shared all that they possessed.

Thu tinda!

(Source: Odaga, A.B. *Thu Tinda*, Lake Publishers and Enterprises Ltd: Kisumu, 1980.)

Orphans

Obong'o and Awuor were orphans. Whenever Obong'o went to war, he would tell his sister not to cry but to stay at home, prepare food for him, and bring it to a pre-arranged place in the forest.

"When you get there," he would say, "wait for me to come and meet you."

One morning, Obong'o left for battle and Awuor stayed behind to cook for him. Setting off with his food later in the day, Awuor had walked some distance when she met some people. She asked them in song:

Joma a Ndere
Joma a Ndere
Unenonae lando.
Lando
Lando
Obong'o omera ago ng'onga
Gi nyango rachar
Koso wuod baba ogo gunda yago?
Kabora lele
Kabora pod ni chien.

(Warriors returning from Ndere,
Where is the brown one?
I pray he hasn't been slain during this bright morning.
Perhaps they've left him among the dead in the wilderness.
There again, he might be following behind.)

The people said that Obong'o was just behind and would be coming shortly. She was happy to hear this and when she reached their meeting place, she put down the food.

Soon Obong'o arrived. They ate together and left for home. The next morning when Obong'o was setting out again, Awuor pleaded with him not to go. "Obong'o my brother," she said, "we've been left alone in this world, and yet you keep risking your life in battle. What would befall me if you were killed? Where would I go? You're all I have."

Obong'o tried to reassure her: "Please, don't worry about me each time I go to battle. Your constant worrying might cause my death."

And with that, he set out once more. Awuor prepared his food and carried it into the forest, all the while singing:

Joma a Ndere
Joma a Ndere
Unenonae Lando ......

They met as before, ate and returned home. This continued for a long time. But one day Awuor, unable to bear the strain any longer, again pleaded with Obong'o not to go to war. He was quite unmoved.

"Don't worry," he said, "let me go now. I'll soon return. I won't die out there."

That day, soon after dawn, when the sun's rays were growing warm, Obong'o was the first to fall in battle. When his companions departed from the field, they left his body behind.

149

Awuor, as usual, brought some food and on her way met a band of warriors. Asking them in song, as she always did:

Joma a Ndere
Joma a Ndere
Unenonae Lando .....

She was deceived with the reply: "Obong'o is just behind." She found no one at the meeting place and, getting alarmed, walked on towards the battlefield, singing and lamenting as she went.

Meeting a second group of warriors, she asked: "Where's my brother, Obong'o?" And they broke the sad news to her. "Alas," they said, "your brother was the first to die in this morning battle."

Overcome with sorrow, and throwing down the food she carried, she wept bitterly and asked, "Where did you leave his body? How will I know where to find him? This place is all dreary forest".

"Just go ahead," they told her, "the body lies where the vultures are fighting. You can't mistake it: no one else was killed today."

Awuor walked on, mourning and singing:

Joma a Ndere
Joma a Ndere
Unenonae Lando ......

Arriving where the vultures fought, she drove the ugly birds away and sat by her brother's side, caressing him, weeping, and saying to herself, "Obong'o, dear brother, what shall I do? I'm here alone. How can I carry you home?"

A great storm was gathering. She leaned over her brother and whispered, "Make yourself small like a cowrie, so I can carry you to the shelter of a tree. A storm is brewing that might kill me also."

She touched Obong'o and was amazed to find that he had grown small like a cowrie. She carried him to a tree, then returned for his "*kuot*" and his "*okumba.*" The storm broke. Heavy rain with hail began to pour. She took Obong'o's "*okumba*" and covered him with it, sheltering herself beneath his "*kuot*".

When at last the rain stopped, their father's brother arrived. He stayed a short time, watching them from a hiding place. But he could not see Obong'o's body. He only saw Awuor weeping and wailing. He offered her no help but quietly turned on his heels and crept away.

Soon after he had gone, Obong'o resumed his natural size and Awuor found him an impossible burden. She asked him, therefore to shrink again: "Obong'o," she begged, "grow small so I might carry you home. If hyenas see me staggering

150

along under your weight, they'll attack us."

Obong'o did indeed shrink back to cowrie size and Awuor was able to carry him in the palm of her hand. Reaching home, she took all their cattle, goats, sheep and poultry, shut them in their house, and set it ablaze. Then she took a firebrand, darted into the granary and set fire to that also. In there she died, after burying her brother outside.

Tinda.

(Source: Onyango-Ogutu, B. and Rosco, A.A. *Keep My words*, EAEP, 1974).

The disobedient wife

In the past when it was time to go to war, all able-bodied men went away to the battlefront.

At the battlefield, bulls were always slaughtered and the meat distributed to the warriors. One time, a warrior called Onino carried home some choice chest meat he had received. He stored the meat in the granary and told his wife, Obunga, "Prepare this meat for me and my mates."

But Obunga did not follow those instructions. Instead, she roasted the meat and ate it all up. When Onino came back and enquired about the meat, Obunga replied in one statement, "I did not cook". Onino was so embarrassed because he had nothing to offer his friends who had come along with their shields and had even carried their own *"kuon"* with which to eat the juicy meat.

Onino checked in the granary and found no meat. He was so furious that he gave Obunga a very thorough beating.

She wailed, wailed and cursed him, "I wish you get killed in battle." As soon as she said that, the alarm sounded summoning the warriors back to the battlefront.

Before Onino left, he told her, "Should I get killed, we shall see what becomes of you." They went to the battle and, as fate would have it, Onino was one of those who fell. But before his heart had stopped beating, he asked his mates to tell his wife that her wish had been fulfilled. Onino then died.

The warriors went back home and announced the tragic news. Obunga was the first to run out shattering the air with a loud wail, mourning her husband. But she immediately lost her senses and ran into the bush where she lived as a wild animal, ever after singing:

Ora noyang'o buoye
Buoch mang'ongo ee
Ma Onino oketo e dero ee
Onino odhi solo yagi ee

Yagi ne oyuoro gi kuodi ee
Ma Onino obuko penja ee
Ma abuko kwero Onino ee
Onino ochako goya ee
Yagi nomuoch gi nyiero to moko noling'aling'a
Ma abuko kuong'o Onino ee
"Onego lweny ki wuogi ee"
Lweny nene owuok Asego ee
Ma gibuko nego Onino ee
Ma Onino ochako kuong'a ee
"Joma dhi dala, joma dhi dala
Ukone Obunga ywak ero awene nyar Ka-Nyamwa".

My in-law slaughtered a bull.
A gigantic bull, ee.
Onino put it in the granary.
Onino went to summon his kinsmen, ee.
They came with chunks of *kuon*.
And others with shields, ee.
Onino began to ask me, ee.
I began to contradict Onino, ee.
Onino began to beat me up, ee.
Some kinsmen laughed while others kept quiet.
I began cursing Onino, ee.
"May war break out, ee!"
War erupted in Asego. ee.
They began killing Onino, ee.
Onino began cursing me, ee.
"Those going home, those going home.
Tell Obunga from Kanyamwa I have left her the mourning.
Tinda.

(Source: Susan Awuor Miruka, Asembo Bay in 1984)

Dhako ma ne wiye tek
(The disobedient wife)

Ne en ndalo lweny koro yawuoyi ne dhi ga ka-lweny. Wuoyi moro ni Onino ne ni gi chiege miluongoni Obunga. Kalweny kuma ne gidhiye no ne iyang'e ga dhok. Onino ne chieng' moro obiro gi ring agoko ma omiyo Obunga ka ochike ni "Ted ring'o wabiro chamo to wadok e lweny. Adhi luongo jowetena". Ka aye to oketo ring'o e dero.
  Obunga to ne okawo ring'o no ochako ng'olo gi pala obulo kendo ohadho nyaka ne otieke ma ok otedo. Ka chuore ne osedwogo gi yagi ma moko oting'o kuonde to moko kuodi to okone ni omigi chiemo. Ne odwoke ni ok otedo kaye oling'aling'a. Chuore ne olimo dero to ok oyudo ring'o ma ne ogoye. Kane chwore goye to ochako kuong'e, "Manego udhi kalweny

152

ma negi". Ka pok dhoge olwar to tung' oywak ma luongo yawuoyi. Onino ne oduoke, " Ee adhi to ka po ni onega to gima notimre ni akia".

Ka ne gidok e lweny to e kaka ne ogoye ma otho. To ka pod ne chunye gudo to noko ni jothurgi ni, "Wach ne uru Obunga ni ywak ero aweyone", kaye notho.

Jogi ne otero ywak dala. Obunga ne owuok ma ogoyo uuwi matek. Kane ogo uuwi mar ariyo to oringo ma odonjo e bungu. E bungu kuro koro ne ower awera:

> *Ora noyang'o buoye*
> *Buoch man'gongo ee*
> *Ma Onino oketo e dero ee*
> *Onino odhi solo yagi ee*
> *Yagi noyuoro gi kuonde*
> *To moko noyworo gi kuodi ee*
> *Ma Onino buko penja ee*
> *Ma abuko kwero Onino ee*
> *Onino ochako goya ee*
> *Yagi nomuoch gi nyiero to moko noling'aling'a*
> *Ma abuko kuong'o Onino ee*
> *Onego lweny owuogi ee*
> *Lweny nene owuok Asego ee*
> *Ma gi buko nego Onino ee*
> *Ma Onino chako kuong'a ee*
> *Joma dhi dala, joma dhi dala*
> *Ukowne Obunga ywak ero awene*
> *Nyar ka-nyamwa*

> *Tinda! adong arom gi nera*

A heinous offence

Whenever their mother was gathering firewood on the hills, and their father out in the fields with the cattle, Obong'o and Awuor, who were brother and sister, used to stay at home and work in the house.

Now one day, Obong'o felt the fires of lust burning inside him and it was Awuor who was the cause. He peeped through a hole in the wall of his *simba* (hut) and saw the compound deserted — except for Awuor who was busy at her work, cooking and making the house tidy. He crept towards her.

Now in Obongo's opinion, all the girls in the neighbourhood were ugly. No. There was nothing wrong with his eyes: these girls just did not excite him. Except Awuor, of course.

She, in looks and shape, was the most beautiful of all. And she was kind. Her good heart envied no one's fortune or success. Morally, she was spotless and would certainly bring honour to the clan when she was married. Her attractions, thus,

153

were powerful and Obong'o responded from the depths of his soul.

He decided he would declare himself, revealing all he had treasured up in his heart. As our ancestors say, such things "are never painted on one's face".

In those days, it was the custom for boys and girls to pay formal visits to each other before they married, a practice sanctioned by their parents. When a young maiden paid a visit, she marched with other girls and sang her lover's praises in chorus. At night, she was taken to her lover's *simba*, where they shared his bed. But their conduct here was rigidly defined. For his delight, the youth could play only on the maiden's thighs and do no more. She, for her part, was forbidden to yield fully to a mere lover, but only to a husband after witnesses had proved her chastity and fidelity.

To return to the path of the story. On this particular day, Obongo's body felt so hot with desire that he found it impossible to control himself and, as we say, he fell on Awuor for support. Without respect, without the presence of witnesses, without the rights of a husband, he stretched her full length and revealed his manhood. Awuor struggled hard to free herself but, much the weaker of the two, her arms were powerless against him. They were like the hands of a baby able to hold something but unable to move it aside.

Obongo swiftly overwhelmed her. But, alas for him, he was unable to withdraw.

Deflowered and defiled, Awuor wept bitterly, lamenting how some other man might do such a thing, but never a brother to his sister. She cried for people to console her, singing:

Obong'o omera ni yaye
Obong'o omera ni yaye
O Obong'o omera odagi nyombo
Odwaro mana Awuor nyamin
Kilindi kilindi Obong'o
Chuk mach e kendo kidumbu

(Look at this mortal crime,
Committed by a wretch who calls himself my brother.
He rejects betrothal because he needs only me, his sister!
Is this really me or another
Whose virginity has been stolen so wickedly,
And by the son of my father and mother?
Obong'o burns for his sister Awuor.
Pity of pities. I'll see him burning like a torch
Flung on a bonfire.)

When their parents returned at dusk, they saw that shame had washed over their home and over all their clan, like rain that showers down on sacred and unholy shrines alike. Sick at heart, they rushed off to fetch *Ajuoga* the diviner to separate

154

their children. Medicine was administered and Obong'o, cast down with shame, withdrew from Awuor.

Because his act was an abomination to his family and his clan, his punishment was heavy. When people who heard of his crime had satisfied themselves that he was guilty, they collected wood from hillsides far and near and built a huge fire. When the tongues of flame began catching at the sky, rising higher and higher in the night, they threw Obong'o into the blaze where he perished at once.

Nor was he mourned as the dead are usually mourned. His body burned and burned until it was a charred heap, and then it burned and burned to ashes.

Tinda

(Source: Onyango-Ogutu, B. and Rosco, A.A. *Keep My words*, EAEP, 1974).

Apuoyo and Apul Apul

A long time ago, there were two very good friends, Apuoyo (Hare) and Apul Apul (the ogre). Both wanted to marry but each of them was interested in the same girl.

Because of his superior cunning, Apuoyo managed to get the girl before Apul who, disappointed, married another girl. After some time, each of them got two children but Apuoyo's daughters were prettier than Apul's.

Apul was very unhappy and their friendship began to wane.

Then there was a very big famine in the country. Apuoyo used to go out every morning to look for food after instructing his children to open the door only after hearing him singing a specific tune which he taught them. Because of the disagreement that had arisen between them, Apul wanted to eat up Apuoyo's children. So he went into Apuoyo's house in his absence and asked the children to open the door. But they did not because the voice was bigger and huskier than that of their father.

So Apul went to consult a medicineman on how to make his voice more pleasant. The medicineman told him to go and eat crickets. But Apul could not get a cricket and decided to eat a frog instead. When he went back to Apuoyo's house, the children declined to open again as the voice was even worse. Apul went to another medicineman who told him the same thing as the first one. So he went on a big hunt and at last managed to catch a cricket which he swallowed quickly and ran to Apuoyo's house, his voice sounding exactly like that of Apuoyo.

When Apul knocked on the door, the elder child wanted to open but the younger one insisted that the voice was not that of their father. But the elder child went ahead and opened the door anyway only to see Apul Apul ready to eat them up. He swallowed the elder daughter, but the younger one disappeared before Apul could eat her too.

155

Apuoyo returned to find his door bolted from the outside. He unbolted it and started inquiring in song:

Where have my children gone?
My two children.

When the hiding child heard him singing, she came out of the waterpot and told to her father what had happened. Apuoyo gave the child the little food he had brought and kept quiet.

That was the same day that the village elders had called a meeting to discuss how they could make rain. Apuoyo decided to attend the meeting at the riverside. He found the other animals already settled, drinking.

The animals were going to entertain themselves by singing in turns. The king of the animals, Sibuor (Lion) insisted that he would sing first. However, his song was not interesting and the animals refused to let him sing on.

Then Apuoyo offered to sing. Apul and his friends protested but Sibuor ruled that Apuoyo be given a chance. Apuoyo took the drum on which he played as he sang:

A-ti-ti-ti nyambla diang'a
See the homestead exuding smoke.
A-ti-ti-ti nyambla diang'a
See the homestead exuding smoke.

This song impressed the animals so much that each of them was soon dancing very vigorously as they got groggier with drink. Apuoyo soon left the ceremony and headed straight for Apul's home. He set it on fire, with Apul's children trapped inside. He then ran back to the ceremony, which was now at its climax.

When the elders saw Apuoyo was back, they immediately asked him to sing his song some more. Apuoyo did so several times. But the mirth with which he did it made Apul suspicious. Apul, therefore, went to a raised spot and looked in the direction of his homestead, only to see bellows of smoke and a big fire consuming it. The sense of Apuoyo's song dawned on him. Apul ran back to the arena to confront Apuoyo but found that his enemy had already left through another route. He tried tracing Apuoyo the whole day but failed.

When it was dark, Apuoyo, who had been running and was tired, lay down to rest. Apul, who could not see properly in the dark, also sat down to rest, not knowing that he was sitting very near his enemy. The next morning, Apuoyo was the first to wake up. On seeing Apul, he began to steal away. But at that precise moment, Apul also woke up and started following Apuoyo. When Apuoyo realised this, he started running again.

After another fruitless chase, Apul sat down to rest again. Then he saw two people walking towards him. The two were Sibuor and Kwach (Leopard) who, on seeing him, asked him what he was doing there all alone. Apul explained that he was chasing Apuoyo who had burnt down his homestead and killed his children.

Sibuor and Kwach told him to return home for Apuoyo must have gone back there. At the same time, Sibuor promised to convene a court session to arbitrate between the two.

When the day of arbitration came, Apuoyo went with his daughter as the witness to all that had happened. As soon as Apuoyo arrived at the arena, Mwanda (Antelope) the runner was sent to summon Apul. On his way back, Mwanda advised Apul to demand as compensation part of the bride-price that would be paid for Apuoyo's daughter.

The animals deliberated for a long time. In the end, they found both Apuoyo and Apul guilty of one felony or another, although Apuoyo was found to have done more damage. Apul was then asked to demand compensation. He asked for what Mwanda had advised, to which Apuoyo readily assented. But when Apuoyo's daughter had grown old enough to be married, the family migrated secretly and went to live somewhere else beyond the reach of Apul Apul.

Tinda.

(Narrated by the late Bala Owade Korguok in Oyude Village, Asembo, Bondo District. Mr Owade was a pioneer Kenyan broadcaster who had a wealth of Luo ethnological knowledge).

Awuor Awuor and her suitors

There was once a beautiful girl who had a peculiar method of testing her suitors. Many came, but could not talk to her directly. They always sent her sister, who sang:

Awuor Awuor,
A guest is calling you at home,
A guest is calling you at home.
Osinde simojro.

Awuor Awuor's younger sister sang insistently. She was calling Awuor Awuor, who was then busy digging in the garden behind their homestead. Then Awuor Awuor sang back in response:

What sort of visitor is he?
Osinde Osinde simojro.

157

What kind of creature is he?
The testing fruits dropped for sure,
And did he pick any up?

Awuor Awuor's sister replied in a song:

The visitor is a tall handsome man.
He is sure a good-looking one.
But the testing fruits,
Fell down and came to his feet.
He picked them up and ate them.

Awuor Awuor replied:

Tell him to go back,
To return to his home.
Osinde Oo, Osinde simojro.

Her song of refusal came out clear and firm.

Another time, a man who looked very presentable came. He was gentle and humbly asked Awuor Awuor's sister to call her for him. Awuor Awuor's sister liked him and said to herself: "I hope he will be strong enough to pass the tests," but even as she thought this in her heart, the man bent down to pick up the testing fruits which came dropping from the tree and rolled to his feet. He began to eat them one after the other.

The young girl was disappointed, but she moved near the back hedge of the home, and began her usual song, calling her sister and informing her about her new suitor. As usual Awuor Awuor was working in the field behind the home.

Awuor Awuor.
He picked the fruits up and ate them.
Osinde, Osinde simojro.

Again, Awuor replied:

Tell him to go away.
To return to his home.
Osinde, Osinde simojro.

Awuor Awuor would not come to see the suitors once she had been told they had eaten the testing fruit. The tall handsome man went away and so did many other suitors who came seeking her hand in marriage. She rejected most of them because they either ate the testing fruit, or laughed at her mother, who was only half a human being.

Only her left side was formed. She had one arm, one leg, one eye and one breast. And Awuor Awuor's conditions were that whoever would marry her must not eat the succulent fruits that grew close to her mother's door, and must also not laugh at her mother.

Then one day, a man who didn't seem very attractive came and Awuor Awuor's sister watched him carefully with suspicion. There was something suspicious about him. Several fruits fell from the tree as he approached and they rolled to his feet. He looked at them with contempt and did not pick up any. He had passed his first test but who was he? Awuor Awuor's sister wondered who he was. Soon the girl began to sing calling her mother for the second part of the test. If the man laughed at her mother, then he could not marry Awuor Awuor. She sang:

Mama, the one-legged one, come
That the guest may look at you.
Mama, the one-eyed one, come
That the suitor may look at you.

As the girl called her mother, the half-woman appeared from the door and began to hop around on her one leg, picking up the fruits that Awuor's suitor had refused to touch. She was quite a sight and few people could contain themselves in her presence. They would either run away in fear or burst out in laughter at her comical behaviour and unnatural appearance. Awuor's suitor tried to keep a straight face, but he couldn't. He burst out laughing. And once again, Awuor's sister began to sing:

Awuor Awuor.
A guest is calling you at home.
Osinde Oo, Osinde simojro.

She sang again and again, repeating the same song until Awuor Awuor heard her and replied:

What sort of visitor is he?
Osinde, Oo, Osinde simojro.

Her sister replied:

He is the son of the secretary bird.
Osinde, Oo, Osinde simojro.

159

And Awuor Awuor asked in a song;

> The testing fruits fell
> And rolled at his feet.
> Did he pick them up?
> Did he eat any?
> *Osinde, Oo, Osinde simojro.*

Her sister sang back:

> No, he didn't.
> He didn't touch the testing fruit.
> *Osinde, Oo, Osinde simojro.*

Awuor Awuor was now eager, singing:

> Did he laugh at mother, yoo.
> *Osinde, Oo, Osinde simojro.*

Her sister answered:

> He did, yoo.
> He laughed out loud and clear.
> *Osinde, Oo, Osinde simojro.*

The man went away greatly disappointed, like others before him that Awuor Awuor had rejected.

When Awuor Awuor had rejected many suitors, a man who looked handsome, well polished and somewhat arrogant came. He passed all the tests. Awuor Awuor's sister became very happy in her heart that her sister had at last found a strong-willed man who would make a wonderful husband for her. She was excited and sang out in a most beautiful voice:

> Awuor, Awuor
> A guest is calling you at home.
> *Osinde, Oo, Osinde, simojro.*

Awuor Awuor asked:

> What kind of visitor is he?
> *Osinde, Oo, Osinde simojro.*
> What kind of visitor is he?
> The testing fruits dropped down for sure.

And did he eat any?
Did he pick up any?
Osinde, Oo, Osinde, simojro.

Her sister answered:

He is Apul
The son of the beautiful woman.
He didn't touch the testing fruit.
Osinde, Oo, Osinde simojro.

Her sister replied and Awuor Awuor came rushing home, carrying her hoe in her hand. At long last, a strong trustworthy man had come along and she would accept him.

It was agreed that Awuor Awuor would go with Apul Apul to his home, which lay many miles away. But first of all, he had to pay some bridewealth. All these arrangements took about two weeks.

Awuor Awuor and her maids accompanied Apul Apul and his brother and cousins to their home.

For three days, they walked along bushy paths and only managed to get shelter in kindly homes. When they at last arrived, there was much jubilation and happiness. The bride and her maids were warmly received.

Amongst the maids, there was a hunchback, and because of the nature of her deformity, she felt pain and discomfort after travelling for so many miles. As a result, she didn't sleep very much at night.

On the fourth night after their arrival, when the other maids were all asleep, the hunchback was still awake. She overheard Apul Apul, his brothers, parents and cousins talking together. They were laying out plans of how they would kill Awuor Awuor and her bridesmaids.

"We shall roll them up inside their sleeping mats one by one and then drown them. When they have died, then we will have a feast. We shall eat them up at our leisure," one of them proposed.

"Yes, it would be better to drown them than cut their throats with a knife," Apul gave his opinion. They talked together and decided on the route they would take to the lake when they would be carrying Awuor Awuor and her bridesmaids. The following night, the hunchback didn't sleep at all. She kept on turning and fidgeting on her sleeping mat. Then Apul Apul, Awuor Awuor's husband, came to roll the girls up in their sleeping mats.

When he had rolled up three girls, the hunchback gave a whining cry, like a person in great pain. Her cry alarmed Apul Apul and he came over to her corner where she was sleeping.

"What is it hunchback? We can hardly sleep, you are crying all the time in your sleep," he said to her.

"Oh, I am dying, but you won't be able to help me. There is only one thing I know which always cures me when I feel as I do right now," the hunchback croaked.

"What's the cure, my sister-in-law? Just name it and Apul Apul will get it for you," he replied with malicious confidence.

"Take the wicker basket. I mean, *osera* used for catching fish. Fill it with the river water and bring it to me. If I drink water carried in *osera*, I'll immediately feel better," she replied, and Apul Apul set off immediately for the river to draw some water with *osera* for his hunchback sister-in-law.

As soon as he went out of the door, the hunchback, using the knife Apul Apul had left behind, cut the ropes that had tied the girls rolled up in the sleeping mats. She woke the other girls, including Awuor Awuor and together, they began to run away towards their home.

The task the hunchback had set Apul Apul was an impossible one, and at daybreak, he returned with an empty wicker basket. He swore that he was not going to talk to the hunchback. But when he discovered she had fled with all the maids, including his bride, he was mad.

He immediately alerted his brothers and cousins and they set out to give chase. They realised that because of the hunchback, the girls would not be able to run very fast. So they gave chase, determined to catch up with them on the way.

On the second day, they caught the girls' scent a few miles ahead of them and decided to use their magic rope to catch them. They threw the rope several miles ahead of them, but every time it caught the hunchback on her swollen back, and then she cleverly took it off and fixed it on a tree stump. When the Apul Apuls pulled and found it tight, they were pleased that they had caught the girls. But when they arrived on the scene, they found the rope securely tied onto a tree stump.

On the third day, they caught up with the girls at the bank of a big river. If the girls did not think quickly, Apul would catch them and they knew very well what the consequences would be. Then the hunchback saw a possible helper. "Mrs Tortoise, please swallow us up. Apul Apul and his big group are after us," she begged Mrs Tortoise, who was sitting on the bank of the wide river. The girls could also see the cloud of dust raised by Apul Apul and his cousins as they came running fast after the girls. They could hear the sound. They were terrified.

"All right, I shall swallow you up," she agreed when she saw great fear in their eyes. She had just swallowed the last girl, her leg just disappearing into her mouth, when Apul Apul, appeared breathing hard, exhausted, angry and hungry.

"Mrs Tortoise, have you seen a group of girls? Which way have they gone?" Apul Apul asked completely unable to speak properly because he was out of breath.

162

"No, I saw no one. I have just been sitting here shaving my husband's head and no girls have passed here. And as you can see, nobody can swim through because the river is too full," Mrs Tortoise said. They looked at the river, then at her, puzzled.

"But look at her, she is enormous," one of the Apul Apul observed.

"Mrs Tortoise you've swallowed the girls. Come on, bring them up," Apul Apul demanded.

"No, I haven't swallowed anybody," she said and added, "I am only expecting."

"All right, I shall take you and dash you on this rock and burst you open," Apul Apul said and caught Mrs Tortoise by her leg. Mrs Tortoise protested spiritedly. Two of Apul Apul's cousins held her by the neck.

Her end was near, but she was brave and clever. She said: "No, if you want to burst me open, then don't dash me on the rock, but instead carry me high and throw me in the middle of this fast-running current which will sure cut me into two."

Mrs Tortoise stared intently at Apul Apul. Awuor Awuor's husband, who was then in rage, got hold of her and threw her right in the middle of the fast-running river.

"Ahaa, look, look," Mrs Tortoise cried, showing the arm of one of the girls. "You have thrown me into my water with my good girls," she laughed! She then dived into the river and swam to the opposite shore. The Apul Apuls looked foolish, but there was nothing they could do.

They returned to their homes, greatly disappointed. Later that day, the tortoise took the girls to their home and when they had related their story to their parents, Awuor Awuor's father gave the tortoise one big cow as a reward for having saved the girls from Apul Apul.

Thu tinda!

(Source: Odaga, A.B. *Thu Tinda*, Lake Publishers and Enterprises Ltd: Kisumu, 1980.)

The man-eater

There was once a man-eating monster called Kaki who ate almost everybody she chose except a certain boy called Obong'o. Although many people failed to trap the monster, Obong'o believed he could.

One day, he took the droppings of rats, went to hide on Kaki's roof. When Kaki had prepared her meal and was ready to dine, Obong'o called out, "Kaki".

Kaki ran out in a hurry to seek out this intruder and do the obvious with him while singing:

En ang'o ma nyaka chak luonga
Kaki ee

163

Acham ji atieko
Ma ti nachami
Kaki ee.

What has been calling me?
Kaki, ee.
I have eaten everyone.
I will eat this one, too.
Kaki, ee.

Having searched in vain, Kaki returned to dine, but alas! The food was half-eaten and the remainder was full of rats' droppings. Kaki said in anger: "What an arrogant rat! What an impudent rat! I can't eat this," and then threw the food away. But Obong'o repeated his mischief every day until the monster became very weak and could only respond in a very slow and melancholy tone:

What has been calling me?
Kaki, ee
I have eaten everyone.
I will eat this one too.
Kaki ee.

One day. when Kaki was asleep, Obong'o climbed down stealthily and slashed off her tail. On waking up, the monster found her sleeping place very wet. She wondered, "Have I wet my bed or what?"

Discovering that her tail was missing, Kaki thought of a plan to avenge herself. So she changed into a very beautiful girl and walked to where the boys were playing *adhula* (a game which has elements of modern hockey and cricket). No sooner had she arrived than she heard one of the players being lauded as "Obong'o the hero who cut the monster's tail".

She ran to him and declared her undying love for him. But Obong'o was reluctant to take her home.

"How can I take you home when I have only met you today and my parents were not informed to expect you?" But she persisted and finally convinced him with her unequalled charm.

After they had had their dinner, Obong'o and the beauty retired to bed. But when Obong'o had fallen asleep, his lover changed into a monster, raging to devour him. He was, however, lucky that his dogs, which were alert, barked at Kaki until Obong'o stirred and woke up. Noticing that Obong'o would discover her real identity, Kaki quickly changed into a beautiful girl once again.

"What have you done to the dogs that they should bark at you?" Obong'o asked.

"Nothing. They just want to bite me. Please, Obong'o, restrain them," she pleaded.

She tried to eat Obong'o up several times but the dogs always barked and scared her. In the morning, she complained that the night had been very cold and asked Obong'o if they could go to the bush to get some dry wood with which to make a fire and keep themselves warm the next night. He agreed, took an axe and released the dogs to accompany them. But the girl protested about the dogs and advised Obong'o to lock them in the house. Not wanting to disappoint his beloved, Obong'o did exactly that and they set off for the bush.

They went right up to the centre of the forest where there was a very tall dry tree. The girl asked Obong'o to climb, promising that she would hand him the axe. But whenever Obong'o asked for it, she only urged him to climb higher. And so he climbed to the very top of the tree.

When he again asked for the axe, Obong'o was most surprised to see that the girl had changed into Kaki and had started cutting the tree.

"Cut! Cut! Cut!" it went.

"You are the clever one who cut my tail. You must die today", Kaki cursed as she cut: "Cut! Cut! Cut!"

With only one cut to go before the tree fell, some three doves appeared and perched on a nearby tree singing:

"Kuu, kuu. What a handsome lad to die just like that!".

This intrusive sympathy infuriated Kaki so much that she chased the doves away very angrily. When Kaki came back to the tree, the stem was again full and round. Kaki resumed cutting with renewed vigour, but the doves came again. This time, Kaki sent them even further away.

Obong'o was mesmerised. He did not know how he would escape death. He began singing the song he always sung to summon his dogs.

Soi soi soso
Soi soi soso
Soi soso ratenge
Soi soso rabuore
Soi soso wuon olang' ma lio lio Kojerma.

Soi soi soso
Soi soi soso
Soi soso the blacks
Soi soso the browns
Soi soso owner of the sharp bell *Kojerma*.

He continued singing until one of his dogs, the blind one, heard his voice.

165

"I can hear someone singing like Obong'o," the dog told the others. But the others who had not heard anything abused it saying, "It must be your blind eye that is making you hear strange things." The humiliated dog kept quiet. But then the toothless one also heard the voice.

"Surely that is Obong'o's voice," it declared.

"It is your toothless gum that is cheating you," the others replied.

Soon afterwards, however, the lame one also said, "I can also hear Obong'o." But likewise, the others reprimanded it, "Shut up with your lame thighs."

It did not take long before all the dogs heard the singing. They chewed at the door, scratched and gnawed until it opened and they came out. They ran very fast to where Obong'o was singing from. When Kaki saw them, she immediately changed into the maiden again pleading, "Please Obong'o, restrain them from biting me. I was only joking." But since Obong'o had known that she was actually a monster, he encouraged the dogs to bite her.

"Bite her; it is just Kaki. Come on there. You brown one, get her; destroy her; tear her to pieces." Kaki was torn into innumerable pieces.

Obong'o then climbed down, took the dogs and the doves and went home. He slaughtered a bull and distributed the meat among the dogs, the blood to the doves and the liver to the toothless dog, to thank them for saving his life.

Tinda, may I grow as tall as my uncle's trees.

(Contributed by author from his childhood memories and repertoire.)

Kaki me ne ochamo ji
(The man-e ater)

Ne nitie ondieg Kaki moro mane ochamo ji duto to ne otamo gi mako. Koro ne odong' wuoyi moro achiel mane oparo rieko mar nyalo Kaki no. Wuoyini ne nyinge Obong'o. Ne oparo mar miyo Kaki kech. Chieng' moro ne okawo chieth oyieyo bas odhi obuto e tat od Kaki. Ka ne Kaki osetedo koro dwa chiemo to Obong'o ochako Iwonge: "Kakiii". Kaki noyie: "Eee". Kaki ne owuok gi ng'wech ka odhi dwaro ng'at ma ne luongeno. Sama ne odhi to nower ni:

> *En ang'o ma nyaka chak luonga*
> *Kaki eee*
> *Acham ji atieko*
> *Ma ti nachami*
> *Kaki ee*

Kaki ka ne osedwero ma ok oyudo ng'atno to oduogo. Ka oduogo to oyudo ka ocham chiembe to modong' oporie chieth oyieyo. Ka noneno chiembe go to ochako wacho, "To oyieyo ni be ki jasungaa! To oyieyo ni be ki ja ng'ayiii! Magi to dak acham nyar ng'ato". Kaye to okawo chiemo opuko. Obong'o ne otimo kamano pile pile nyaka ne Kaki odhero ahinya ma koro ka iluonge to ower mana mos ni:

En ang'o ma nyaka chak luonga
Kaki eee
Acham ji atieko
Ma ti nachami
Kaki ee

Chieng'moro kane Kaki nindo otero to ng'atno ne olor oa e tado ma odhi ong'ado iwe. Kane ochiew to oyudo kama ne oninde ka n'gich thithithi. "To alayo koso an'go motima?"

Ka ne ofwenyo ni iwe onge to oparo gima dotim ne ng'ama ne on'gade no. Ban'ge ne olokre nyako maber miwuoro kaye to ochako wuoth odhi kuma yawuoyi ne goye adhula. Ne owinjo ka ji pakre kendo ka ipako yawuoyi ma tugo. Nopo mana ka owinjo ka ipako wuoyi moro ni "Mano Ọbong'o wuoyi mane ong'ado iw Kaki ma otamo jimako!" Ne oringo ma odhi otwere kuom Obong'o ni ose here kendo nyaka odhi olime. Obong'o ne otemo tamre ni, "To ere kaka adhi kodi dala to akiayi to bende jo-dala ok on'geyo wendoni?". Kata-kamano ne ochwere mit Obong'o be ka ne oneno berne gi kaka yawuoyi moko be ne dware to oyie okawe.
Ka ochopo otieno ma gisechiemo to gi dhi nindo. Ne orito ka Obong'o osenindo to olokre Kaki. To Obong'o ne opidho guogi mang'eny. Guogi gi ne oneno ka Kaki dwaro chame kendo ne gigweye matek ma Obong'o ochiew. Kaki ne olokre nyako kendo.

"Itimo guogi gi nade?" Obong'o nopenje.

"Gi dwa mana kaya. Yawa Obong'o kwergi". Kaki nohombo kamano.

Kinde duto mane odwa chamo Obong'o to guogi go gweye nyaka ne piny oru. Ka piny ne oru to okone Obong'o ni koyo ne ochame gotieno mondo gi dhi gitong'yath moro ma otwo ne oneno e bungu. Obong'o ne okawo le to ka ne odwa dhi gi guogi to nyakono nokone ni guogi to gilorne gi e ot matek. Ne gitimo kamano kaye to gidhi. Ne gidhi adhiya nyaka e chuny thim kuma ne nitie yath mabor ma otuo. Ka aye nyakono nokone Obong'o ni mondo oidhi obiro gamo ne le. Obong'o ka idh idh to ka okwaye le to oko ni, "Pod idh aidha abiro gamo ni le". Ka ne ose idho malo mogik to nyakono olokre Kaki kendo ochako ton'go yath "Tong'! Tong'! Tong'!" kowacho ni "In ema ing'eyo ng'ado iwa nyaka anegi". Tong'! Tong'! Tong'!

Ka ne yath chiegni chot to akuche moko adek opiyo machiegni kanyo. "Kuuu mano wuod wegi maber ma dwa tho nang'o?" Kaki ne oriembogi to ka oduogo to oyudo ka yath mane otong'o cha ochomre. Kendo ka ochako tong'o kendo to akuche ka ochako oduogo kendo ne oriembogi to oduogo oyudo ka yath ochomre. Obong'o piny ne ochamo e wi yath kendo ne oparo gima dotim. Ne ochako luongo guogine gi wer;

Soi soi so so
Soi soi so so
Soi soi so so Ratenge
Soi so so Rabuore
Soi so so Radiere
Soi so so wuon olang' ma lio lio kojerma

167

Ne oluongo aluonga nyaka guoge ma wang'e otho owinjo.
"Ng'ato awinjo ka wer ka Obong'o!"
"Ok wang'i ma othono ema wuondi" jowadgi ne odwoke gi gero.
Bang'e to marafuok be owinjo.
"Ng'ato adier wer ka Obong'o!
"Ok fuoki no ema bwogi".
Rabam ne owinjo.

"Kata an be awinjo ka Obong'o wer"
"Ling'nwa gi bam moko".
Bang'e to ne giwinjo duond Obong'o giduto. Ne gimuodo dhoot gi mirima nyaka giwuok. Ne giringo aringa ka gichiko itgi nyaka gichopo ir Obong'o. Kaki kane oneno gi to olokre nyako kendo ochako hombo Obong'o: "Kwer gi kik gikaya an bende ne atugo atuga". Obong'o to koro ne oseng'eyo ni en mana Kaki kendo omedo mana siayo guogi ni:
"Kaye uru akaya en mana Kaki. Sia! Sia!
Rabuor make. Chode uru! Kidhe uru!"
Ne gikidhe matindotindo ka nanga nyaka otho.

Obong'o kane oselor to okawo guogi ne mane okonye go gi akuche ka bende. Ne odhi ma oyang'o ruath. Guogi ne omiyo ring'o, akuche ne omiyo remo to rafuok ne omiyo chuny.
Tinda! adong arom gi bao ma ka nera

The man who went to establish a new homestead

In the olden days, a certain man called Obong'o came of age and went to put up his own homestead. He left his mother with his daughter, Awuor, in their original homestead. Because his mother had a wounded leg and could, therefore, not move around much, he slaughtered a bull whose meat was preserved so they could feed on it during his absence.

One day, Awuor took with her a leftover bone to chew on her way to the well. Her grandmother tried to persuade her against it but Awuor was very adamant. She pretended that she had left the bone behind but hid it inside the pot she was carrying to the well. On reaching the well, she sat down and started chewing on the bone. And then Apul Apul the ogre appeared.

"Awuor, what are you chewing?" she asked
"It is just the bone of a chick," Awuor answered.
"No bone of a chick can be so big."
"I am only chewing the bone of a lamb."
"Which lamb's bone can be so big?"
"I am only chewing the bone of a kid."
"Which kid's bone can be so big?"
"I am only chewing the bone of a cow."

"Which cow's bone can be so big."
"I am only chewing the bone of a big bull."

"Now you have answered correctly," said Apul Apul. She then asked Awuor to carry her baby so that she could carry the water pot back to Awuor's home.

Awuor's grandmother, who was resting under the house's eaves, was dumbfounded when she saw Awuor's company. "My grandchild, what have you brought home? Didn't I warn you?" she asked.

In the meantime, Apul Apul had entered the house and cooked herself a very delicious meal. She cooked and ate without giving Awuor and her grandmother anything. She only let them feed on the remnants she scraped from her teeth after eating.

After some time, the meat Obong'o had preserved got finished. The day after the meat was finished, Apul cooked the *kuon* as usual. Awuor's grandmother wondered what Apul would use to eat the *kuon*. She therefore asked, "Daughter of the bush, what shall you eat the *kuon* with now that the meat is finished?"

For an answer, Apul told her, "Sit down. Stretch out your leg". Then Apul plastered the *kuon* on the woman's wound before removing and eating it. The old woman knew exactly what would follow when Apul tired of this. So she asked Awuor to take some simsim with which to summon birds she could send to call Obong'o back.

Awuor took the simsim, started singing to summon the birds and promised to reward the best singer. Awuor asked each bird to show how it would call Obong'o. All the birds which came tried their best but none impressed Awuor as much as the chaffinch, who said that she would call Obong'o back by singing:

Sisio ka Nyigilo
Nene iweyo ne ng'a meru?
Nene awee ne Oremdiere
Oremdiere ma ka ng'ano?
Oremdiere ma ka meru
Tiend meru ma lokre amunglu
Tieko dero go mana ligala.

(Sisio of Nyigilo,
Whom did you leave your mother?
I left her with Oremdiere
Whose son is this Oremdiere?
Oremdiere of your mother?
Your mother's leg becomes a stump
For finishing a granary
Just go on building

Awuor liked the song so much that she rewarded the bird and sent it on its errand. The chaffinch flew very fast to where Obong'o was building. It sang for a

169

very long time before Obong'o's helpers discerned that it had a message. When Obong'o himself heard the song, he pulled down the structures he had erected and headed home.

Back home, Awuor had climbed to the top of the hut with Apul's baby while Apul busied herself grinding flour for the next meal. When Awuor sighted her uncle matching home with his cattle, she burst into a iubilant song:

> Radier aneno ti agone sidika.
> Rateng' aneno ti agone sidika.
> Rabuor aneno ti agone sidika.

> (I see the multi-coloured one, let me play the lyre.
> I see the black one, let me play the lyre.
> I see the brown one, let me play the lyre).

Apul heard the song and got a bit curious. "What is that you are singing?" she asked Awuor.

Awuor replied, "It is the child I am rocking and lulling." Apul went back to what she was doing.

When Obong'o had come very near home, Awuor dropped Apul's baby. Apul heard the thud and cry of her baby but before she could do anything, she saw Obong'o entering the homestead and started to pretend that she was up to no mischief. Obong'o also did not act in any way that would make her suspicious. He instead slaughtered a bull and gave a piece to Apul to roast. Apul put the meat on the fire and went to sit outside where Obong'o was. After a while, he sent her to check on the meat. When Apul had gone into the hut, Obong'o followed with a forked stick with which he held her neck and pinned her to the fire. Apul was burnt to death.

Tinda.

(Source: Narrated by Susan Awuor Miruka in Asembo Bay 1984).

Wuoyi mane odhi goyo ligala
(The man who went to establish a new homestead)

Ndalo machon wuoyi moro ni Obong'o notuk odhi go ligala to owe min e gunda gi nyakware miluongo ni Awuor Awuor. Ne owe ka oyang'o dhiang' michamo nyaka oduogi nikech min tiende ne otimo adhola. Chieng'moro nyakware nene okawo chogo ni omuodo ka odhi e kulo to dane ne okwere ni Apul Apul nitie kuro. Awuor nowuondore awuonda to osoyo chogo e agulu. Kochopo e kulo to obet ochako muodo nii to Apul Apul ochopo.

> *"Awuor to mano chok an'go mimuodono?"*
> *"Amuodo chok nyagweno".*
> *"Chok nyagweno manade matin kamano?"*

170

"Amuodo chok nyarombo".
"Chok nyarombo manade matin kamano?".
"Amuod chok nyadiel".
"Chok nyadiel manade matin kamano?".
"Amuodo chok dwasi moro modhero".
"Chok dwasi modhero manade matin kamano?"
"Amuodo chok buoch moro mang'ongo".
"Eeero! Koro eka iwacho maber".

Apul Apul ni ne en monyuol. Ne otuomo pi kaye okelo nyathine Awuor oting'o to en oting'one pi ka gidhi dala. Ka gi chopo dala to dan Awuor ohum nono, "Aa Awuor nyakwara nende akweri. Neye gima ichopo go!"
Apul to ne odonjo e ot otedo kuon mochamo gi ring'o. Awuor gi dane to ne ogweno ne gi lake ema·gichamo nyaka ring'o orumo. Chieng' moro kane ring'o oserumo to Apul notedo kwon. Dan Awuor ne ochich ma openje, "To nyar'bungu an'g nicham kuon gi an'go?" En to nokone ni, "Bed piny. Rie tiendi". Koro nondhino kuon e a dhood dan Awuor to ochamo. Dan Awuor to nong'eyo ni Apul biro chamogi ma ne oko ne Awuor ni okaw nyim oluong go Obong'o. Awuor ne odhi ma ochoko winy ni mower mamit to omiyo nyim. Onge mane ower mamit. Gikone to Hundhwe ne obiro mochako wer.

Sisio ka Nyigilo
Nene iweyo ne n'ga meru
Nene awe ne Oremdiere
Oremdiere ma ka ng'ano
Oremdiere ma ka meru
Tiend meru ma lokre amunglu
Tieko dero go mana ligala

Wendni ne mit ma omiyo Hundhwe nyim. Hundhwe nochako ng'wech nyaka kuma Obong'o ne gede monuoyo wendno. Joma konyo Obong'o ne owinjo ma giling'. Obong'o to ka ne owinjo wendno to nochako mana tuk kendo obiro abira sano. To Awuor Awuor ne oidho wi tado gi nyathi Apul. Kane oneno ka ner mare biro gi dhok to ochako wer:

Radier aneno ti agone sidika
Rateng' aneno ti agone sidika
Rabuor aneno ti agone sidika

Apul mane rego ne owinjo mopenje, "Awuor iwero ang'o no?"
"Aa nyathini ema ywak to ahoye ni Adhiambo ling' aling'a.
"Mano ber".
Ma ne nergi ochopo machiegni to noweyo nyathi Apul piny ni pangla! Apul nolokre to oneno Obong'o koro ochako wuondre. Obong'o ne okawo dhiang' oyang'o. Ne omiyo Apul ring'o mondo obul. Bange ne okone mondo odhi olim ring'o to oluwe gi ragwar. Sama ne Apul olung're ni loko ring'o nii to osire gi ragwar e mach ma owang' nyaka otho.
Tinda, adong arom gi bao ma ka nera.

171

The bargain

There was a great famine in the land where Obunde and his wife Oswera lived with their many children. The only creatures who had some food were the hyenas and before they would part with it, they demanded a lot of things.

One day, Oswera went to one hyena's home and asked him for some food. Her children were almost dying of hunger and want for food.

"I have no more food except sweet potatoes," the hyena told her.

"I shall be happy to have the potatoes. We have nothing, not a grain of food at my home and the children are starving. Please, let me have some and I shall repay you after the harvest."

"No, if you want food, you must exchange it with something right now. Will you give me one of your children in exchange for my potatoes?"

Oswera hesitated. Her children were dear to her, but then they would die without food.

"Yes, I shall let you have one of them for a meal, if only you could let us have some potatoes," Oswera answered. Then she took a big basket full of potatoes and told the hyena the exact time when he could go to her home to collect one of her children. It had been a big bargain and she started wondering how she was going to stand and watch one of her children eaten by the hyena.

Oswera thought hard and decided she would not give a single one of her children to the hyena for a meal. She, therefore, chopped young banana stalks, cooked the plant nicely and dished it in a large bowl. When the hyena came, she gave it to him and the beast ate greedily and went away satisfied that he had eaten one of Oswera's children. Soon, the potatoes were finished and she had to go to the hyena again.

Oswera and Obunde, her husband, kept on cooking and preparing banana stalks for the hyena each time he came for one of their children, until one day she had no more banana stalks to cook for the beast.

"You have now eaten all my children, yet we still need potatoes. What shall we give you now?" Oswera asked in despair.

"Then I shall come for you and your husband," the hyena replied angrily as he helped Oswera to load a basket of potatoes on her head.

"Yes, come tomorrow at the usual time, at three o'clock and get me. I shall have cooked myself for you." Sweet Oswera said calmly.

The following day, the hyena went promptly as Oswera had told him and he found the home almost deserted. He looked everywhere, but apart from Obunde, there was no trace of anyone else. Then he looked at the usual place and found a huge bowl full of a big meal Oswera had cooked for him. The hyena did not realise that a meal of dog meat had been prepared instead of Oswera. When he had eaten, the hyena told Obunde he would come for him the following day. Obunde got very

172

worried, but had nothing to do. He had been too lazy to watch how and what his wife cooked, so the following day, he started crying.

"Ah, Oswera my wife, how did you cook yourself and how shall I cook myself for the hyena." He sat down under a big tree in his compound and wept. Oswera was very annoyed with her husband.

"You, you stupid, foolish man. Why sit and cry there all day long? How do you think I cooked myself? Take one of the dogs and quickly prepare it for the hyena and stop being silly," she castigated him.

Very quickly, in fact, within a short time, Obunde had caught, killed and prepared a dog for the hyena. Then he joined his wife and children in a huge hollow of a tree in his compound, where they had hidden.

That day the hyena knew he was going to have his last meal of human beings. Therefore, he brought many other hyenas. They were going to feast on Obunde. As they ate, they heard Obunde singing. At first, they were puzzled, then they realised that Obunde was boasting of how they had cheated the hyenas.

The greedy hyena ate banana stalks,
Not my family.
The greedy hyena ate a dog,
Not Obunde Magoro ....
The greedy hyena ate banana stalks,
Not my children.
Now come and get Obunde,
His children and wife ....

Obunde sang these provocative words and the hyenas got very mad. The first hyena rushed into the entrance of the hollow on the tree, but Oswera had heated a long piece of iron until it glowed red. She thrust this into the hyena's mouth and pushed it deep into his chest. The beast fell down, dead. The next one, who was outside the hollow also rushed in and Oswera repeated her performance.

In this way, she killed all the hyenas and saved her husband and all their children. Then they came out of the hollow, and were happy together. They had eliminated the greedy and oppressive hyenas. They could now go and get the sweet potatoes from the hyenas' garden without fear.

Thu tinda!

(Source: Odaga, A.B. *Thu Tinda*, Lake Publishers and Enterprises Ltd: Kisumu, 1980.)

173

Cutting a middle finger

Aloo and Obong'o were orphans. Everyone else in their family had been killed and they were left alone in a remote house in the forest.

They owned a few cows which Obong'o grazed at night. By day they stayed in bed, for they lived in fear of *Hono*, the monster that had killed all who once lived in those parts. This hideous creature roamed the forest by day, reluctant to hunt by night because its eyesight was poor; and it feared being trapped by *ochung' tir* (the human being). With its weak eyes, it was better that it avoids the forest at night.

Whenever Obong'o came from grazing his cattle, he asked Aloo to open the door in a tune neither man nor beast could imitate:

Aloo nyarma yawna.
Aloo nyarma yawna.
Koth biro tinigoya okoo.
Nadhi Konyango ayudo ka jojuogi.
Ido e sigalagala edipo.
Ne gi neg ruadha marachar achar.
Ruadha charo ji ka nyinge.
Aloo nyarma yawna.

(Aloo, my mother's daughter open the door.
The rain is going to drench me.
I visited Onyango's place.
and found wizards in the court casting spells.
They killed my white bull.
You know, the one that scares everybody.
Aloo, my sister, open the door for me.)

Now, in another part of the forest lived Apul Apul. Through careful observation, this ferocious creature had discovered that Aloo was left alone at night, opening the door only when Obong'o returned and sang his song. Aloo, he noticed, was beautiful and he wanted to sink his teeth into her flesh.

And so, anxious to imitate Obongo's singing, which never failed to get the door open, Apul Apul left the forest and consulted a medicineman who gave him this advice: "Never dance when you see star-grass dance; never sing when you hear a bird sing; never crack beetles when you see them fly."

But Apul Apul, really a stupid fellow, paid no heed. He danced when he saw star-grass dancing in the breeze; he sang when he heard the birds in chorus; he snapped at beetles when he saw them flying about.

So when he sang at Aloo's house, his voice was hoarse, and the door remained shut. Again Apul Apul called on the medicineman, but again disobeyed his orders and the door remained shut. After a third consultation, however, Apul Apul grew ashamed of his obstinacy and carried out the instructions he was given. Then, standing outside Aloo's house, he opened his jaws and sang:

174

Aloo nyarma yawna ....

When, to his delight, Aloo opened the door, he began to beg for bread from her, and it was given him. Then he begged for chicken, and this was given too. Then he begged for goat meat and this also was given. Finally, he begged for milk and this Aloo also gave him.

Inside the house, he was given more food and when there was nothing left, the greedy beast leapt on the girl and devoured her. He wanted to flee into the forest, but his belly was so heavy now that he could only stagger away and hide behind the house.

When Obong'o returned, he sang his song, but Aloo did not open the door. Forcing his way into the house and finding, to his dismay, no trace of his sister, he quickly seized his weapons.

He sharpened his spear.
He sharpened his sword.
He sharpened his dagger.
He tested his shield.
He tested his club.
He bent his bow.
He sharpened his arrows.
And set out to search for Aloo.

He first searched about the house and soon found Apul Apul — *ka ogoyo gari*, as we say - fat, swollen, and paralysed.

"Where's Aloo?" Obong'o demanded.

"I don't know," Apul Apul replied. "Unless you tell me, I'll cut you to pieces," Obong'o swore.

"Don't do that," pleaded Apul Apul, "just cut my middle finger and you'll soon find your sister."

Obong'o slashed the finger and Apul Apul screamed with pain. But only blood appeared, spurting red all over the green grass. And now the pain grew. It grew so sharp that the beast could bear it no longer and confessed to Obong'o that it was the last finger on his right hand that he should have cut. Obong'o cut through this, too, and out leapt Aloo, falling onto the grass alive and well. Filled with rage and disgust, Obong'o hacked Apul Apul to pieces. And forever after, nothing grew on that spot except star-grass.

Tinda

(Source: Onyango-Ogutu, B. and Rosco, A.A. *Keep My words*, EAEP, 1974.)

A problem of breasts

It happened in the old days that a certain wife bore her husband four children, all of them girls.

But sad to relate, when the girls came of age, their breasts had still not bloomed; instead they were flat like a man's. Yet every other girl in their age-set had fine full breasts, their nipples jutting out threateningly, as though warning oncomers not to collide with them.

These girls ridiculed the four daughters, calling them snakes, since snakes are round and breastless.

Good breasts are alluring. How can a girl hope to attract a man if she is only half-beautiful? Sad at their daughters' plight, their parents approached a diviner, who advised that a hut be built for the girls deep in a distant forest. "Leave them locked up there," he said, "and soon, one after the other, they will grow good breasts."

Impressed by this advice, the parents built a hut, locked in their daughters and returned home. But it is hard for a mother to resist visiting her daughters, and several times, she called on them, carrying food. To be admitted, she would sing in a tongue none could imitate, and on hearing her voice, the girls would open the door. This was her song:

Lang' lang' la
Lang' lang' la
Lili liyo liyo
Lang' lang' la.

On her first visit, she sang, the door opened and she sat down with her daughters to eat. Incredibly, while they were eating, the breasts of one of the girls began to bud; and after the meal she was proudly taken home by her mother.

But Opul had also heard her singing. Anxious to imitate the mother's voice, gain access to the hut and eat a feast of human flesh, he asked a medicineman how he might add sweetness to his hoarse cry.

He was advised as follows: "Once near the hut if you see *obiya* grass dance, don't laugh; if you see flies, don't eat them; if you see a tortoise, ignore it — just go your way."

Opul swore he would obey these instructions but he had hardly walked a couple of steps before he saw *obiya* grass dance and laughed; saw flies and gulped them down; saw a tortoise and attacked it. Then he went merrily on his way, practising his song for the girls. The sound was not exactly harmonious, but Opul was an optimist. Arriving at the door, he raised his voice and sang:

LAANG' LAANG' LAA
LAANG' lAANG' lAA
Lili lili liliyoo liliyoo....

He was recognised at once. "We know it's you, Opul," the girls chorused. "Who else has so dreadful a voice?" Hyena was furious at this and quickly rushed back to consult his doctor.

The next day, the girls' mother came again, sang, went inside and shared her food. The meal eaten, she noticed the breasts of yet another daughter growing fast; and once more, full of joy, she took up her basket and returned home with the lucky child. And now Opul approached the house again but still unable to obey instructions properly, he failed to sing correctly and was refused entry.

On the next occasion when she brought food, the girl's mother once more saw the breasts of one of the two remaining daughters beginning to develop. But she was sad at leaving her last daughter there alone and took her way homeward sorrowing. That same day Opul arrived, but greedy and disobedient as ever, he had rejected advice and failed to gain entry.

The following day, mother came as usual and sang her song:

Lang' lang' la
Lang' lang' la
Lili liyo liyo ....

Her daughter opened the door and they sat down together to eat. But this time alas, there was no sign of growing breasts, and mother left for home sad — but still hopeful. Left alone in the gloomy forest, her daughter was filled with terror. It was all so silent, except for the forest beetle which she could hear droning mournful, never ceasing his eerie noises. Every moment she expected to hear her mother returning. But Mama had long left and lonely waiting lay ahead before a new day could be born.

Now Opul was a very determined beast. Despite his earlier failures, he went again to his doctor, who earnestly counselled him this time to heed his advice. Besides renewing his suggestions for sweetening Opul's voice, he told his ugly patient to cover his eyes with blinkers of skin.

"Off you go now," he said, "and when you reach the hut, strip off your blinkers and start singing. This time, I'm sure you'll succeed."

On this occasion, instructions were obeyed to the letter. When Opul's head bumped against the door, he stopped, tore off his blinkers, and sung in perfect imitation of the mother's voice.

The girl approached the door but then hesitated, saying to herself, "That voice sounds like Mama's but I can't be sure."

Sensing her hesitation, Opul shouted: "I usually sing only once before my daughter opens the door. She hasn't stirred yet. Has Opul got her, I wonder?" These final cunning words did the trick. The poor girl seized the door, and swung it open. Opul was on her in an instant, tearing her from limb to limb, ripping out her bowels, and greedily devouring her belly with all its contents. What few bones remained, Opul carried deeper into the forest, where his mighty jaws could be heard crack-crack-cracking in the gloom.

Soon after Hyena had gone, the girl's mother arrived, bearing food and drink. She sang loudly, confident that all was well:

Lang' lang' la
Lang' lang' la
Lili liyo liyo....

On and on she sang, but alas, to no avail. Finally, she glanced at the earth near the doorpost and noticed, to her horror, traces of wet blood. She screamed, overwhelmed with sorrow and fear, "Oh what's gone wrong! What's gone wrong! Has Opul slain my daughter?" She continued singing, now mournfully:

Lang' lang' la
Lang' lang' la
Lili liyo liyo
Aliya mar ringo
Lang' lang' la
Aliya mar ringo
Lang' lang' la
Masira nodhieri ka thuno odagi biro.

Aliya mar ring'o
Lang' lang' la
Aliya mar ring'o.

Lang' lang' la
Masira nomaka ka thuno odagi biro ee
Lang' lang' la
Nyani yawna ee
Lang' lang' la.

(Lang lang la, lang lang la,
Lili lili liyo, lang lang la.
Like some dried piece of meat their
breasts failed to sprout and misfortune
befell me. Daughter,
please open the door.
This is your mother calling.)

178

Lang' lang' la
Nyani yawna e
Lang' lang' la

Convinced now that her song would not be answered, she struggled with the door and forced it open. Then throwing wide the shutters and seeing in the light wet patches of blood staining the floor, she uttered a heart-rending shriek of sorrow, as though she was calling to the very forest to help in her grief:

Lang' lang' la....

Growing calm once more, she walked away, leaving her food but carrying a heavy heart. At home, she lit her pipe, took her walking staff, and set off for the forest, quietly singing a lament for her poor dead girl. Further and further into the depths of the forest she walked, until, reaching the forest's very heart, she slew herself out of love for her murdered child.
Tinda

(Source: Onyango-Ogutu, B. and Rosco, A.A. *Keep My words*, EAEP, 1974).

Forest full of meat

There was once a forest that was supposed to abound in meat. No other animals knew of its whereabouts except Othin.

He used to go to hunt there almost daily, and each time he went out he returned with a lot of meat. As a result, his family was well-fed and was never in need of meat or any other provisions because he often bartered some of the meat for the other commodities the family needed.

One day, Othin's friend, the Zebra, went to pay him a visit and as usual he made food, lots of it, in order to impress him. "From where do you get so much delicious food?" Zebra, asked with admiration. He went on: "Most of us can't feed our families right now because it is too dry and we can hardly get meat or any food with which to exchange for whatever food we need."

"Come tomorrow morning and I shall take you to the part of the forest where the meat abounds. You'll be able to carry as much meat as you desire," Othin replied maliciously.

The next day, Zebra came early to call on his friend. And Othin was ready for him. They walked towards a deserted spot in the forest bordering a big river. When they reached a cliff, where rocks formed a sort of stair descending from a kind of platform, Othin told Zebra to lie down on the lower stair of the rock while he climbed up to the top of the cliff to get the meat.

"When you hear a lot of commotion, don't stir and don't open your eyes. This will be the meat rushing down the slope. It will fall down and we will collect it at our leisure," Othin explained cunningly.

Othin then climbed on top of the rock while his friend remained lying prostrate at the bottom of the cliff. Othin hoisted a big piece of rock and hurled it right on to Zebra's head and the small pebbles it disturbed came rushing down the slope at the same time. Othin kept on shouting all the time, telling Zebra, "Keep your eyes closed, the meat is coming."

The rock burst Zebra's head and he died on the spot. Othin was pleased and laughed with glee as he danced happily down the cliff. "Where do you think Othin gets the meat?" he said mockingly as he bundled his dead friend and carried him home to feed his family.

Othin tricked many animals, who he purportedly treated as his friends, small and big in the same way. The elephant, the squirrel, the giraffe and others all fell victim to cunning Othin's trickery.

One day, Leopard came to visit him and after an elaborately prepared meal, he asked him how and from where he obtained his provisions and such good food for his family.

"I shall take you there my friend, if you care. I know the spot where meat is plentiful," Othin boasted.

"Take me to the place tomorrow. My family is starving," Leopard pleaded.

The next day, Leopard came and together with Othin, they set off almost immediately, both in very high spirits. They went to the usual spot and Othin gave Leopard his usual instructions, which he had given to his other victims.

"The meat will come stampeding down the slope, but don't open your eyes. Lie still until I tell you to get up. Then we shall collect it at our leisure," he said.

"Is that all I have to do? Just to lie on my back with my eyes closed? Funny really," the leopard remarked, surprised.

"Yes that is all you have to do. I am a clever animal and I always make meticulous plans," Othin replied boastfully as usual.

Leopard lay at the bottom of the steep cliff and closed his eyes while Othin climbed up the cliff laboriously. Soon he uttered his usual cry to warn Leopard to keep still with his eyes closed. He hoisted the rock and dropped it on Leopard's head; but Leopard had opened his eyes and had seen the stone coming. He had shifted his position, so the stone did not drop on his head and he did not die. But he lay still pretending to be dead.

Othin came and as usual bundled and carried Leopard, praising himself and bragging about his unbeatable wit. Leopard got annoyed and clawed Othin's back.

Othin shifted his load and said, "Ehummmmm, the son of Amolo, the clever one, this time, I have killed the bitter-blooded leopard that will for sure pronounce

180

my doom. I thought I killed it, yet it has put its evil claws on my back. Perhaps it is a ghost."

He spoke to himself and once again, Leopard clawed not only his back but his forehead as well. This was beyond endurance. Meat or no meat, Othin threw the bundle away and began to run.

Leopard got up, broke the ropes that were binding him and ran faster than Othin. He reached Othin's home long before him. By chance, Othin's family was away. They had gone to visit his mother and nobody was at home, not even his wife. Leopard had gone in rage intending to massacre the whole lot in revenge. He decided to hide and wait.

Othin arrived at his home late that day and was suspicious. He was clever and wanted to check whether anybody was in the house.

"Can I get into my house." Nobody replied. He asked: "Can I enter my house." No reply was forthcoming still.

"What is the matter. My house, you've often welcomed me home. What is wrong today, can I come in?" Othin repeated again standing astride at the entrance. "Come in," a clear voice came from the abyss of Othin's house.

"Ahahaaaaa. This is the first time I have heard an empty house talking to the owner," Othin said as he ran away. Leopard who was hiding in the house rushed out to catch him, but the cunning Othin had beaten him to it. He had escaped through a thicket behind his home.

Thu tinda!

(Source: Odaga, A.B. *Thu Tinda*, Lake Publishers and Enterprises Ltd: Kisumu, 1980.)

A marriage in the sky

Once upon a time, there was a group of people who lived in the sky. The chief of that kingdom had a beautiful daughter whom he was very proud of.

Every year, the chief and his daughter came down to visit their relatives who lived on earth. During one of the visits, a small cunning animal called Othin (Hare) saw the chief's daughter. He thought she was very beautiful. He fell in love with her and asked her to marry him. The chief agreed to let Othin marry his daughter, provided that he produced all the gifts he needed as bride price.

Finding the gifts for his in-laws presented no problem to Othin because he was very clever and imaginative. To the chief, he gave ten granaries of corn and one hundred head of cattle. He gave his bride-to-be a beautiful skirt made of sisal fibre.

But Othin could not take the girl right away. He had to go to the sky to meet her mother and the rest of her family, who also had to approve of the marriage. If they

181

did not like Othin, the marriage could not take place in spite of her father's consent. This was the custom.

As a matter of expediency, therefore, a visit was arranged when Othin could go to the sky to see the chief's people and seek their consent to marry the chief's daughter.

Othin had to travel far up to the sky and he took some of his friends with him as companions, so that he would not be lonely on the way. He took the elephant, the rhino, the lioness and her cubs, the leopard, the hyena and the spider whose web was used to pull others to the sky.

The party spent several nights in the caves on the mountain. It took them five days to reach the sky and they were all very tired after their long journey. Nonetheless, they were excited since none of them had ever travelled that far from earth.

The chief and a big gathering of his people met the visitors outside his home. Amongst them were his wife and daughter. Othin was very happy and pleased to see his pretty bride-to-be.

The visitors were led through the chief's homestead, into a special house where they would stay. But Othin was warned that before he could receive the approval of the tribe to marry the beautiful girl, he would be put through a test which had been planned and arranged by the chief. Then there would be an impressive party for Othin and his friends to crown their visit.

Othin listened carefully while the chief told them what the test was going to be. First, they were told that any food brought to Othin and his group, in the name of visitors, would be eaten by Othin's friends only, Othin would not touch it. For Othin and his friends to eat together, food would have to be brought for both the visitors and the son-in-law. The procedure was that whoever brought the food would announce for whom it was intended. It sounded simple indeed.

For the first three days, food was brought for the "visitors" and the "son-in-law". And so everybody ate and drunk happily to their fill. They were entertained by the sky girls who sang and danced for them. The girls wore rainbow-coloured skirts and looked attractive, young and fresh. It was all very enchanting, beautiful and oh! how exciting. Oh! how happy they all were.

After Othin and his group had spent three days in the sky, things changed and food came for the son-in-law only. So Othin ate all the food by himself for two consecutive days while his friends went without food or drink. Naturally they began to complain among themselves as they were becoming very hungry.

"Rrrrr ..." roared the lioness. "My cubs are starving. I shall have to return to the plains if we are not given food by sunrise."

Fortunately, the following day, food came for the "visitors" only and not for the son-in-law. How glad they were! They ate and drank till they could not move. Then they lay down in the shade to rest. Othin was not happy at all, and this state of affairs went on for four days. So this was the chief's plan! He wanted to starve him to death, Othin thought quietly. How long could Othin do without food? Would he persevere to the end and pass his test?

On the fifth night, Othin felt very hungry and tired. That night, while his friends slept, he crept into the chief's fold and killed the fattest ram. He ate everything and left only the bones. Before he went to bed, he carefully cleaned his hands and mouth on the back and face of the hyena, who was then fast asleep and snoring. He also made sure there was blood on the claws and paws of the hyena.

Next morning when the chief discovered that one of his rams had been killed, he called the whole village and immediately summoned the best witch-doctor around. He would do all in his power to find the guilty person who had killed his prize ram and eaten it all.

After some time the witch-doctor made his findings known. The ram had been killed and eaten by Othin; his medicine had assured him that the culprit was Othin! All eyes turned to Othin who, for a moment, did not know what to do. He denied vehemently that he ever killed and ate the chief's ram. He had been fast asleep and couldn't they all see how thin he was, he had not eaten for days! There was silence. The chief liked Othin and wanted him to marry his daughter. As such, he could not let him down.

Finally he convinced the witch-doctor that Othin was innocent. He ordered an examination of everyone in the village. The examination was to be thorough and every part of the body was to be minutely examined. Soon they found a clue which led to a new culprit.

Blood was found on the hyena and he was arrested at once. According to the laws of the sky, the punishment for such an offence was very harsh. After the trial, which took one whole day, the hyena was found guilty and since he was not a member of the chiefdom, he was dropped from the sky to the earth below.

Oh! What a cruel animal Othin was! But by his cunning trick, he had passed the test and was allowed to marry his bride. They were given an elaborate party at the chief's home. Everyone enjoyed himself tremendously. The following day, after the wonderful party, Othin, his bride, together with those who had accompanied him to the sky, returned to earth.

What happened to the hyena? Surely he had been cruelly treated by Othin — he had been used as a scapegoat. He felt very badly hurt and as a result, he turned into an ugly cynical animal.

Nowadays, he seems to run crookedly and can neither lift his head nor neck up. He was embarrassed after his fall and ran to the bush where he has remained ever since, living in caves and hollows in trees.

He only comes out at night to look for Othin and to tell the world, by screaming and laughing, that he did not kill the first ram in the sky, but that since that day

Othin gave him ideas. Nowadays he walks about at night hunting for animals such as rams and goats to kill and feed on.
Thu Tinda

(Source: Odaga, A.B. *Thu Tinda*, Lake Publishers and Enterprises Ltd: Kisumu, 1980.)

On the art of friendship

Strange to relate, Hare and Eagle were close friends. Then one day Eagle invited Hare to dine at his house. Hare arrived and Eagle cooked the food.

Now Hare was astonished to find that Eagle had cooked only bread: there was no other dish to go with it. Great friends, of course are never embarrassed about discussing domestic matters. Thus, Hare remarked, "I say, Eagle, I can't see what we are going to eat your bread with. Are we to have it without vegetables, meat, and chicken?".

Eagle reassured him. "Don't worry," he said, "that's a simple matter. Just relax and see what happens."

With the bread cooked and placed in its basket, Eagle flew off to the next village, where he swooped from the sky and hooked up a chicken, carrying it home to be cooked. The problem of a second dish was solved.

Hare was not impressed. He knew, or pretended to know, all things. He was convinced that nowhere in the world could anyone be found managing affairs better than himself. On this occasion, therefore, he coolly observed, "Yes quite good; but that's what I usually do."

Given the rules of friendship, it was soon Eagle's turn to dine with Hare. He arrived early and was mildly surprised to find that Hare, too, had cooked only bread, with no accompanying dishes. Asking Hare what else would be served, he was given a lofty reply. "Friend, that's a trivial matter. Be patient, you're going to enjoy a really tasty dish." And with that, Hare ran to the nearest village intent on catching a chicken. In the village square chickens were pecking about while their owner sat by his door pulling maize seeds from their cobs. Hare chased the chicken, but was spotted by the farmer, who began hurling maize cobs at him. He fled for his life.

Eagle, who saw his host scamper home dripping with sweat, asked what was wrong. But Hare avoided the question. Instead, he kept talking loudly to himself, hiding the truth under the cloak of sudden and unexpected events. "I'm tired of these mishaps which befall me when I've got an important guest here. I went to get a chicken for our meal, as I always do, but today the farmer was there. Would you be kind enough to bring one yourself before this bread gets cold?"

Eagle flew off, swiftly hooked a chicken, and fetched it squawking in his claws. Hare felt ashamed. No sooner had his guest left than he loudly lamented, "Eagle's an embarrassing friend, no matter how nice it is to have him calling on me." And so ended their friendship.

Hare next visited his friend Tortoise, who cooked a dish containing no flour, even though a basketful of millet stood by the fire. "I say, Opuk," he ventured, "where's the flour for the bread? Must we eat unground millet? Look, the water in the bread-pot is nearly boiling." Tortoise told him not to worry. "Relax," he said, "I know what I'm doing." And when the water began to boil, he called his daughter to bring the millet and a grinding stone. Then lying on his back, he told his daughter to grind the corn on his flat undershell. And soon, she had ground enough flour to make the bread. Hare of course refused to be impressed, merely observing, "Very interesting, that's just what I usually do."

On the return visit, however, it was once again Tortoise's shell on which the corn was ground, Hare's belly being much too soft for milling purposes. He screamed with pain when his daughter started to grind, shouting, "Stop! Stop! Things just don't seem to work out properly when visitors come. You grind corn on my belly everyday, yet now because there's a visitor present ...."

And so the corn was ground on Tortoise's belly. The bread was cooked, the guest returned home, and their friendship ended.

Onyoso, the fat-bellied insect, was Hare's next friend. When Hare called on him for dinner, Onyoso cooked his usual meal of bread and *akeyo* vegetables. But Hare was alarmed to find that the vegetables had no oil in them!

"Onyoso," he said, "I'm surprised that you've cooked the *akeyo* without any oil. Does it taste sweeter that way?"

Onyoso replied that it did not, but told Hare to be patient and all would be well. Onyoso now told his child to bring a potsherd so that he might heat it and press it against his stomach to make the oil flow. *Akeyo* always tastes delicious soaked in oil.

The potsherd was brought and heated. Onyoso pressed it against his stomach and soon the fat poured forth, filling a bowl to the brim. This was then poured over the *akeyo*, drenching it thoroughly.

Hare's response was typical. After witnessing the impossible, he merely remarked. "Well done, Onyoso, you're very clever. But you know I always cook this way myself. Until now, I didn't know anyone else knew the trick." On their walk back home Hare issued a return invitation.

On the day of the visit Onyoso arrived and Hare began cooking bread and boiling *akeyo*. When the vegetables had been pounded and were ready for the oil, Hare called for a potsherd and heated it. He squatted down on it, but it was far too hot and badly burnt his backside! He leapt up howling in pain. No oil appeared of

185

course: Hare had never in his life brought out oil from his belly. Incredibly, he kept on trying; and with each delay, the bread grew colder. At length, greatly humiliated, he asked for Onyoso's help.

"Please, Onyoso," he begged, "help me out with some of your oil. The bread's going cold, and I can't understand why oil won't ooze from my stomach today." And thus, once more, the end of a meal brought to an end a friendship. And by this time, Hare was so ashamed that for a while, he stopped making friends with either animals or insects.

But eventually he tried again. Akuru, daughter of Obondo the dove, whose voice is all music, became Hare's friend. The couple quickly became close friends and it was soon agreed that Hare should pay the customary visit. The weather promised to be fair on the appointed day: the sun shone warm, and rain clouds were visible only far away in the distance where the sky ends behind the hills.

When the friends had finished eating, however, the sky grew stormy — an ominous sign since Akuru had that day laid out to dry all kinds of grain. Rain now would be disastrous: many hands would be needed to gather in the corn. Yet Akuru showed no sign of alarm. It was approaching that twilight hour between the end of the day and the onset of night when, from clouds as black as fish cooking pots, a steady drizzle began to fall.

Seeing this, Hare said, "Akuru, whose voice is so sweet, when are you going to bring in the grain from the drying mats? Call your friends to help us before the rain washes it all away!" But Akuru told him to stay calm: she was not in the least worried. As soon as the rain began falling heavily, in big drops and with hail, she sang a magic song, telling the grain to come back to the granaries and sort itself out:

Kuuu
Kuuu
Madonjo e dere odonji
Madonjo e udi odonji
Madonjo e agulni odonji

Kuuu
Kuuu
Grain for the granaries enter!
Grain for the houses enter!
Grain for the pots, enter!

Amazingly, the grain came in from the storm untouched — it was as dry as stone. Hare who saw this, said, "How interesting, this is precisely what I usually do!"

The day came for Hare to entertain Akuru. He had been out begging for grain from as many houses as he could. He dried it in his courtyard so that he could

186

perform the same trick as Akuru. It was a fine warm day and the grain dried out early. Hare left it in the sun, hoping and praying that the sky would darken and drench the earth with rain.

His prayers were answered. Late in the evening, a mighty wind blew up soon followed by a torrential downpour. Hare panicked. He rushed out, singing *Kuuu, Kuuu, Kuuu, Madonjo e dere odonji....*" but was mortified to discover that nothing happened. He called Akuru to help, and she arrived singing once again:

Kuuu
Kuuu
Madonjo e dere odonji
Madonjo e udi odonji
Madonjo e agulni odonji

It was useless. The rain poured down and the grain refused to move. It was too late — the grain, soaked through, was ruined. Now Akuru had warned Hare to bring the grain in earlier. She was angry at his stupidity and when she left that evening, she took her friendship with her.

Hare's last friend was Onyang' Onyang' the crocodile. Since Onyang' lives in the lake, he prepared a meal of fish when he entertained Hare. The friends also drank fine beer which Onyang's wife brewed for the occasion. The evening ended with a hearty toast drank to the health of Onyang's great ancestors and those of his wife, and finally with a toast to Hare himself.

Now Hare was invited to stay the night, and at his own request, slept on the verandah, where Onyang's wife had laid her eggs. At midnight, when his hosts were asleep, Hare crept from his mat and began gorging himself with Onyang's eggs, roasting them before greedily swallowing them. When they were nicely roasted, they would break open with a popping sound, which was the signal for Hare to burst into song praising the sweetness of his hostess's eggs:

Tong Onyang' Onyang' omera
Tong Onyang' omera
Loyo tong duto gi mit
Ago piny ni THUP! tamuonyo.

(The eggs of my brother Onyang'
Onyang' are sweeter than any. I give
them a knock and THUP, they're gone!)

Now Hare, careless in his merriment, disturbed Onyang'. He called from his bed, asking Hare what he was singing about. The clever glutton replied untruthfully, singing:

Agoch Onyang' Onyang' omera
Agoch Onyang' Onyang' omera
Loyo agola duto gi liet
Anindie kuok chotna.

(The verandah of my brother Onyang'
Onyang' is warmer than any. When
I sleep out here, I sweat all over.)

Only half-awake, and his mind free of suspicion, Onyang' heard the song, smiled to himself, and went back to sleep. Early next morning, before anyone began sweeping the house, Onyang' woke Hare because he had planned to escort his guest back to his home on the lakeshore. Half way over the water, Hare, whose ears are long and sharp, heard Onyang's wife and children calling: "Onyang' Onyang' Yo! Hare's eaten your eggs!" Onyang', whose hearing was poor, asked what was being said, and Hare explained that they were being warned to swim ashore as fast as an eye blinks before an approaching storm would find them still far from land. Onyang' sped through the water as swift as lightning when it tears the sky and instantly sews it up again.

A second call came. "Hare's eaten your eggs! Hare's eaten your eggs!" But again Onyang' heard only faintly. A third call, however, he heard most clearly, and at once seized Hare's hind leg in his jaws.

"Let go!" cried Hare. "Catch my leg. That's a log of wood you've got. What on earth are you trying to do?" With this, Onyang' withdrew his teeth and sank them instead into a thick log floating in the waves.

"That's it!" called Hare. "You've got me now. Hold tight!" And he swam off with all his strength, escaping death, but once more losing a friend.
Tinda

(Source: Onyango-Ogutu, B. and Rosco, A.A. *Keep My words*, EAEP, 1974.)

The story of Ojwajni

Many years ago, there was a very severe famine that people named *"Ang'ieng Laki"* (I make you bare your teeth). In one location, there was a young man called Ojwajni who had a wife and a child.

One day after the famine, Ojwajni's wife went to Adhiegra Market and bought three *Obambla* (sun-dried) fish. On that particular day, Ojwajni and his kin had gone to a marriage feast where they were very well fed on chest meat and other delicacies. But when Ojwajni returned home, he again ate *obambla* in the *duol* where all male members of the family gathered in the evening.

188

After such gorging, Ojwajni suffered a stomach upset, was belching stinking gas and began chewing several medicinal herbs for relief but to no avail. By late evening, Ojwajni was so uncomfortable he could hardly sit. He left the *duol*, went to his house and sat on the sleeping mat. His belly was so distended now that he could hardly lie down. Soon after, he could not even breathe with ease. In fact, he could only gasp like one suffering an asthmatic attack.

Ojwajni was now very worried and began appealing to his wife to push and topple him onto his side so that he could sleep. But because of his full stomach, Ojwajni's words could not even come out audibly. All his attempts to speak ended in mere whistles. "Uu u u, uu u uu uu u" he whistled meaning to say, "Nyamgutu, push me to lie on my side". His wife, who was shocked by this strange behaviour, wondered: "Eh, Ojwajni, what arrogance has come over you that you can only speak in whistles?"

Ojwajni could not clearly hear his wife's question and continued "whispeaking". Perturbed by her husband's strange behaviour, Nyamgutu finally bent down to examine him closely and try to comprehend what he was attempting to say. Ojwajni was in such bad shape that only the whites of his eyes could be seen. Still unable to hear Ojwajni's words but alarmed by his state, Nyamgutu dashed off to call her brother-in-law because Ojwajni's condition was beyond her.

When Ojwajni's brother rushed to the scene, he was equally amazed by the whistling. He placed his ear next to Ojwajni's mouth so that he could discern what his dying brother was trying to say. That is when he heard, "Push me onto my side; topple me onto my side." The brother acted swiftly and pushed Ojwajni with such force that Ojwajni began to vomit and diarrhoea simultaneously.

He soon got some relief and could breathe normally again. But Ojwajni had learnt his lesson about over-eating.

(Source: Translated from Shadrack Malo's *Sigend Luo Maduogo Chuny*, Lake Publishers and Enterprises, 1989.)

Yieng'o olokore tho
(The story of Ojwajni)

E higa moro nenitie kech miluongo ni Ang'ienglaki. Keni nochamo ji ahinya, to ne ok oriwo piny duto kaka keye ma moko. To kaka pile bang' kech ma kamano, chiemo ja chandnga ji. Ka piny nochiek, nenitie wuowi moro miluongo ni Ojwajni: jali nonwang'o osekendo mi koro ne en gi nyathi achiel. Ka piny nochiek chiege nowuok odhi e chiro miluongo ni Adhiegra mi nong'iewo obambla adek. To chieng'ono Ojwajni gi yagi nodhi mokelo agoko kendo gichuto ring'o kaka kit yawuowi obet. To kuom yawuowigo, Ojwajni gi jowetene noduogo dala, mi odhiambone, negimedo chiemo moko e duol kama gibudhe, eka bang'e chi Ojwajni nokelo obambla mi giduto negichamo gi kuon ohiya.

189

To bang' chiemogo duto, Ojwajni nochako jiero gwe, kendo nochako nyamo yedhe moko mondo okwene iye to ne ok okwe. Ka piny noyuso moromo kar sa achiel gi dire, koro Ojwajni ne ok nyal bet piny maber, nikech mano nochung' oa e duol modhi ode. To ka ne en e ode, noneno ka iye otamo wang'e eka nodhi mobet e pien. To nikech iye nokuot ahinya, nomedo nindo gi ng'ete, bende koro nogamo mana yueyo. To bang'e ka noneno ka iye okadho kare, nochako nyiso chiege mondo odhire ogore gi ng'ete mondo onindi. To nikech iye nokuot ahinya, ne ok onyal wuoyo, to nonyalo mana liyo matintin eka bang'e nochako liyo ni, "U,u, u", tiende ni, "Nyamgutu". "U, u, u, u,uu, U, u, u, u, uu," tiende ni "Nyamgutuu, dhira agora piny." To chiegeno ka nowinjo koliyo kamano, nopamore kowacho ni, "Ma joodwa, to Ojwajni yo, ruoth manadi ma tinde omaki ma iwuoyo mana gi liyoni?" To en nomedo mana liyo to wang'e ema medo tagore. Ka Nyamgutu nokulore mong'iye mos, to noneno ka Ojwajni yueyo mayore kendo iye bende koro nomedo kuot moloyo. To en noringo modhi ir yuore maduong' konyise ni oreti piyo nikech Ojwajni otamo wang'e. To yuoreno ka nobiro nobuko penjo Ojwajni gima chame. To Ojwajni nomedo mana liyo to en nochiko ite machiegini mi owinjo gima Ojwajni nedwaro, modhire mogore piny gi ng'ete. To mano ema nodoko yath mokonyo Ojwajni, nikech e kindeno ema Ojwajni nochakoe ng'ok ma dhoge kelo to kabang'e kelo.

Siganani nyisowa ni onego kik wapiemre gi chiemo

(Source: *Sigend Luo Maduogo Chuny*, Shadrack Malo.)

Rading's wife meets her match

One day, a very good friend of Rading' Awang'mach called on him at home. Rading' then instructed his wife, "Make for us some tea. My friend is on his way somewhere."

His wife informed him, however, that she and other women were to go and prepare the fish they had left in smoking and that she was already late and was keeping her mates waiting. Rading' heard this but all the same assumed that she would make the beverage. His wife, on the other hand, joined her colleagues and they went their way.

Rading' waited for the tea in vain. After an uncomfortably long wait, his friend left while Rading' remained, fuming. He could not understand why and how his wife could embarrass him like that.

In the evening, when she returned from fishing, Rading' controlled his anger long enough to ask her why she did not serve them and thus embarrassed him. His wife surprised him by rudely asking, "Where were your hands? Why didn't you make tea for your friend?"

Rading' could not believe it. How could a woman, least of all his own wife, answer him with such contempt? Did she actually mean he should have gone into the kitchen and prepared tea?

Rading' grabbed his walking stick and began to beat his wife. But she was not going to let him have his way. She got hold of the stick, threw it away and caught

Rading' in a bear-hug. She twirled him round her hips, lifted him above the head and slammed him down before sitting astride him in victory. Then she burst out in a self-praise song, "Ah, everyone has witnessed Odoro's sister triumph."

Infuriated by this scorn, Rading' abused her. "She has triumphed over your mother? I only slipped on cow dung." His wife got off him and the two again engaged in combat. Once again, she threw Rading' headlong on to the floor and shouted in triumph, "Ah, all have again witnessed Odoro's sister triumph." Rading' again abused her: "Odoro's sister triumph over your mother. It was my shoes that made me slip. Get off me you demon, I am not your bicycle."

As soon as she released him, she began wailing loudly and claiming that Rading' was intent on killing her. She fled towards her brother-in-law's hut with Rading' hot on her heels and looking very dangerous. When her brother-in-law saw Rading' pursuing his wife and brandishing a heavy club, he intervened and restrained him, beseeching him to spare the woman. Meanwhile, the woman continued yelling that Rading' had already broken all her ribs.

Then her brother-in-law's wife, whose child was sick, begged Rading's wife to stop wailing and disturbing the sick child. As if that was an invitation for more howling, Rading's wife continued with the claim that her husband had smashed her ribs. The child's mother was incensed by this nonsense and began to drag the wailing woman towards the door. "Go and fool around with your husband, not with me," she warned as she gave Rading's wife a sound beating, felling her twice before sympathisers arrived to save her.

(Source: Translated from Shadrack Malo's *Sigend Luo Maduogo Chuny*, Lake Publishers and Enterprises, 1989.)

Amen
(Rading's wife meets her match)

Chieng' moro osiep Rading' Awang'mach nobiro lime, to Rading' nonyiso chiege ni mondo olosie chae nikech jalo ne en ng'at ma kadho. To dhakono nodwoke ni owuok odhi teng'o rech gi mon wetene kendo sa noserumo. To Rading' ka nowinjo kamano, noling' koparo ni chiege loso budho gi osiepneno. Matin to bang'e jalo nodhi.

To e kinde mago duto Rading' nobet ka iye owang' motamore nono. To ka piny nochopo odhiambo, chiege noduogo oa teng'o. To ka Rading' nonene nopenje marang'o a okuodo wiye mak otedo ni wendo, to dhakono nonyohe ka wachone ni, "To in a lweti odhi kanye mak a itedne gi nyoho nyoho moko." To Rading' Awang'mach ka nowinjo ni dhako e ma onyohe, nokawo luth eka ochako goyogo dhako. To dhakono ka noneno kamano nogamo luth e lwet Rading' mowito kucha, eka bang'e nomako Rading' gi amen, mi noting'o Rading' e wiye mochwado piny mochunjo kuome kowacho ni, "Aa, kuneno nyar gi Odoro". To chwore nodwoke ka wacho ni, "Nyar gi Odoro ma dor meru to ineno kowuoyo e ma okiera". Eka

191

bang'e dhakono nochung'ne eka gichako girwako kendo, eka dhako otero tiende momenogo dichwo moloko mochwado piny mopakore ni, "Kuneno kendo nyar gi Odoro". To dichwo nodwoke ka wacho ni, "Nyar gi Odoro ma dor meru to ineno ka wuoche e ma okiera, ayena we karrori kuoma, jachiendni."

To dhakono ka noa ir chwore, nochako ng'wech kogoyo nduru ni chwore goye nege. To noringo modonjo e od yuore maduong' mondo okonyree, to chworeno nemirima ohewo kendo nomedo lawe gi mirima. To owadgi maduong' ka noneno kobiro gi mirima koting'o luth maduong' noromo kode e dhoot mogeng'e eka nochako hoye mondo koro owe dhaw. To e ot manodonjoeno, nyathi netuoe. Dhako mawuon odno nokwero dhakono mondo kik omed ywak e ode nikech nyathi tuo, to dhako ma nodhawo gi chworeno nomedo ywak ka owacho ni chwore oturo kore gi luth maduong'. To dhako ma wuon ot iye nowang' ahinya ka noneno kaka dhakono medo mana ywak mi nogore e lwet dhakono koywaye oko, mi gikanyo dhapgi nomoko ka owachone ni, "Tug mana gi chwori to ok an". Eka dhako ma wuon ot noting'o dhakono mogoye piny eka jothek obiro othegogi.

Siganani nyisowa ni teko mar mon romre chutho gi teko mar chwo, to gin ndalo duto githoro miyo chwo duong' kendo gidhengore ni gi.

(Source: *Sigend Luo Maduogo Chuny*, Shadrack Malo.)

Arum Tidi

A long time ago, some young men from Kakrera once went out into the plains to hunt. As they hit the shrubs to scare out the animals, they came upon the bird *Arum* (marabou stork) and hit it.

One of the young men, Kibwon Nyawanga, hurled his club at the bird and hit it as it flew away. The bird grunted in pain but did not seem to have been severely hurt. Kibwon's colleagues were very cross with him because *arum* is regarded as a bird of ill omen.

"Kibwon, you hurl sticks even at creatures which you know are taboo!" they reprimanded him. "One time you will regret your rash actions."

But he told them off, saying, "The marabou stork is a bird just like any other. Forget about those ancient taboos that only old men believe in these days."

They went on with the hunt and soon ambushed some rabbits. They set their dogs on the rabbits and pursued them into the thickets where the rabbits had sought safety. The hunters frantically hit the bushes in order to drive the rabbits out.

They were in the meantime unaware that a buffalo had been napping in the bush. The commotion startled the buffalo, which came out fiercely and started chasing the dogs. When it saw the young men, the enraged buffalo changed course and turned on the already fleeing hunters. As fate would have it, the buffalo seemed to have chosen Kibwon as its main target. Luckily, however, Kibwon was able to scramble up a tree just as the buffalo caught up with him. But he did not escape the swipe of the great horns which gored an ugly wound into his thighs.

Kibwon reached the top of the tree and clung to it for dear life. The enraged buffalo, as buffaloes usually do, urinated on its tail and swished the itchy urine onto Kibwon up the tree. Kibwon scratched his scorched skin furiously but would not let go of the tree. The angry animal therefore decided to wait for him under the tree. When night fell, Kibwon was still up the tree and the buffalo still under it. The buffalo eventually got tired, lay down under the tree and soon went to sleep. Kibwon also fell asleep still holding on to the tree.

As he slept more and more, so did Kibwon lose his grip on the branch. He came hurtling down, landing smack on the buffalo's back. The animal woke up in a panic thinking that a lion had landed on it. It shot off into the forest at supersonic speed with Kibwon himself sure of death when he fell on the buffalo, off in the opposite direction. Kibwon ran so fast that he even forgot to branch into his home when he reached it. He instead branched off into another homestead where he stayed speechless for a whole week.

(Source: Translated from Shadrack Malo's *Sigend Luo Maduogo Chuny*, Lake Publishers and Enterprises, 1989.)

Arum Tidi

Yawuot Kakrera moko buora nowuok odhi pedho e thim. Ka negipedho ne giicho arum tidi, to wuowi miluongo ni Kibwon Nyawang'a norikni mobayo arum gi rungu mogoyo kore mi arum ochur. To katakamano ne ok ohinye. To kuom jo-apedha kata kuom jodwar, mano en hawi marach icho arum kendo baye gi rungu. Jowetene nochako dhawo kode ka wachone notimo marach kendo jomoko kuomgi nowachone ni, "To in Kibwon gimoro kata mana gi ming'eyo ni kuero, chieng' niromgi mak mari."

To Kibwon nodwoko yagi ka wacho ni, "Weuru weche mang'eny, arum en mana winyo kaka winy moko. Weuru ketoru e weche mag jodongo." Bang' mano ka negidhi nyime matin gi pedho, negiicho apwoyo eka negiweyo guogi bang'e to gin bende negiling' bang' guogi gi apudha. To apwoyo noringo modonjo e bungu mochido gi guogi kaachiel mi negichiewo jowi ma thwon ka nindo. Ka jowi noneno guogigo, nochako lawogi mi weg guogigo nogore kuome, mi noweyo guogi mochako lawogi. To ka gir kirage, nochiko mana Kibwon Nyawang'a tir. Ni Kibwon nyon ka to onyon ka. To ka jowi nechiegini juke noyudo yath maduong' moidho ka diemo wang'. To ka ne pod oidho, jowi nobaye mogwaro thoche.

Ka Kibwon nochopo e wi yath, nomako yath tatata, mi e kinde mago jowi ne mirima ohewo moolo pi e yiwe mokiro e wi yath kuom Kibwon. To pi jowi yilo ji ahinya, mi kibwon nochandore ka pi jowi yile mi kamoro koro nochiegini gore piny. Bang'e jowi nomedo chung' e tiend yadhno nyaka piny noyuso korito mana Kibwon, to Kibwon nonag'ore e yath tatata. Ka piny noyuso, jowino noninodo e tiend yadhno. To bang'e kar sa adek nindo notero Kibwon e wi yath to jowi bende ne nindo otero e tiend yath. Ka nindo nonyoso Kibwon ahinya noa e wi yath mogore piny e ng'e jowi ni thup, mit jowi nochiew ka paro ni mita sibuor e ma ogore kuome, mi jowi nochako ng'wech kochiko bungu to Kibwon bende nochiew machoka ng'wech

193

kotony. To Kibwon noringo mokalo dalagi modonjo e dala moro machiegni gi dalagi, mi nobet kaka momo nyaka juma achiel mangima.
Siganani nyisowa ni jarikni jacham um, to marariyo onyisowa ni onego waluor gik ma jodongo oluoro.

(Source: *Sigend Luo Maduogo Chuny*, Shadrack Malo.)

Friendship ends but kinship is permanent

Long ago there was an old man called Opiche Radiek who had three sons: Radiek, Ochwich Nyawang'a and Akich Rapenda.

Sadly though, these brothers were always at loggerheads. Among them, Ochwich was the most provocative. After their father died, the feuds between them became more frequent and brutal. One day, Radiek and Rapenda teamed up and roundly beat up Ochwich. Ochwich was so bitter that he decided to migrate to Kabondo.

Ochwich settled in Kabondo and became a great livestock keeper. He was so prosperous that he even forgot his former homeland. Besides, the people of Kabondo loved him so much and he reciprocated this by inviting them to drinking parties now and again.

During the marriage ceremony for one of Ochwich's daughters, his brothers, who had got wind of the event, decided to attend. When Ochwich saw them, he not only abused them, he also set his dogs upon them. From that time on, his brothers, who were equally prosperous, gave up on him.

After living in Kabondo for six years, Ochwich decided to find out just how much people of Kabondo really loved him. He decided to feign death.

His wives spread word that he was ill. After two days, the whole village was abuzz with the news of his illness.

On the fourth day, Ochwich's wives burst out in loud wailing announcing that he had died. They then uncovered pots of rotting blood that had been stored in the "death chamber". The room was instantly filled with a stench. When the people of Kabondo came to mourn, they attempted to enter the death chamber but turned away holding their noses, for the stench was unbearable.

As custom demands, messengers were sent to inform Nyawang'a's brothers of his "death". When the brothers arrived, the stench had become worse with the passing days. The whole company of brothers and their wives arrived moaning loudly. When they got to the door, they were hit by the smell but they braved it saying that they had to see their kinsman as he lay in state. They went right into the death chamber in deep mourning.

When Nyawang'a saw this, he decided to stop the joke. He let off a great sneeze and shook as one awaking from a deep coma. He got up to the great shock of the

194

kinsmen who, however, started rejoicing at this "resurrection". Ochwich had now established beyond doubt that kinship is permanent because his brothers had disregarded their past differences and braved the nasty smell in the chamber to mourn him, something which his surrogate kinsmen could not do. He, therefore, decided to return to his original homeland where he lived with his kinsmen ever after.

(Source: Translated from Shadrack Malo's *Sigend Luo Maduogo Chuny*, Lake Publishers and Enterprises, 1989.)

Osiep tho to wat to ok tho
(Friendship ends but kinship is permanent)

Chon gilala nenitie jaduong'moro ma nyinge Opiche wuon Radier. Nonywolo yawuowi adek: Radier, Ochwich Nyawang'a gi Akich Rapenda. Yawuowi adekgo ne ok winjre, to kuom yawuowi adekgo, Ochwich Nyawang'a ne kwiny moloyo kendo ne ojawang'o wach. To ka wuongi notho, dhaw nomedore e kindgi mi chieng'moro Radier gi Akich negigoyo Nyawang'a mi Nyawang'a nokecho mi nodar modhi Kabondo. To Nyawang'a nobet kuno ndalo mathoth mi koro nobet kaka jakuno chutho, mi nobet japith maduong' mi wiye nowil gi owetene to owetene bende wigi nowil kode. Jo Kabondo duto nohere ahinya kendo ka nonywowo kong'o to oluongogi.

To chieng'moro noluwo bang'nyare maradek mi nonego rwath bwoch. To jowetene ma nodong'Nyakach nowinjo mi nobiro mondo ocham ring'o. To Nyawang'a ka nonenogi, noyanyogi mi nosiayo nigi guogi mi guogi nokayogi mi noriembogi chuth. Nyaka a chieng'no, chuny yagi ariyogo noa kuome chuth. To ji ariyogo ne gin gi mwandu ahinya to moloyo wuowi maduong' nenigi pith mogundho.

Bang' higini auchiel, Nyawang'a nedwaro ng'eyo kaka Jo Kabondo ohere. Eka nonyiso monde mondo oikre ni goyo nduru ni otho. Ka noseloso wach gi monde, noboro remo mokuogo e ot kama nene entie ka otuo. Nonyiso monde ni chieng' ma gigoyo nduru ni otho to giel agulni mondo mibuolo mar remo opong' ot eka ong'e kaka jogo ohere ka di gichopi kama onindoe.

To bang' ndalo ariyo tuo mare noromo gweng'kendo osiepene nebironga lime. To bang' ndalo marang'wen kogwen, nduche noywak mi gweng' notimo koko, to monde to nonyiso ywak mana gi oko, ka gichopo e dhoot to umgi e ma gimako. Chiege maduong' to neywak ka rendore e dhoot to omako ume. To osiepene ka nochopo gi dhok okinyi mang'ich negitemo donjo e ot to ne ok ginyal nikech tik remo notamogi gi ng'we mi gin bende negirendore mana e dhoot. To monde nooro jaote odhi luongo ominene ariyo kande, to gin ka negichopo odhiambo, koro remo neng'we mokadho.

To Radier ka nochopo, noywak kogore piny to owadgi machielo bende mana kamano. To yuoche duto ka nochopo neywak malich kendo giduto negiringo ma gidonjo e ot mi negigore kuome pep, ne ok gidewo tik mar remo, kata umgi ne ok gimako ngang'. To e kinde mano koro Kabondo nodhier nono. To bang' ywak ma kamano, kendo ka Nyawang'a noseneno pogrwok man e kind wat gi osiep, nowuondore mogir diriyo, ni, "thiyo, thiyo". Bang'e ji noling' nikech chunye noduogo. Nyaka a kanyo Nyawang'a nong'eyo ni osiep tho to wat ok tho, mi nodar odok thurgi.

Siganani nyisowa ni osiep tho to wat ok tho.

(Source: *Sigend Luo Maduogo Chuny* by Shadrack Malo.)

196

BIBLIOGRAPHY

Ayany, S.G. *Kar Chakruok Mar Luo*, Kisumu: Lake Publishers and Enterprises, , 1989.

Malo, S. *Sigend Luo Maduogo Chuny*, Kisumu: Lake Publishers and Enterprises, 1989.

Mbuya, P., *Luo Kitgi gi Timbegi*, Anyange Press, 1938.

Miruka, O., Nairobi: *Encounter with Oral Literature*, East African Educational Publishers, 1994.

Odaga, A.B. *Poko Nyar Migumba*, Kisumu: Lake publishers and Enterprises, 1978.

Odaga, A.B. *Thu Tinda*, Kisumu: Lake Enterprises Ltd, 1980.

Odaga, A.B. *Luo Sayings*, Kisumu: Lake Publishers and Enterprises, 1994.

Ogot, B.A. *The Jii-Speakers,* Kisumu: Anyange Press, 1996.

Ogot, G. *Aloo Kod Apul Apul*, Kisumu: Anyange Press, 1981.

Ogot, G. *Ber Wat,* Kisumu: Anyange Press, 1981.

Ominde, S.H. *The Luo Girl,* Nairobi: Kenya Literature Bureau, 1952.

Omolo, L.O. *Wasomuru Sigana Mamit*, Kisumu: Lake Publishers and Enterprises, 1984.

Onyango-Ogutu, B. and A. Roscoe, *Keep My Words*, Nairobi: East African Educational Publishers, 1974.

Osadebey, D.C., "West African Voices," *African Affairs* 48 (1949).

INDEX

199